COMEDY

COMEDY

COMEDY

DRAMA

COMEDY COMEDY COMEDY DRAMA

A Memoir

Bob Odenkirk

RANDOM HOUSE
New York

Published in the United States by Random House,
an imprint and division of Penguin Random House LLC,
New York.

RANDOM HOUSE and the HOUSE colophon are registered
trademarks of Penguin Random House LLC.

LIBRARY OF CONGRESS CATALOGING-IN-PUBLICATION DATA
Names: Odenkirk, Bob, author.
Title: Comedy comedy comedy drama : a memoir / Bob Odenkirk.
Description: First edition. | New York : Random House, [2022]
Identifiers: LCCN 2021020154 (print) |
LCCN 2021020155 (ebook) | IBSN 9780399180514
(hardcover) | IBSN 9780399180521 (ebook)
Subjects: LCSH: Odenkirk, Bob | Actors—United States—
Biography. | Comedians—United States—Biography. | Television
comedy writers—United States—Biography. | Television producers
and directors—United States—Biography.
Classification: LCC PN2287.O26 A3 2021 (print) |
LCC PN2287.O26 (ebook) | DDC 792.702/8092 [B]—dc23
LC record available at https://lccn.loc.gov/2021020154
LC ebook record available at https://lccn.loc.gov/2021020155

Printed in the United States of America on acid-free paper

randomhousebooks.com

2 4 6 8 9 7 5 3 1

FIRST EDITION

Book design by Simon M. Sullivan

For Nate and Erin—
and, most of all, Naomi,
my biggest break of all

So sometimes, when the car that is life drives into a tornado, the storm could fling you away, but you could land in paradise. And that right there is a fantastic thing to remember.

—CHARLIE BOE, "Essay"

Contents

Introduction

———

How does one begin a book? A letter, a word, soon a sentence, then another, and suddenly a paragraph is begotten—a two-sentence paragraph. Dickens, Melville, Odenkirk—all have faced the same query, and only one has failed. Melville. "Call me Ishmael." Talk about giving up.

How about starting with an intention? I will attempt to identify the "big breaks," wormholes of opportunity that allowed me to move ahead five or ten spaces, or that simply sent me in the right direction. There are obvious ones—getting hired as a writer at *Saturday Night Live,* being given the plum role of Saul Goodman on *Breaking Bad*—and lots of not-so-obvious ones. I'd like to point to some of the less obvious ones especially, to drive home the cold fact that these breaks come in all sizes and often don't look like breaks when they happen. Most of this book is about my time in the comedy trenches, but then there's the part about drama and acting with a capital A, bereft of buffoonery.

How about starting with a warning? You hold failure in your hands, dear reader. The "bad breaks," if you will. Don't look away! I want your eyes to behold my floundering, and I invite you to laugh at it. Go ahead, mock me! Because the sheer amount of failure is worth a sneering chortle. I will grace your eyeballs with a bunch of words about projects you've never heard of. Pilots. Outlines. Presentations. Stumbles. Dead ends.

Moon shots that ended up under a pile of rocks. Some were worthy, some less so. Often they just got weaker as they were pursued and ended up neither here nor there. Misfires! Some of them delight me to recount; they still bring a wistful smile. Others leave me red with shame, shaking my head at myself still: What was I thinking? I wish I knew. These projects that went off the rails are a big part of my slog through the muck of showbiz. I am writing about them because of all the lessons I learned from them. Did I learn any lessons from them? I believe William Goldman nailed it with "Nobody knows anything." Let me add to that "Nobody learns much, either." But I will regale you with as many of these dead ends as I can recall— "Keep 'em coming, Gleep Glop!" I promise that if I can ascertain a pithy truism, I'll cough it up onto these pages so you can append it to your secret success journal. Also, why is your success journal a secret? Tell everyone about it—we want you to win! I'm on your side.

Here's what I can admit to right out of the gate, and it's tragic: I tried just as hard at the stuff that didn't work as I did at the stuff that worked.

What's the Upshot?

In writing this ink guzzler, the biggest shock to me was to discover just how single-minded I was. For decades, I pursued my love of sketch comedy like a cartoon horse chasing a carrot. And what d'ya know? I actually got a couple bites out of it! After enjoying that sketch-comedy carrot, I went looking for other carrots. *Clop-clop-clop* went my dumb ol' hooves until one day, out of nowhere, dramatic acting opportunities came along. Drama turned out to be a weird carrot that I sort of like and that sort of likes me. This carrot analogy is now over, and I am not sad to see it go—it was a burden for both of us.

So, now I find myself in "drama," of all things—comedy's enemy. In the past decade or so, I have been called upon not to mock but to empathize with humanity, to discover dignity in every character, even when the character's most notable quality is his lack of dignity. It's a new kind of challenge, approaching humanity's foibles from a sympathetic stance, my work is turned inside out. For the first thirty years of my career, I did nothing but compromise my character's dignity—kissing elephants' asses (see *Mr. Show*—"Prenatal Pageant"), turning Charles Manson into Lassie (*The Ben Stiller Show*— "Manson"), and scripting the brief heartbreaking tale of a motivational speaker who lives in a van down by the river (you know that one). So, from laughable indignity to tear-jerking dignity (maybe not tear-jerking . . . how about tear-welling) to . . . a touch of ultraviolence. This, then, is the strange trajectory that my journey has taken, and I'll try to make some sense out of it in these pages and give crazy luck its due.

Hey Bob, sorry to interrupt, but why are you writing a book about yourself?! You're not dying, are you?

Some people might think it's a bit premature of me to be writing a memoir. I hope it is. Here's what happened . . .

Ben Greenberg, a big-time New York editor (*he* made me put that in!), called me out of the clear blue. It was an afternoon in L.A. and I was sitting on my porch, gazing at the barbecue, thinking, *I should probably clean that thing sometime this decade,* and he planted the seed: "Why don't you write a memoir?" I'd recently read a showbiz memoir by an actor I respected. It was chock-full of stories about Broadway shows, movies, and classic television shows. I enjoyed it, but also it made me feel kinda bad. I knew my kids, then in their late teens, wouldn't know a bit of what he was talking about. Not a single project, even though some of them were true classics. Culture moves incredibly fast these days. I figured that if I wanted anyone in the general public to have even a passing knowledge of the projects that would fill my harangue, I'd better get to gettin'. Look, most of the greatest stuff I've done is classified under "cult hits," and that is using the word "hit" brazenly. So I had to write this thing now, before my reference points got smothered under the stream of fresher cultural gloop that cascades upon us all, day and night, from our "devices."

But also . . .

Just two days before that fated phone call, I'd had a conversation with an actress who told me about auditioning for an improv team at a hotshot L.A. theater school (this was before coronavirus temporarily shut the doors on live theater). She was in line with more than one thousand hungry-for-stage-time performers. "One THOUSAND?!" I asked, alarmed and daunted. "That's too many people lining up to make stuff up." I thought about when I was starting out, about how mysterious showbiz was to me then, how far away and impossible—if I'd been asked to get in a thousand-person line just to improvise, forget it. I would never have stood in that line. But the conversation brought me back to just how unknowable a career in showbiz was to a kid from Naperville, Illinois. It was just a completely ungraspable pursuit. *How is it done?* I wondered. *I just want the nitty-gritty, and please focus on the gritty.* Maybe by writing about my journey I can give some young hack a sense of making a career happen, calm their nerves, or maybe drive them away or—who knows—provide someone with a shortcut to fame.

I like shortcuts, big breaks, and showbiz memoirs.

Also, I'm dying . . . in the sense that we all are. And on that bright note—buy the book already, your plane and/or toilet seat awaits.

COMEDY

COMEDY

COMEDY

DRAMA

Chapter 1

A Madman Leads Me Astray

———

A young ME is walking, determinedly, down Wells Street on the Near North Side of Chicago—a lively strip of bars, restaurants, and porn emporiums. The brutal wind whips, cold enough to hurt your face *and* your feelings. White snow blankets the street, gray slush devouring the edges. I'm twenty and in my fourth year of college. The great maw of my future looms. It looms like a maniac. Enough with the looming! At this point I've been writing and performing comedy, mostly on the radio, at Southern Illinois University with my madcap friend Tim Thomas, the first of many comedy partners to come, and after months—years, really, of writing short comic satires and curiosities, I am wondering: How does it work?

"It" being showbiz. Hollywood. A career making television, movies, what have you. Seriously, *what have you*? I'll take anything. It's all such a blind guess at this point, it all seems so impossible, knowing what to aim for, what to commit to, where to step next. Nasty gray slush and potholes abound; in fact, forget what I said about white snow blanketing streets. There's no white to be seen—it's all gray, all foreboding.

A few months before that, I was sitting in an empty classroom in Carbondale, Illinois, writing bits for my weekly radio comedy show, *The Prime Time Special.* Tim and I had a theme each week, but really it was just random "comedy" indulgence. I would write bits, type a few up, we'd record them, then we'd riff *live* on the radio for an audience of no one. But, at some point while filling pages with comical jottings for the show, it occurred to me that *this* is what a comedy writer does for a living: fills the page, gets some laughs, fills another page. I'd been doing this kind of stuff since my early teens. First doing my comedy into a Panasonic tape recorder, then scripting stuff on my mom's typewriter, all through junior high and high school, and now college. By age twenty I'd been steadily pumping out the blithering idiocy for over a decade. I suppose if I'd grown up in Hollywood it would have been obvious that this was my calling, but where I was, in the particular family that I was in, it was far from obvious, and making comedy didn't qualify as a "calling" or a "job" or "work," much less a career. But college was ending and a choice would have to be made. This awareness of what I'd been actually doing with my time made me curious if I should, I don't know . . . *try?*

My interior monologue was the good old midwestern, glass-half-empty view:

"Young man, what are you gonna do with your life?"

"I could maybe be a comedy writer . . . ?"

"A comedy writer!! Help me out here, I can't see so good. Who do you think you are? Mr. Bill Shakespeare?!" I scowled at these hopes and dreams. It's how I was brought up—scowling—and coincidentally, it's one of the keys to writing comedy, being critical/skeptical. Even being *mean* at times. The world deserves a swift kick in the pants. I believed that then and still do.

But it was ludicrous to imagine going into showbiz. Beyond

insane imagining it. Yet what the hell else would I do? Find work in an "office"? Honestly, I wasn't real sure how you do that, either.

I'd used my college-radio credentials to get an interview with the great Joyce Sloane. Joyce was "den mother" of Second City theater, in Chicago. She had shepherded the lives and creative choices at that legendary comedy theater for decades, and she did it with a personal touch. Like if your mom ran a theater, but also if your mom liked theater and if she merely rolled her eyes at the smell of pot. Joyce was the best and would one day give me my big break. She was so nice on this consequential day (for me) that she gives me an hour of her time.

I sit in her office and pepper her with names, asking her to tell me of paths to greatness: John Belushi, Joe Flaherty, Bill Murray, Dan Aykroyd, Gilda Radner . . . the list is long and I easily kill an hour with it. I want to hear a story that sounded like something I might duplicate; someone coming out of nowhere, trying and failing, and eventually, through dint of toil and sucking, getting *somewhere*. I'm sure she thinks she's giving me what I want as she reels off the "legend" versions of each person's story. The fan-friendly touch-of-magic tall tales. The one I remember specifically was about Joe Flaherty. I loved Joe's giddy characterizations on *SCTV*, best of all Guy Caballero and Sammy Maudlin. Go look them up. So, he wasn't the most famous of the performers on my list, but I figured I might hear a story that might sound like something I could aspire to. Joyce's version went like so:

"Joe Flaherty? Joe was in Pennsylvania and he packed himself a sack lunch and got on the train to Chicago. He came right to the theater and walked in and said, 'Give me a chance,' and we did, and he was wonderful!"

Seriously, she mentions that he'd made himself a sandwich

before getting on that train ride. I guess it was a talent sandwich. Where can I get one of them? All the stories she was telling involved the performers' innate self-confidence and undeniable talent. Success on this renowned Chicago stage was a three-step process at most:

1. Enter Second City theater
2. Ask to be put on the stage
3. Be gifted

"John Belushi? He showed up to the theater one day and said, 'Put me on that stage right now!' and I said, 'You get up there, mister!' and he was absolutely a riot and just tore the house down!"

"Billy Murray? He was here with his brother Brian and he was making everyone laugh and we said, 'GET ON THAT STAGE right now, you!' And he went up there and we all said, 'Yayyyy!!'"

"Wow," I sputter, sadly, to Joyce as our hour wraps up. She really was one of the greats, the heart of the theater, and like I said, she actually would, one day, give me one of my biggest career breaks, but at this moment, inside, I am dying. "Shit. Okay, I can't do this. I'm just a regular person, I'm not 'gifted' or 'special' or 'worthy.'" After all, I've been sitting in her office for an hour already and no one has said "You get up on that stage right now, mister!" I thank Joyce and try to keep my head from falling too far down my chest as I walk out into the February day that has somehow gotten even colder, grayer, more Chicagoey than it already was.

I walk down Wells Street, past the cigar store, past the Zanies comedy club, with headshots of someone named Jay Leno, a stand-up comic who wore a prank oversize chin for yuks. I am pondering my fate and the question of how cold a city *should* be. Not *this* cold, I can tell you. I duck inside a bookstore because I like books and there was less wind inside.

I pick around in the "theater books" section, not that I feel comfortable there—at this point I'm years away from feeling comfortable with the "theater," or calling myself an actor, without giggling in embarrassment. I thumb awkwardly through books on something called "improvisation," which, as I understood it (and to this day, forty years later, I don't completely understand it), is related to sketch comedy, because sketch comedy is the thing I love most in this world beyond my brothers and sisters (all six of them).

At this point in my life I am in love with all things labeled "sketch comedy," Monty Python above all, but also Woody Allen, Steve Martin, and some really obscure stuff. Improvisation seemed a way *in* to this world of sketch, and to sweeten the pot, improv seemed a *swift* way in. With improv there's no need to "hone" skills, but rather, simply learn some "exercises." *A shortcut! I'll take it . . . Except, nah, I should just give up on this whole thing . . . I ain't got it.* Isn't that what had just been drilled into my brain? The universe was very clear just now: *Stop, go back.*

So I'm leafing through two books: Viola Spolin's hefty tome *Improvisation for the Theater* and Keith Johnstone's slimmer, idiosyncratic *Impro*. I'm leaning toward the shorter, more soulful of the two when into the store ambles a jabbering mound of clothing with a human being inside. He appears to be some kind of down-on-his-luck wizard, muttering incantations. And, actually, I will find out, the man is a WITCH, and he will change the course of my thinking and even my life on this very day.

A WITCH, ladies and gentlemen. He calls himself that with pride!

The woman behind the counter calls him Del. "No, Del,

that book isn't in yet." "Yes, Del, you can use the washroom, but please try to hit the *inside* of the toilet." I don't remember exactly what she said to him, but she used his unique moniker multiple times: Del. Del . . . where did I know that name from? It rang a bell, but it shouldn't've. I'd seen it before, maybe twice. Maybe. In the program for a Second City revue that I had attended when I was fourteen, six years earlier. Or possibly as one of the final credits on the long scroll at the end of *Saturday Night Live,* where Del Close had briefly worked as an "acting coach." It doesn't make sense, except if you knew, if you only knew, just how intensely my prefrontal cortex had stored any and every tidbit about sketch comedy I'd watched in the past ten years. I did not know what Del Close looked like, and I certainly didn't know his legendary status as a guru of sketch-comedy performers, because that *hadn't happened yet.* Still, despite the obscure and threadbare connection of that name to my favorite thing, this next thing happens . . .

I step up to this unkempt, some might say "seedy-looking" stranger and ask, "Are you Del Close?"

"Yes."

"Can I interview you?" I say, waving my tape recorder in the air to show I mean business.

"Well, I just quit Second City, again, yesterday, and I just quit cocaine and heroin and *Saturday Night Live,* too, so, fortuitous timing, this is a good moment to look backwards, and forwards, and . . . *inwards.*" Then he laughed, which turned into a cough. He was always saying things cleverly and portentously, and coughing. Del was at a juncture and I was, too, and so our junctures junctured.

Our next stop is a bar where Del orders a Bloody Mary—a blast of nutrition after what he's been putting in his body the past few years. Then we walk up the cold wind tunnel of Wells

Street and down an alley to his penurious digs. A one-bedroom, cluttered-on-the-verge-of-hoarded-level, smoke-stained pad. He talks the whole time. I listen, happily.

Signs and Portents in the Sky

This "Del Close" fella, as I come to learn over his two-and-a-half-hour ramble, is a survivor of nearly every edgy comedy scene from the past thirty years: the Compass Players in its St. Louis and New York iterations, and The Committee in San Francisco, and an important decade at Second City teaching Belushi and Murray and Ramis and everybody good. He is the grand master, the oracle—someday his name and legend will be known far and wide. He is also, by appearances, in dire straits: fresh out of work, his cramped apartment cluttered with books, pulverized furniture, rampant ashtrays, and picture this—the octagonal window in the front door lacks a pane of glass. This is February in Chicago, and the wind is barging in like a boorish jerk.

"It was a jealous husband that broke my window, last year, January first, and I've left it open as kind of a memorial." He explains to me (and this dialogue is verbatim, from my tape), "It was the coldest day of the year, twenty-six below zero, and I suddenly didn't have a front window! So, this is balmy compared to twenty-six below! But the cats like it, to get in and out of," and then he laughs and coughs at the memory of it all. As I sit, transfixed, turning down repeated offers of a wizened brown roach, the demon February wind grapples with the gasping radiator heat . . . and the wind wins, and THAT'S the last you'll hear from me on the temperature in Chicago in February . . . YOU keep bringing it up.

Del was only forty-nine at the time, but he looked much

older because of DRUGS. The usual suspects: caffeine, pot, heroin, cocaine, peyote, LSD, psilocybin, mescaline, but *also*, back when he was traveling with "Dr. Dracula's Den of Living Nightmares," a traveling show in the 1950s, he would visit flea markets and pick up old, outdated medicines collected from private stashes and swallow whatever was inside the little brown bottles, ingesting random substances from the early 1900s. He very likely ate polio. This regimen had left him a physical wreck, but his mind was as sharp and feverish as a college student on shrooms. I couldn't be more entertained by his scattershot ramblings if it were Shakespeare himself spinning a tale. It's funnier than Shakespeare, that's for sure.

Here's Del, abridged a bit. I've edited out the coughing spasms. "And the soberer I got, and the more successful Second City got, the more we all realized that we were just repeating ourselves over there, and so it finally came to a head—Bernie [Sahlins] has directed the last two shows over there . . . and there has been a great—I mean for us, for the public, it's a trivial little disagreement, for us, a great crisis of artistic vision and it was mutually decided that, since I was so heavily into experimentation and the use of improvisation to find out more and more about what constitutes a human being, and Second City is more into success and auditioning for television, that I am no longer the director that they need over there."

On and on. He talks about doing off-off-Broadway, about his medicine show/sideshow beginnings, about the Compass and Second City runs in New York, about The Committee and trying to create a long form of improvisation he called "The Harold" (which would ultimately be his greatest artistic legacy). He talks about drugs. He likes talking about drugs, almost as much as he likes doing them.

"I was taking a lot of methedrine on those days!" and "Tim

Leary was saying that he's going to send me some ketamine in the mail. I've gotten to know Tim in the last few years, and he says it's great!"

And he talks about being a witch.

"I had been accused of practicing shamanism for so long—that's what led me to practice witchcraft. They accuse you of practicing these things, so you figure, *I'd better go out and find out how it's done,* and the only way to find out how it's done is to do it. Shamanic journeys out of the body . . ."

You'd think his mad ramble would put me off. Me, a fairly good suburban, Catholic boy. A Boy Scout, no less! Proud of it! I had great times in Boy Scouts. So what is this witch doing? Puttin' a spell on me. All I can say is that it drew me in and shook me by the collar and screamed in my face, "YOU CAN DO THIS! THIS IS GONNA BE GREAT!" I trembled in the presence of his galloping mind. This stinky old dude in this cluttered apartment—one entire wall stacked with books about halfway to the ceiling, which, he explained, he bought with excess money he now had because of quitting cocaine. Del had wild gray hair, tangled and oily, and his short-term memory was shot, hence the repeated offerings of tiny, twizzled turd-brown joints . . . but his long-term memory was astonishing. He was a gnarled, shaggy Sasquatch of a man, spouting a run-on sentence that Jack Kerouac would struggle to follow, but I loved it so much. AND, understand this: it was *reassuring.* Del's disconnected monologue made everything I secretly hoped for seem possible.

I was so happy afterwards. I wanted that. I wanted lots of people and ideas and offbeat things to happen to me in my life, more than I wanted to play golf or drive a big car or tell people to take their shoes off when they came into my house.

I'm from a very nice town called Naperville, which is what

it sounds like: a small town in Illinois named after a determined white man of upstanding, righteous self-certainty named
(no kidding) "Joe Naper." Nothing against the old dude—he
got a town named after him; good on ya, Joe. Every morning
as I headed off to school, my mother would lean out the door
and shout, "Be good!" And basically, I try to do that. Please do
not send me ketamine in the mail. I think it's illegal. But here's
the thing: I'd never met a person anywhere near Del's age (he
looked sixty-something to me, but, like I said, he was forty-
nine)—anyway, an "old guy"—who talked with excitement
about what he'd done in his life and *what he was going to do
next.* Del was burning with inventive energy. He seemed wildly
entertained by his own saga, *even by his failures,* of which
there were many. He'd lived an unmoored, precarious, and
sometimes genuinely dangerous life. But it was also full of new
chapters, surprising moments, and now here he was, an abject
wreck, but still in love with the possibility of something amazing happening tonight or next week.

In fact, he was right then planning a show for a club called
CrossCurrents that would be his home for the next few years.
"Signs and portents in the sky! Eclipses of the moon and fireworks! I belong in struggling organizations, I'm just not comfortable with successful operations, and so the show at CrossCurrents
is certainly struggling, I mean, it doesn't even exist yet, it's going
to be a monthlong struggle just to get the first half hour out,
we're going to have to figure out how to work together . . ."

His words, plans, grandiose pronouncements, the hacking
coughs poured forth, filling my soul. I stare at his chattering
head and think, *And if I did everything that* you *did, except for
the drugs, I wonder where I might get to? I bet I could afford
glass in my windows.*

That night it was settled. I was committed. I left college at the end of the semester, three credits shy of a degree, and headed to Chicago to make my way into writing, making funny things, and not doing drugs.

Me in my most elemental form.

Del's journey to icon status as a trailblazing improv guru was just beginning, but he would inspire many, many others in the years to come—even, despite his legendary misogyny, many great female comic voices. He did a lot of good in the end, and all while fighting demons few others knew about, though they could be guessed at—self-hatred, frustration, resentment; a lot of hurt feelings inside that guy. As Janet Coleman, author of *The Compass,* the best book on those early years of improvisation in American comedy, told me, "You know what Del did that was truly amazing? He didn't commit suicide. He figured out other things to do."

Chapter 2

My Funny, Angry Dad

———

A tale as old as time. Daddy issues. The end.

My dad, Wally Odenkirk, could get mad at a rag that he was using to dry the car. If he dragged it across the hood and it slopped against his pants and left a wet mark, he could burst into a rage.

"Goddammit! What the HELL?!" He would curse the sky, the rag, and its unruly wetness. The universe would stare back, not giving an inch. It was funny if you weren't too close to the unjustified intensity of his emotional outburst. I inherited this "thermonuclear emotional latitude" from him. I can go from zero (calm, grinning, friendly) to eighty (sputtering, red-faced, dynamite) in zero-point-zero seconds. This can be useful in acting. In real life, it can be unnerving. It's amazing to me how often it's unintentional and doesn't reflect my actual state of mind, but is to me some kind of fun-house mirror exaggeration of my actual feeling. And I suppose it's about as fun as a fun-house mirror to see this distorted rage spring forth unexpected, as in "not very fun at all."

Wally Odenkirk was also, surprisingly, when he wanted to be, *intentionally* funny. Making wisecracks—derisive, blunt, contemptuous ones—or just being cruelly sarcastic to someone's face. One time he pulled over to get directions from a stranger, and the guy gave a confusing grunt in return, and my dad said, "Well, thanks, pal, you're a real help! Glad I pulled over!" I was about nine, and the way he said this, out loud and with a big smile, it just killed me. His point of view, that midwestern hard-nut attitude, was to cut everything and everyone down to size, and like I mentioned earlier, it's actually a very good POV for a comedy writer.

My father made business forms for a living. Read that sentence again . . . yes, you are asleep now and you will do my bidding. He told barroom jokes and liked to watch *Hee Haw* and *The Benny Hill Show* (the British *Hee Haw*—he basically loved *Hee Haw* in any language). This is humor that hits you over the head, and it hurt my head.

Generally speaking, my dad was rough and too intense, and those were his good qualities. He was never around, and when he was, there was tension in the air. The older I got, the more thankful I was that he was gone most of the time. When my parents finally separated for good, when I was fifteen, I was delighted. My heart leapt and rays of light shone from my eyes. I could exhale. I would only see my dad a few scant times until I got a call, when I was twenty-two, telling me that he was dying. His life was nothing but tragedy, and fairly small-potatoes tragedy, a life barely lived. Saying goodbye to him was a shrugging affair.

My mother was and is very dedicated to Catholicism and its tenets. If I had a nickel for every time someone told me "Your mother is a saint" when I was a kid, I'd have lots of stupid nickels. Saints are great on prayer cards, in person, though, they are hard to know what to do with. Perhaps some of the scandals within "The" Church rocked her boat a bit, but let's hide that back under a thick blanket of distraction, shall we? The Church was her rock, she was our rock, and, boy, we needed a rock. She was steady. The buck stopped with her, and

I'll just say it, because it'll make her happy: *Thank GOD for that*. My mom is also very funny, but she doesn't know it. She was always a big fan of not thinking too highly of yourself, or anyone else for that matter. This is a base component for good comedy thinking and writing—a lack of respect for the world and one's place in it. Thanks, Mom.

The Odenkirks. Seven kids! Can you believe it?! What's with those Catholics, huh? We were considered a clan by the neighbors. And it's true that we hung together tightly. We kids got closer as things got more tenuous and wobbly. There was a gloomy, existential uncertainty that hung forever in the background—accompanied by a crackling sense of imminent doom. It was a sense based on info collected directly from the horse's mouth.

"Boys"—my dad had taken me and my older brother, Steve, aside—"we're about to run out of money." We were standing in our new bedroom in our new house in a suburb that was being built around us, with new bunk beds and desks just offscreen, heck, it almost seemed like the beginnings of some kind . . . hope. Yet here was Wally telling us everything was about to come to a dark, scary end, and soon! We'd be "out in the street" was the phrase bandied about during these semiannual morale boosters. I was five, so I didn't have a lot of good counsel for him. My brother Steve was six—maybe he had some ideas about the job market and financial planning. (Steve ended up being a banker, and I ended up going into comedy to make fun of the people in charge—so I think that moment, and the many other moments just like it, impacted both of us.) I remember staring into the silence and metaphorically shitting my pants.

These little doom-laden rambles from the Cap'n were striking, frightening, and irregular enough to have maximum impact. Once, when I was around nine, this troubled tippler got my brother and me up at 2 A.M. and told us he would be leaving soon and would mail us money with which to pay the bills. I recall wondering: How would I write checks? At the time I hadn't yet mastered cursive writing.

I've always been a reader, and at some point I just started thinking of my dad as a character in a book—Dickens, I suppose. Like he wasn't really real, and all the things he was doing or not doing—draining money from bank accounts, losing his business, getting into car accidents, disappearing for long stretches—it was all happening to some imaginary screwup and I was safely hearing about it, all made up for my listening pleasure. I would overhear the latest tattle of pathetic behavior and just append it to the sorry tale I was "reading." That worked well for me. This kind of healthy disassociation from reality may even be considered a skill for a future actor.

Meanwhile, I was confused a lot by life, and especially by important aspects of growing up, sex being number one. I spent a lot of time in Boy Scouts looking for male role models and found a few. I lucked out when one of the offenders in that organization skipped over me, but I know friends who later told me some rough stuff they'd been through. Other bad things happened. Catholicism did not help, not even a little, in navigating the pea-soup fog of adolescence.

Can I be done with "the darkness" now? I think we've all had enough of this kind of sad tale, and I share mine here just to say what you are already thinking: they're nothing special, my psychological crevasses. I enjoyed a deeply unspecial suburban upbringing.

So . . . Let's get on to the comedy.

Two things made life good in our house. First, my brothers and sisters, every one with a good sense of humor and kindness toward one another. We relied on each other and we laughed

Look at this kid . . . What could go wrong?

together, a lot. They were my first audience, at the dinner table when Dad wasn't home (most nights). My brother Bill, smarter and funnier than me, would eventually join in, and this was my first "open mic night." Good thing my parents had seven kids—we had the primary requirement for a theatrical enterprise: asses in seats. I was the headliner. Mostly I would stand up and act out some idiocy from the day, make fun of people I'd met, or just be a clown.

Interestingly, teachers encouraged and indulged my constant farting around. In fifth grade, the science teacher let me read the newspaper in class and even allowed me to teach one lesson. I offered a silly riff on the lesson plan, got my laughs, and got back in my seat. In middle school, three amazing teachers conspired to let me put on comedy sketches for my projects. I did a piece on the African nation of Ghana, one on Abraham Lincoln, another on the Great Chicago Fire . . . all with scripts, and a classmate named Jerry Hinck, crude sets, costumes, and well rehearsed . . . and I got As and applause for all of it. They even sent me to perform these pieces around the school in other classrooms. Do you think this left an impression on me? It fucking did. Big-time. This was my first big break. *Teachers change lives,* so thank you, teachers!

And then . . .

In middle school an angel was sent from England above to save me. An angel named Monty Python. You know what, let's get far away from religion and put it like this: Monty Python was the hip-hop that saved my life.

Every Sunday night on Channel 11, the PBS station in Chicago, Monty Python episodes were shown, and the firmament cracked wide open. Here was a grand statement about life on earth. A hilarious, undermining, smart-silly swipe at humanity, at false dignity and rules. It was comedy with a kick. It never winked or suggested that "We're all in on it." Instead it maintained its point of view and said, "We're in, and *whoever doesn't get it* is out." It felt great to find my people.

In his autobiography, Python member Eric Idle says he had a similar reaction when he saw Beyond the Fringe, the classic sketch group that included the greatest comic mind of all time, Peter Cook, and also Dudley Moore and Alan Bennett and Jonathan Miller . . . a genius club. Eric says in his autobiography that as a young man he saw the Fringe's live show and recognized a deeper quality to the comedy: "This was anger, but it was being used for laughter."

"Yes" to "Anger" being mixed in there. And I'm glad he said it, not me.

To me, the best comedy has an anger in it, and I still don't like comedy that lacks a touch of that anger. It's like "smooth jazz"—a waste of jazz.

Of course, this anger, in Python, is buried within thick layers of silliness. Sketches like "Arthur 'Two-Sheds' Jackson," "Nudge Nudge," "Cheese Shop," "Upper Class Twit of the Year," "Olympic Hide-and-Seek Final," "Bicycle Repairman," "Déjà Vu," "Timmy Williams Interview," "Argument Clinic," and on and on describe the world at large as one big clusterfuck of idiocy. Picking out favorite sketches of Python would also miss the real greatness of that show. The best thing about Python was *the whole thing put together,* the way a great episode had momentum and ideas, lines, themes. Gilliam's animations were the key. His animations did more than connect up these sketches and allow for truncated endings, and sketch writers know that endings, really satisfying endings, for sketches are often the least fun/funny part. And there was never that American apology for the comedy, that closing credit smile and wave and sing-along that said, "We didn't really mean it, all that comedy—it's just friendly joshing!"

Python did mean it.

"Life's a piece of shit, when you look at it," as Eric Idle beautifully put it. This tied a bow on it for me. Python was like my Bible, and in many ways it provoked contemplation just like that ratty old book. Also, it was kinder and more truthful.

My friend Steve Meisner, whose father put my father to shame in the Bad Dads Hall of Shame, also had his circuits lit up by his first viewing of Python. These smart Brits were whispering to us, in our sad living rooms on Sunday nights right before another dark week began, "Yes, you're right: it's all a big, dumb lie, and you don't have to respect these people, you can laugh at them." Fucking beautiful, and we could finally exhale. Steve and I bonded over Python—their shows, records, everything we could get our hands on in the barren wasteland of pop culture at the time.

Popular comedy in the early seventies was weak. I'll never forgive my dad for liking *Hee Haw,* but in his defense, he spent part of his childhood in the Deep South and had a bit of bumpkin in him. It's crazy, but *Hee Haw* will make its way back into this memoir later. We also watched the grotesque, twisted "comedy" of Benny Hill and his "friends." It made us laugh. But it was "off" to me, as so much comedy of that era was. It made me uncomfortable, being, as Holden Caulfield would put it, "phony," and phony in an extreme way. The bulk of the comedy of that decade (when it was still sold in bulk) even had a "creepy" underside to it. The niceness was a mask. A cheap plastic Halloween mask of John Denver's bland face barely secured over the horrified, rotting, post-Vietnam, post-Altamont culture. A con job that everybody—the conned and the cons— was helping to carry on. TV featured lots of performers "breaking" into laughter and then feigning embarrassment—which is the worst. Everything was feigned, half apologized for, artificial chemical substitutes for the real thing. K-Tel and Ron Popeil products, throwaway culture that showed up already broken and disappointing. We all related to that great scene in *The Graduate:*

> MR. MCGUIRE: "I just want to say one word to you. Just . . . one word."
> BENJAMIN: "Yes, sir?"
> MR. MCGUIRE: "Are you listening?"
> BENJAMIN: "Yes, I am."
> MR. MCGUIRE: *"Plastics."*

The film might be set in the previous decade, but that word said it all about the culture of the seventies. A synthetic polymer molded to distract briefly and then be tossed aside to poison the ocean. And if you don't know what I'm talking about, please order yourself a pet rock, eat a Space Food Stick, watch video of Sammy Davis Jr. getting "roasted," and enjoy a good squirm.

Deep Cuts

The Monty Python Matching Tie and Handkerchief was a three-sided album. One side of the album had two side-by-side intertwined grooves—they were unafraid of "meta" humor like this, fucking around with structure, something my future *Mr. Show* writing partner, David Cross, also loved to do. Comedy emanating from England was better; even the soft stuff, like *The Goodies* and *The Marty Feldman Comedy Machine,* seemed bolder and miles ahead of anything in America. This was the comedy that molded my mind.

John Locher, my one friend with a great dad (I gotta call out a good one when it comes along, they're so rare!), had even more offbeat stuff. Number one being his collection of Bob and Ray shows on cassette. Bob Elliott and Ray Goulding had a radio show for eons somewhere on the East Coast, and they delivered the best American comedy before *SNL.* Drier than the Sahara in September, Bob and Ray also delivered their idiocy without winking, "breaking," or flop sweat. No *pandering* allowed. John Locher also had Derek and Clive recordings before anyone else I knew, and that . . . well, Derek and Clive were black-tar comedy. Pure essence of funny. "Derek and Clive," played by Peter Cook and Dudley Moore, were semi-improvised character riffing done in Electric Lady recording studio, in New York, at 2 A.M. after the two had already spent their night doing their off-Broadway stage show. They would get really drunk, which was okay because the characters were drunk, too. Then they'd just start blabbering away. One of their bits, "This Bloke Came Up to Me," is still, to me, the smartest, simplest example of the improvisational rule of "Yes, and" that exists.

I'd saved up my allowance and money from mowing lawns and bought a Panasonic cassette recorder at Kmart for thirty bucks, and immediately started scripting comedy bits to record with my brother Bill. It was my prize possession; playing things back, silly bits, made them more of a performance, made it all somehow "produced," intended, more than just farting around. AND I could record all the cool, offbeat albums that my friend John Locher kept acquiring.

Albert Brooks's albums were a small ray of sunshine, and also hard to find, and then there was the Credibility Gap. "The Gap" lit up my comedy circuits and made me realize Americans could be hard-laugh funny/smart, just like Brits. For the record, the Gap included a fresh-out-of-college Michael McKean, a Harry Shearer, a David Lander, and a fella named Richard Beebe. That's two-thirds of Spinal Tap right there, and of course McKean would later be Charles McGill on *Better Call Saul*. This is an insane, improbable phenomenon. Anyways, the Credibility Gap version of "parody" was unique, as their pieces were more than the sum of their riffs. We would get a run at this kind of thing years later on *The Ben Stiller Show*. For those who care (and everyone should), in the late seventies they recorded a hilarious masterpiece album called *Floats*, wherein they built comedy bits around the actual Pasadena Rose Parade—check it out.

One more element to my comedy underpinnings was a "crazy DJ" on Chicago radio named Steve Dahl. Except . . . Steve was actually NOT a crazy DJ. He was sophomoric, but too "self-aware" and cantankerous to be one of those glib creeps. He was actually making fun of the "crazy DJs" of that period. Steve and his newsman partner, Garry Meier, made fun of all this cheap, plastic, disco-based late-seventies culture, and I think Steve's simple, homespun piss-taking has never left my heart. Later, David Cross and I would build *Mr. Show* around Monty Python's example, but our version retained some of the low-falutin', sophomoric, comic kick that Steve had in his heyday. Steve's show was where I first heard Albert Brooks, too. Albert was smarter, dryer, and more adventurous with comedy than anyone, though Steve Martin came close.

I used to ride my bike through the placid, quiet, still-building streets of Naperville, past the abandoned Nike missile site, and lock her up outside the Jewel-Osco grocery store, where I would quietly attend Komedy Writer's Kamp at the magazine stand. That's where *Mad* magazine was. *Mad* was good at teaching you comedy writing because it wore its mechanics on the outside. It's easy to imagine the pitch sessions that may have gone into an issue of that fish wrap: "What if we do *M*A*S*H* and call it *S*M*A*S*H*E*D,* and Hawkeye and Trapper John and the whole gang are drunk the entire time?" "Sure, write it up." I used to read it without laughing out loud, but inside my head I was nodding, "Uh-huh . . . I get it. That's *sort of funny*. It's a start, anyways." I rarely paid for the inky blather, but the mechanics of *Mad* are good circuitry to burn into any future comedy writer's brain.

Naperville, Illinois, had a big "Sesquicentennial" celebration in 1976 . . . one hundred and fifty years of quiet, subdued, pleasant living. The celebrations were typical Americana and perfectly wonderful, but here I was, fourteen years old and seeing only empty artifice. I was yearning for comic troublemakers who would call BS on the parade of hoopla and hogwash around me. And, on cue, here she be!

SNL was the quantum leap in American comedy, but Steve

Martin's album *Let's Get Small,* which came out in 1977, was the booster rocket on that quantum leap. Steve was quickly my favorite stand-up comic, and it only bothered me a little that lots of other people liked him, too. His appearances on *SNL* elevated that show. No other host brought such energy and a cohesive point of view to the proceedings. I think it's because Steve's stand-up act was, also, sort of a sketch-comedy version of a stand-up comic, so he fit in every way. Those episodes of *SNL* were stupendous, thrilling, electric, and still, I think, the best the show has ever been.

I was a good student, even when I was goofing around. My brothers and sisters and my mother kept things together at home . . . but with that wonderful, nerve-racking backdrop never leaving us, always unsettling us, and I gorged myself on comedy. You might think I'd be planning for a career in comedy already! No way. Come on, man, this was the Midwest, and I was a good, humble, in fact self-doubting clown . . . I figured I'd work in forestry, since I like the outdoors. In fact, in high school I filled out some kind of career-planning assessment and it said just that: *Go into the forest and don't come back.* One reason it is hard for kids like me to imagine a career in showbiz is that you've never seen anyone, *any adult,* doing this work in person . . . but that changed thanks to being in Chicago, where Second City theater was still thriving.

Second City Plants a Seed

When I was fourteen, a friend from school invited me to join his family on a trip to see the Second City revue. I'm surprised I agreed to go, as the theater itself was so foreign to me at that time, and the newspapers and my parents had certified Chicago as a big, scary place. Chicago was having a rough time of it in the seventies, but it still had spirit. It was a *Dog Day Afternoon* kind of place, it seemed to me, and I think my parents liked that fear factor. Still, I agreed to go see this comedy show, even though I had no idea what I was agreeing to. We had seven kids running around our house; my mom probably didn't even notice I was gone.

Second City Theater, on Wells Street, was dirty, dark, and stank of stale beer and nachos. It was jam-packed with adults smoking, drinking, and, once the show began, laughing. I don't remember the sketches that well, but there was one mashup where Don DePollo played R2-D2. It was very silly, good and dumb. Don was a legend at Second City, a supremely funny fellow. The sketch was broad and silly, a real crowd-pleaser, full of zeitgeist references. But there was also a quiet sketch about two pals reminiscing over a dead guy they both knew. It was kind of dark, played real. And there was swearing! The show made me happy, but more than that, the experience— being in that *place*—felt like a glimpse behind the curtain of adulthood. People letting off steam. That experience stuck with me, as did a name on the program . . . Del Close.

A few years later, when the notion of pursuing a career in comedy came hesitatingly into my consciousness, I would think about those actors I saw on the Second City stage. They were getting paid to be silly. Hmm. They were real people, I'd seen them with my own eyes, living, breathing, they were three-dimensional—the best quality in a human being! If they could work this angle, maybe . . .

Premature Matriculation

When I was a tot, my mother sent me to school a year "early," and I left high school a year early, so I was sixteen when college was the only option besides "working." I chose college. It helped that my awesome, hardworking grandfather had left enough money for my family to survive the collapse of my father's business and the subsequent divorce and leave some funds for each of us to go to college. I was quite aware of the age and maturity gap between me and the other young people headed to higher education, so I chose a local college to contemplate existence and put a few credits under my belt. Basically, for me college was a good place to hang out, navigate my awkwardness, and start cranking out the clownery. Or rather "colleges," plural, as I went to four in all—I'm including the one class I took at Columbia College in Chicago to obtain a degree from SIU. After my first year at the College of DuPage, I forged ahead to the big time: Marquette University, in Milwaukee. Marquette had amazing, mind-blowing professors, but I was looking for amazing, mind-blowing students . . . or at least a warmer city to goof off in. So in 1981 I bummed my way down to Southern Illinois University, in Carbondale, a sleepy town three hundred miles south of Chicago, and that let me get perfectly lost. Academically, SIU left my brain plenty of room to daydream, and I had access to film and television equipment, plus nobody was watching or judging, so I could try and fail a whole lot in secret. I met this crazy genius named Tim Thomas, and he and I got along like two hopheads, cracking each other up with rude riffs on the local countrified vibe of the place and its culture. We soon had a weekly radio show in which to spread out and be ridiculous; we called it *The Prime Time Special* because it was not on in prime time and it was not special—it aired on Thursdays at midnight. We wrote sketches all week, prerecorded some and riffed others, and played a few songs to kill the four hours. No one was listening—we knew this at the time and we didn't mind a bit; in fact, we liked it that way. I feel bad for the young people doing what we did but putting it all up on YouTube, where it will live forever to haunt them.

Thanks to the freedom and resources I had at SIU, by my third year of college, comedy was becoming the most important responsibility in my life. I found myself sitting in an empty classroom, behind the teacher's desk, a pile of blank typewriter paper on my left, a page in front of me for jotting brainstorms down, and, on my right, a small stack of comedy material ready to perform for no one's ears. Looking at the pages in front of me—blanks on the left, notes in the front, scripts in the "outbox" (to nowhere) on the right—and thinking, *Maybe, just maybe . . . this is how Hollywood works!* Wouldn't that be something? And I thought of Second City and how those were professional grown-ups (they were maybe five years older than me at the time) doing comedy and, I assumed, doing it for a living. Hmm. Maybe *I* could . . . That was when I called up the theater and Joyce Sloane was kind enough to say yes to regaling me with magical tales.

And there it is, the first five thousand hours of my "ten thousand hours" (actually, closer to twenty thousand) that I would need to get good enough to get paid to write comedy. It was 1983, I had had my come-to-Del moment, and it was time to drive to Chicago, have my car break down, live in a basement apartment with a mentally fragile communist, and perform for no one in the big city! And, possibly, get mugged a few times. Let's do this!!

Chapter 3

The Chicago Funny Company

In Chicago in the early eighties, improv was already being taken too seriously. (In about twenty years this humorless sanctity would infect an entire generation.) Del and his teachings would become enshrined more and more over the next few decades, and as hard as I would work to undermine this preciousness, I would not make a dent. Improv was, for me, just a version of sketch comedy—a *weaker* version, but I will admit, the speed with which you could generate it, and the forgiving quality of the audience toward it, were big pluses. Working alongside the community of hardcore improvisers, including Del and his worshippers, gave me plenty of opportunity to learn and grow toward what I really loved.

Del had acolytes. I wasn't one of them, I just liked the guy. All the pot smoking and the ceaseless coughing kind of put me off. But there he was, striding amongst us uncertain newbies, living the bohemian life of a scowling, crotchety, indulgent artist for all to see, and *that* I dug. He had great plans for improv to become the only and best and most honest kind of theater ever attempted by man. He taught upstairs at CrossCurrents, a jazz club that was moving toward more comedy with Del and his classes and shows. Upstairs was blank space, perfect for an improv classroom. Del's classes were unfocused in a great way, full of experimentation and discovery and rants. Dave Pasquesi, who was one of Del's closest followers, characterized his greatness and struggle this way: "Here was a man who can't manage having a telephone, who can't 'operate life,' but there was another quality. He was willing to give you anything, there was nothing he withheld, and most of what he had was information. He would answer any question, so long as you're not an idiot." Dave developed improvisational skills and focus to the level Del aspired to his whole career—worthy of the price of a ticket. I was skeptical, even as a student, of Del's high hopes for "making shit up." Robert Smigel, who also took some of these same classes, said "eighty percent of class was Del talking and saying very interesting things, but I was impatient and I just wanted to get up and do things." Me, too.

In one class, Del himself got up and improvised, and it left a deep mark on me. He was so *wholly present,* it was a revelation. The way he stood, moved his body—he brought an entire universe to life. This was the first real "acting" I ever saw up close. In the end, I think Del was really just a great actor with a restless intelligence and some powerful demons. But as an actor he shone, fully committed, "in the moment"—all that magical, actorly shit. I would have liked to see a lot more of him as a performer. But just seeing him work for a few seconds on that day stuck with me. "That's what acting is!"—lose yourself in the part, bring an entire world with you onto the stage. Inhabit that imagined world fully and the audience will join you there.

Del was always chasing "long-form improv," something more than the short, loud "games" that are the bread and butter of most improv shows. One time, talking about how kids play cops and robbers, he observed, "Shouldn't the whole game abruptly end when the cop catches the robber? It doesn't, though. It goes on and on." The kids, he explained, have an innate sense of keeping the tension alive, keeping the story going, and if you can connect with that kid logic, maybe you can create scenes that go on, relationships that allow for stories that mutate and grow, telling a longer story rather than just finding the first conceptual joke of the scenario and beating it to death. Del hated "jokes." He allowed that laughter could come only from character. I only half agreed with him on that. I was too skeptical to become anyone's disciple, I had authority issues, even when the authority was an "anti-authority" as Del.

I was also lost in Chicago. It took me a long time to get my bearings.

The first job I had, before becoming a terrible waiter, was in Elmhurst, way north of the part of the city where low-budget theater was happening. Someone told me the temp jobs there were better than anywhere else, or easier, anyways. There I was, standing on an "L" platform at 5:30 A.M., waiting for that early-morning train to take me to the bus to take me to some office building an hour and ten minutes away, where I would shuffle papers and deliver mail around the office for eight hours, then another hour and a half returning. Dumb.

I eventually figured out easier jobs that let me have more time for writing comedy, which was all I wanted to do. Filling pages with nonsense. Mostly working toward sketches, but occasionally jokes came out that might work okay in a stand-up venue.

"I was raised Catholic, which means I'm an atheist now" was the first line I wrote for my stand-up act. Chicago has a large Catholic population, so I figured that people could relate. My mother would have been appalled, but also a little proud to hear me get laughs. The important thing is that I got tired of saying it after saying it one time. This would be one of the reasons I could never make it as a real stand-up. You can't be sick of your own act that fast. Most stand-ups take a few weeks to really hate their material, yet they have the stamina to keep pounding it out. It is, maybe, the key to doing that particular art form.

There was a lot of opportunity, even for an unseasoned performer such as myself. Chicago theater was then and is now a hotbed of creativity and trying. All credit goes to the audiences, who actually show up. They show up even for offbeat, fringe stuff, featuring up-and-comers and risky endeavors that challenge your expectations of what theater can be. If you want to make a lot of money as an actor, head to L.A. If you want to do a lot of acting, head to Chicago. You'll thank me. Try the Italian beef at Al's while you're at it.

Slowly, I sorted out a cool artistic life, the one I'd been dreaming of for years, with lots of freedom to write, perform, and sit around talking about writing and performing. The last bit was my favorite part, and possibly where I learned the most. I found a low-paying, low-stress, clean job in a bike shop. I discovered new ways to mix beans, rice, and hot dogs, which I ate from my official Boy Scout mess kit. Using what was left of my grandfather's college gift, I purchased a series of shitty cars, and every one of them pooped out on me sooner than later, so for two winters I rode my bike everywhere, a ten-speed with thin tires carving its way through the ice-sculpted roads of Chicago in winter. (It is cold there, have I mentioned?) I even found a young lady who would tolerate me, who gave me her good heart and support. An actress and artist who, like me, was just starting out, but who had real, respectable schooling in thespianism.

There was no single scene in Chicago. Steppenwolf was the cutting edge of drama acting, Second City had its system in place delivering crowd-pleasing comedy, and then there were, and are, lots of little storefronts and even basements with performance spaces. Chicago was cool like that, and it still is. I wanted to perform NOW and resented establishment anything, so I was very happy with the sewer-adjacent performance spaces. I wasn't getting in line at Second City . . . Classes, then touring, then satellite shows, then maybe, after eight years, the coveted main-stage revue.

Nowadays there are classes for comedy at many colleges. Some even have degrees in "Absurdist Joshing" and "Character Japery," and one offers a master's degree in "Kooky Behavior." My advice to those colleges: *Combine* the Setup 101 and Punch Line 101 classes—you'll save time and it'll all make more sense.

Does anybody believe you can become a great comedian in a classroom situation? The stage is the place to fail and learn, and I got lucky moving to Chicago in 1983, because stand-up was about to go boom and suddenly there would be so many stages. All the stages a boy could wish for—places that gave me "stage time," more precious than gold to a young performer.

The Stand-up Boom was absolutely nuts, a textbook *fad*—you can find some sources for it, but nothing really explains the appetite for this most limited of comic forms (limited especially in that particular heyday). And there's no particular reason why it happened, either. *An Evening at the Improv* started to run on television in 1982. The show was a cheaply produced grab bag of performances from the Improv nightclub, in Los Angeles. Then you had the late-night shows: they'd always had comics, but suddenly this particular type of performer drew all the focus. Chicago went from having three clubs to having way too many. And every disco and smelly ol' bar had a comedy night—and they paid you money to perform, and you didn't even have to be good at it. You didn't even really have to do it;

you just had to tell something that roughly sounded like "jokes," and be willing to suffer the audience's stares and ignore the simmering bad vibes, and they'd hand you a dirty twenty-dollar bill. And that, folks, settles that. You are a pro the second you take that crumpled, sweaty, possibly counterfeit twenty.

This fad seemed to have been ignited by the clinically superior "comic stylings" of Jerry Seinfeld and Jay Leno, and good for those two, who are naturals at it. They were just standing up and telling jokes, and suddenly everyone wanted to see THAT. To be clear, very specifically, this audience wanted Seinfeld or Leno or something exactly like them, please and thank you. Steve Martin's ironically distanced and hilarious act of only a few years before would have been ignored off the stage in these clubs. Okay, there were some outliers who made it big with smart, conceptual material—Emo Philips and Steven Wright, to name two greats. But mostly, ninety percent, it was observational comedy, performed by nice young men in polo shirts wearing a jacket with the sleeves pushed up to the elbows, that the mob clamored for, and if you were anything but that exact thing . . . Get outta town, ya jerk!

Still, while I and most of my friends were never going to fulfill the very narrow desires of this new crowd (all the people who just simply *looooved* disco music only a few years earlier), this explosion had its benefits. Suddenly there were ten thousand stages, and they'd have to settle for my craziness, or the weirder, more random acts that were willing to suffer in the spotlight. Lots of funny people came out of the woodwork, and we were happy to disappoint audiences, so long as we could make the other comics in the back of the club laugh.

The mob mentality of this scene was oppressive, because I was just never going to give them what they wanted. Speaking of the mob, one of the clubs with a "Komedy Nite" that paid cash, the Stay Out All Night disco, had a 2 A.M. show on Sunday night. The comic stood on their well-polished dance floor, right next to a money chamber (one of those clear booths that blew air up and you would grab at dollar bills blowing around in it, and even if that's not true, please picture it), and you told your jokes, and you ate it—you absolutely ate it, no matter who you were—in front of a grumpy, annoyed gathering of current and future AA members huddled in a scowling scrum around the bar. Monsters. Luckily, they were far enough away that they couldn't hit you with an olive. But it paid good— forty bucks! It had to be a money-laundering deal for someone. I'm not pointing fingers at any mobsters here. I like my fingers—I need 'em to finish this book.

My act was a mishmash of absurd trifles, relatable whimsies, and comical musings.

Absurd trifles: "Pot these days is stronger than it used to be—either that or they're just making the bongs shorter."
Relatable whimsies: "Has anyone else noticed how nasty porn has gotten lately? I'm talking since last Thursday at around 2 A.M. It really turned a corner."
Comical musings: "I'm kinda bummed out. I tried to join a gang—the Blackstone Rangers. I submitted an application. I knocked on doors. I killed a man. Nothing worked. Finally, I got a couple of them cornered in an alley on the South Side. 'Why don't you want me?' I asked. 'What's wrong with me?' They said I just wasn't what they were looking for 'at this time.' I pressed them, but they just said, 'Nah, you're just not . . . what we're looking for.' 'Is it because I'm white?' 'No, never,' they assured me. Then they beat the living shit out of me."

In what felt like an hour, fifteen minutes would pass and I could get my twenty beans and drive quickly to the next gig.

The comics that filled these glorious holes were a motley assortment. The run-of-the-mill, misogynist, canned-act bros were kings. They may have dressed and presented themselves as faux Seinfelds and Lenos, but their material was nowhere on par with the real deals. It couldn't really even have been accurately described as "material." A few years later, as this phenomenon was winding down and its gruesome bones were beginning to show, Robert Smigel wrote a recurring sketch about the phenomenon for *SNL* called "The Stand-Ups." Check it out: it's a document of truth and shame.

In the end, what did I get from being a bystander to the Stand-up Boom? Simply this . . .

Blame the Audience

As usual, it was all the audience's fault. Performers, especially young performers, may want to try something new and offbeat and against the grain, but you'll be rewarded if you give the audience what they paid for. And in this Stand-up Boom, what they paid for was "THAT THING WE SAW ON THE TV!" Anything else was a frustration to them, even when they liked an act—if it wasn't "that thing," they didn't like it! And this was where I learned about audience expectation and how powerful a force it is, and how you have to work with it, not against it. A friend of mine, Tom Johnson, had the most interesting, absurd, smart comic lines, which actually got solid laughs. Even Tom's headshot was funny: under his photo was printed TOM JOHNSON "FAMOUS" IN "EUROPE." One night I watched Tom kill it in front of a club crowd. It made me happy to see the crowd liking his alternative approach. Afterwards, I asked some audience members who'd been loving his act who their favorite comic of the night was. They named a different comic, who had executed a virtual tribute to Eddie Murphy, quite possibly even plagiarizing outright. Why did they go for this copycat crap? Because he gave them what they paid for. Expectations are almost everything. Besides writing good stuff and presenting it well, you have to give some thought to how the audience comes to it, and what they signed up for. They're good people, that ol' audience, but if they paid for a greasy hamburger, then a deftly seared steak will only bum them out.

Anyway, I knew very quickly that I wasn't built for stand-up. For me, it was just a place to trot out some comic premises, maybe do a "voice" (not an impersonation), take a riff and push it around, and get some nice chuckles. Also, I didn't care enough to try that hard. The stand-ups I know who succeeded all absolutely love the form; it's their favorite thing, almost an addiction. Often one addiction among many. Lucky bastards.

Also, take note: I like audiences. I like them to get what they paid for. I just needed to find a stage where my particular brand of idiocy belonged, where they expected it. Not easy to find.

Beyond Chicago's Fringe

These were unfocused, trying times, with plenty of good times along the way. I got to burn through a lot of strictly amateur silliness.

Sunday nights at Who's on First?, a suburban nightclub, was the comedy workshop to end all workshops. Who's was a typical comedy club of the time . . . Wait a second, let's call it what it was, a shack with a PA system and a toilet or two nearby. In this crumbling shed was held one of my favorite and longest-running workshops of comedy. It attracted no

Me doing my godforsaken act at some
godforsaken Komedy Nite.

audience, so we had no one to satisfy but ourselves, and the
most wonderful lunacy was on display. Steve Rudnick and
Leo Benvenuti, a comedy team, presided over the once-a-week
night of random experimentation. Doing your act on Sunday
nights at Who's would've been redundant, as we were playing
to each other and we'd already seen each other's acts. We all
brought our latest inspirations, and we all were inspired by
the funniest, most natural and unforced comic improviser I'd
ever seen, Leo Benvenuti. Leo provided his own sound effects,
scoring a scene as he was doing it. I'd never seen improv so
playful. It was what Del taught: find that inner kid who wants
the game to keep going. Leo could be physical and big, but

also precise, and he transformed scenes on a whim, moving through time and place—whatever it took to get somewhere fun. Until I saw the Groundlings alumni at work years later in Los Angeles, I've rarely seen such unforced comical improvisation. I was surprised to discover that Leo had studied with one of the original teachers of improv in America, Viola Spolin. So Leo knew the basics, and, as he described it, that was all he ever needed.

LEO'S RULES OF IMPROV

1. Remember to "Yes, and." (Avoid stage denial.)
2. Focus your energy.
3. Face the audience.
4. Project so they can hear you.

That's it. Sorry about the massive debt you owe on your Masters in Improvisatory Sciences.

Beyond that, Leo was led solely by his instincts. I asked him about it and he humbly agreed to having the knack. "It was transcendental. I never knew I was doing it, I was just in the scene. Sometimes, when we did blackout scenes"—scenes that end abruptly, usually off a big laugh—"I would think, *What just happened?* I was really, really present and lost in the scene." Personally, I wouldn't experience performing on this level until many years later, in *Breaking Bad*. I needed great writing to take me to another place.

Steve and Leo as a comedy team helped to make this night work, and as experimental as it was, it was funny and not completely random. We had repeat (elite) audience members who knew a good thing was happening. Somehow, Steve and Leo struck the perfect tone, opening up the audience's minds to something different, and even entertained comedy club drunks with bits like this genius turn on the old "Who's on First?" comedy classic.

Steve and Leo's "Who's on First?"

STEVE AND LEO ONSTAGE,
À LA ABBOTT AND COSTELLO . . .

STEVE: Well, Leo, it's baseball time again.

LEO: I know, Steve, I'm a big fan.

STEVE: So am I. You know, my favorite team of all time was the '69 Cubs. But I can never remember the names of the players.

LEO: Oh, that's easy. Let's see . . . you had Santo on third, Beckert was on second, Banks on first . . .

STEVE: That's what I'm trying to find out, the first baseman's name!

LEO: Banks—

STEVE: The guy playing first.

LEO: Banks—

STEVE: The man on first base.

LEO: Banks—

STEVE: Look, all I'm trying to find out is, is Banks on second?!

LEO: Banks is on first—

STEVE: I'm not asking if Beckert's on first!

LEO: Beckert's on second.

STEVE: Ron Santo.

LEO: Oh! He's on third!

STEVE: (*flabbergasted*) How'd we end up on third?!

LEO: You said the man's name!

STEVE: If I said the man's name, did I say Banks is on third?!

LEO: Banks is on first!

STEVE: I'm not asking if Beckert's on first!

LEO: Beckert's on second!

STEVE: Ron Santo.

BOTH: Third base!

It was scripted, memorized, perfectly delivered, and stream-of-consciousness absurd. Jeff Garlin would come over to me backstage and suggest something like "Let's put our coats on backwards and tell everyone we're the Jimson twins and we are no longer sponsoring this show."

"Why?"

And, really, there can be no reason, but he would immediately come up with one. "It's because we're insulted by the acts they've booked."

Now there's a logic to it! Well, enough logic for me. A very low bar. "Okay. But why do we have our coats on backwards?"

"We had no mother. We raised each other."

Sold! A solid premise, rich backstory—Shakespeare himself would approve. Jeff treated every room, the most mainstream, the most fringe, with no respect at all. It was an open canvas for whatever came into his head, and the audience could follow along or not—it wouldn't slow him down. For someone who loves stand-up as much as Jeff does, this is a unique approach, and he made it work. This was another thing that separated me from "real" stand-ups: their brazen disregard for being liked. The hardcore stand-ups I know all have proud stories of "walking the room," performing their act to an unappreciative or hostile audience and *digging in* on it until they all disperse. I lack that particular gene.

I liked Bob Newhart's stand-up and thought I could do something like that—if I could find a crowd with the patience for something so thinky and scripted. I saw a one-man show by the New York cool guy Eric Bogosian entitled *Sex, Drugs, Rock & Roll* at the tiny theater behind the Second City main stage—it was made up of monologues, acted out with blazing commitment, that were at times funny, and sometimes simply intense and edgy. I thought there might be some crossover between these two styles, Newhart and Bogosian, and that I could get some laughs out of the confusion. But bringing either of those two more theatrical presentational styles to the clubs as they existed in the Boom era would take a bullheadedness that even I didn't possess.

This Sundays at Who's group would all have successes in the impossible-to-predict distant future. Steve and Leo wrote *The Santa Clause,* among other popular family films, Lew Schneider became a writer and producer for *Everybody Loves Raymond* and *The Goldbergs,* Tom Gianas directed the *Tenacious D* short films for HBO, Ken Campbell became a voice-over actor in Los Angeles, and Jeff Garlin was, and still is, Jeff Garlin.

A big break was on the horizon, but in my efforts at the time I was not plotting and planning, trajectorizing or strategorizing. There was no obvious route to fame, or even a "career" . . . Every day was just *Write something funny today,* then see what happens.

I guess I passed one audition in my life. I got hired by Scott Vehill, a local theater impresario who was willing to try any damn thing, for a sketch show to be written that already had a title, *Yuk-Shak.* Our indiscriminately assembled group was charged with writing political commentary, but we ended scripting a mess. A comically tinged mess. I remember playing a bunch of drastically exaggerated human beings. A sloppy entertainer, a preteen kid with a chip on his shoulder and a small mouth and a high-pitched voice . . . brazenly inane. However, it "played." This unhinged, unjustifiable show ran for a few weeks inside a handsome tavern at Southport and Belmont in Chicago. The audience mostly filled the theater for our run, and they mostly paid for their tickets. Again, Chicago is great like that.

One person in that audience was Robert Smigel. I had met Robert when we were both taking classes at the Players Workshop, and we hit it off right away. He came to see me in this screwball show, and I imagine he liked my commitment. Commitment is key! Still, it can be overrated. Deranged conspiracists are also gifted with commitment; only a select few become highly regarded actors. Robert probably dug just how intensely silly I was.

Smigel was as sketch-obsessed as I was, going so far that he had ditched college and a brilliant future as a dentist to pursue it. While I was gazing at Python like a hypno-wheel, Robert had had his eyes locked on *Saturday Night Live*. *SNL* was still struggling, and although Eddie Murphy had supercharged the show, lately it was dragging again. Expectations for the show still remained way too high, but expectations were dropping fast.

A few months earlier, Robert had run into Tim Kazurinsky in New York and recognized him from the current *SNL* cast. Tim had been in only three episodes at that point, so he was justifiably shocked that Robert recognized him and knew his name. Kazurinsky, famous for being both funny and nicer than you need to be, told Robert about Chicago and a school of improvisation there called The Players Workshop. Robert's eyes lit up and a dental school lost its finest student.

By the time we crossed paths, Robert had already formed a group that was performing sketches, with him overseeing the writing. The show they did got good, solid laughs throughout. Relatable concepts, surprising choices, performance fun—the perfect mix for the best sketch comedy.

His sketch group was called All You Can Eat, and the show he wrote, *All You Can Eat and the Temple of Doom,* would become a bona fide hit in Chicago. Robert admits it was written to be a crowd-pleaser: "Todd Lambert [a cast member and the producer, too] wanted to make the show commercial, so it ended up being a little like *SNL*. I wasn't doing every pure idea I had; I was sort of tailoring the show to being the smartest, funniest version of what I perceived *SNL* to be." It played in Chicago for a year and a half, and was his entrée to the big time.

Soon after we met, Smigel and I became roommates in an apartment above a pie restaurant with the Dale brothers, Doug and Joe. It was a real comedy commune, with two cats and a library of videotapes featuring the best, most obscure, most important comedy and films playing 24/7. Comedy nerd central. It's where I first saw . . .

1. Albert Brooks's *Real Life,* a watershed moment in comedy cinema.
2. Andy Kaufman's less well-known, weirder stuff—yes, even weirder than the weird stuff he was known for.
3. The movies *All That Jazz* and *Lenny.*
4. *Cold Turkey,* an offbeat comedy film by Norman Lear. (It's not great, but it's indicative of the obscure, experimental work a comedy aficionado should know.)
5. Forgotten classic TV shows that I didn't care for but that the Dale boys loved.

Doug and Joe had assembled these lost comedy moments and screened them for us on glitchy videotape. Andy Kaufman's talk show parody where the host desk is about fifteen feet higher than the guest's chair is a beautiful thing; it's hard to believe there was a time when something that strange could be produced . . . And there was no sense that that kind of golden experimental age would ever come again.

The Big Time Comes into View

"It's *Saturday Night Live*, with the Not for Ready Prime Time Players!" misspoke Don Pardo on that very first episode in 1975, back when it was handmade and strikingly fresh and a bit out of control. The cold open on that first episode was a Michael O'Donoghue sketch featuring Michael himself (a writer, not a cast member) and John Belushi, in an absurdist comic set piece: a "blackout" bit, nonsense, not topical, but very well played and, most of all, genuinely funny. The kind of thing they stopped doing when O'Donoghue, a master at absurdist humor that is genuinely funny, quit in a huff. There was so much promise in that little bit. Anything could happen, the audience would have to pay attention so as to "get it," and occasionally they did. The audience was excited by something dangerous, and I was right there with them.

So many people have gotten their hopes up for *SNL* and all its promises. *Live comedy! On a Saturday night! Anything could happen!* My tale of working there, being disappointed and let down by both the show and myself, is one more on the pile. Everybody gets disappointed in their own way, but that has changed as, with time, fewer people get their hopes too high. It's live and on Saturday night and . . . that'll have to do.

My first real interaction with the show was season 11, episode 4. John Lithgow was the host, and a redundant band called "Mr. Mister" sang their ditties. I was living in Chicago still, but I went to New York to follow my friend Robert Smigel around, pitching him jokes and trying to find the fun part of working at *SNL*. I never really found the fun part, because the stressful part always seemed to overwhelm everything else. Over time I would find that I was not alone in feeling this way—more painful and strenuous than fun.

At that point in the show's storied history, a high degree of tension was probably warranted. Things were beyond rocky. The wheels were coming off. The cast included Anthony Michael Hall, Joan Cusack, Jon Lovitz, and Terry Sweeney, funny and good actors, not necessarily both of those things concurrently. I think it's safe to say that cast didn't "jell," though everybody was working real hard to make that happen. Jelling, it seems, cannot be forced. Pressure never eased, and no stride was hit. My buddy Robert was scrambling madly to deliver for the show—his dream gig. He spent all his time at the offices, rarely slept on a Tuesday night before Wednesday's read-through, so that he could get more writing done, and on some weeks he skipped snoozing on a Thursday or Friday night, too, because he was often producing a packaged pre-tape. I could barely keep up with him, and that remained the case in the years ahead.

Rockefeller Center is imposing, its intimidating grandiosity resplendent with supercool art deco style, but once I got up to the seventeenth floor I found nondescript, functional offices with no personality. Lorne's private office was a beauty, and the views all around it great, but I was surprised what a downer the rest of the place was. It had the vibe of an insurance office, the kind I'd briefly worked in doing temp jobs, which is to say, no vibe. Where were those bunk beds I'd heard they installed for all-night writing sessions with Aykroyd and Belushi? Where were the cocaine troughs rumored during the "lost years"? Where was the fun, loutish, backstage-at-a-comedy-club, competitive-but-collegial sniper's den that attracted America's best, hippest young minds to sit on their high horses and throw stones from? I knew it was a professional organization, but it shouldn't feel like they were producing *Good Morning America*. This lack of clubbiness/funkiness was an even bigger disappointment to me than my own weak writing talents, and that's saying a lot. Creating a comedy show with the rock-band-on-the-road team spirit that I dreamed of was years away, and I would do it, far from New York and glorious 30 Rock, on a mean, tough, smart, and stupid show called *Mr. Show*, but first I had to put in my time in the trenches.

A certain amount of *SNL*'s nauseating tension in those years can be written off as the show's trying to find itself again. By this point, *SNL* had been up and down and back up and now down again. I factored this in and wanted the show to find its way, because, folks, it was the ONLY sketch show in America. So . . . I'd be a fool to *want* it to suck. But it didn't help one engineer comedy, this palpable desperation. Frankly, even the laughter seemed desperate, like the audience members were also trying to prove themselves. There was so much *trying* going on, it really undercut the chance that something genuinely and simply fun and funny could happen.

Would *SNL* ever be as good and dangerous and new as it was in those first five years? *No!* Oops . . . I spoilered myself. How about if we just limit this yearning for glory days to the first sketch ever on the show: O'Donoghue and Belushi doing an English lesson—"I want to feed your fingertips to the wolverines"—basically hip young wiseasses entertaining themselves. The show peaked right there, and it's been downhill since. Lorne has heard this ten billion times, but he shows up and makes the show with the army he's got and the damn thing'll have to do.

I did enjoy aspects of the big time, and most of all I loved watching Robert Smigel work. He already excelled at sketch writing before he'd been hired. The guy really had it down. When I sat in a room with him, even over the phone when I was still living in Chicago, pitching lines, Robert showed me by example how to find the best part of a comedy idea and make the most of it.

I should note that both Robert and I made it into the orbit of *SNL* via another friend of ours, Dave Reynolds. Take note, a lesson looms! Young writer/actor/entrepreneur, very often your opportunities come via your friends' achievements, so *make a lotta good friends who are talented.* My career is based on Dave Reynolds having done a great audition. Thanks, Dave! What happened was . . .

Back in Chicago a year and a half earlier, Dave, a member of Robert's group All You Can Eat, had auditioned for a teen-date movie called *Just Another Saturday Night* (a title later changed to *One More Saturday Night*) and he got the part! This meant I could play Dave's parts in the stage show while he shot in Hollywood! Working alongside Robert in All You Can Eat solidified our friendship. It was also mind-blowing to be making enough money to live on by doing a stage show, with no burger grease involved. The movie Dave was making, one that almost no one saw but that changed so many of our lives, happened to be written and produced by Al Franken and Tom Davis. So . . . Dave invited Al and Tom to see the sketch show he was in, hence they saw and appreciated Smigel's solid sketch writing and *bingo*—they hired Robert when they were made executive producers for season 11 of *SNL,* and, la-di-frickin'-da, I grabbed his coattail and got my foot in Rockefeller Center's golden revolving doors.

I certainly never counted on getting a job at *SNL,* but I took every opportunity to write with Robert and to share my own work with him. It meant a lot to me to even be in proximity to real show business. I did feel excited that real comedy writing pros were glancing at my feeble scribblings. I can remember I was running food to a table one Saturday night, at the restaurant where I did that, when I looked over my shoulder to watch Dennis Miller read one of my jokes on "Weekend Update." The television's audio was drowned out by the sounds of chewing and tired fifties hits (this was a burger place with faux fifties decor), but the picture of Bob Hope over Dennis's shoulder told me my joke had made it on: "The statute of limitations on respecting Bob Hope for his earlier work ran out this week." I loved that Dennis had got it and liked it enough to perform it. Oh, and the audience did, too—they laughed at it—the people actually grasped my snarly little jape. I delivered the hamburgers to the right table and restrained myself from gushing to the customers that I'd just had a joke on "Weekend Update."

Smigel was kept on the staff into season 12, justifiably, but still amazing, because there was such a big changeover. Gradually, the show was developing some . . . momentum, character, goodness, with a new cast that were on the same wavelength, now including Dana Carvey and Kevin Nealon and the great Jan Hooks. Robert was delivering amazing stuff, including all-time classics like the scene at the Star Trek Convention, and the Steve Martin "I'm Not Gonna Phone It in Tonight!" showstopping cold open. Robert explains away his excellence at penning sketches to simple relentlessness. "I was obsessed with *Saturday Night Live*. It was a Rupert Pupkin effect. You know, he was not bad in *The King of Comedy*—I mean, Rupert Pupkin, himself. When he actually got the opportunity he was good. It was not an exciting kind of good but he was completely competent . . . I was obsessed with *Saturday Night Live* when it was bad, with Jean Doumanian. That year I watched it, I was just fascinated by the craft and I wanted to see if it would ever get good."

When Robert recommended me for a spot on the writing staff, I was summoned for an interview with the great and powerful Oz.

A Chip on My Shoulder as Big as the Ritz

I may have been penniless, but at twenty-four years old, in 1986, I was also a loud and proud comedy snob when Lorne Michaels graciously wasted his time meeting me. Like everyone ever, I thought the show had been better when I was thirteen. The purist that I was would have said: "*SNL* hit its high point in the planning stage."

I was a Python fan first, but those first five "classic" *SNL* years were stuck in my head and heart, just like they were for everyone else who'd experienced that phenomenal beginning. Early *SNL* had that unapologetic swagger—"We're doing *our* show for *us* over *here* . . . If you want to join the fun, catch up." I liked that blazing "try to catch up" approach, and I thought everyone else, especially Lorne, wanted to rekindle it. This was wishful thinking supported by no evidence at all.

I don't know if Lorne had a grand plan, but after all the ups and downs of the first decade, maybe he was consciously pursuing something more reliable and sustainable. The audience for the show had become broader, and this less pissed-off, far less hip audience had expectations now, unlike with the first incarnation. Me, I prefer Steve Jobs's philosophy: "People don't know what they want until you show it to them." But Steve and I were outliers here. Good ol' Steve.

Leaving my apartment in Chicago for the big job interview— you'd think I'd get on my knees and beg to work there. But no. I maintained my cool demeanor. Flying to New York, I had plenty of time to let the intimidation factor stew, but did I even like *SNL*? The corny hosts (in between the cool hosts). The corny bands (and sometimes unbelievably cool musical heroes). Entering the orbit of the actual show itself was the most intimidating thing ever, and possibly the most embarrassing thing ever. It was both. Of course, I wanted the job. But I wanted a time machine first, to take me back to the beginning, to discover a show with a bunch of like-minded scruffians and troublemakers.

I had still more time to ruminate on how not to be hired as I sat for my two-and-a-half-hour wait period (this waiting outside Lorne's office is legendary among prospects; one pal of mine claims she owns the record at six hours). I considered, briefly, kissing ass, praising the glory years, maybe dropping a Derek and Clive reference, as I knew he loved British comedy . . . but I landed on the following game plan. I would be critical, distant, and unappreciative. He probably hated having his ass kissed, I figured, after all those years. Talk about not being able to read a room.

Here's a reenactment, paraphrased from watery memory. Lorne goes first:

"So Robert tells me you're a good writer. What are your favorite comedy shows?"

"Well, mostly Monty Python . . . *SCTV* was great, at times. But this show you're running . . . not so much."

"Hmm . . . Well, we're thinking of hiring some new writers. What do you think about working here?"

"Not interested. Definitely not. I would be . . . not bummed out, but let's say *miffed*, to be asked to work here. This show is soft, unsatisfying, weak, not very funny—it's in a death spiral. Do you appreciate my blunt forthrightness?"

"I prize cold, hard truth above all. And what do you think of me?"

"Well, you're the boss, so you must be out of touch. I find you to be distant, cold, imperious, unnecessarily intimidating."

"Your honesty is refreshing. *Beyond* refreshing—it's a comfort and a balm. Thank you for taking the time to come to New York. It's been wonderful to meet you. Good luck waiting tables."

"Oh, I'm not a waiter yet. Currently I'm just running the food to the table."

"Wonderful. All the best on that."

"Yep. And good luck with your not very good TV show."

I did not get hired immediately after that meeting.

A few months later, I did.

Why he hired me despite suffering my high-horsiness, I cannot say. What is true is that this meeting set the table nicely for the deeply awkward energy of all our forthcoming interactions. We got off on the wrong foot and stayed on it. I'll take the blame. But should I have said no to the job? Of course not! It was the biggest break of all the breaks I would have up until Vince Gilligan's assistant handed him the phone in 2009, twenty-three years later. Everything I would learn about sketch writing and how to do it, everything that would someday help me write and produce the best show I had in me, *the show I was dreaming of when I was scoffing at SNL*—all of that I learned in my three and a half seasons at *SNL*.

Looking back, I am not sure if my derisive attitude from the get-go was powered by moxie, or if I was just scared of this big beast offering to swallow me whole. I guess I'd say it was both. But the good thing is that working at *SNL* would make me good enough to write great stuff in line with my high hopes. Unfortunately, this didn't happen *while* I was working there.

Chapter 4

A Bright, Shining Nanosecond

———

ROBERT: I was like, definitely Bob, I can get Bob
hired and I would never regret it; he is a genius and
there is no way that they wouldn't be lucky to have
Bob.
ME: You were wrong.
ROBERT: I was wrong. I was very wrong. You
alienated. But *they* were wrong, too.

—ROBERT SMIGEL, interviewed by me in *The
Believer,* vol. 7, no. 4 (May 2009)

November 1987. The Rockefeller Center Christmas tree is lit
up before me, the strap from my duffel bag digging into my
shoulder. Inside are all the clothes I'll need to look like a real
comedy writer: two flannel shirts, one extra pair of jeans, three
underwears. People spend their whole lives in this costume
without washing it once. Great people, legends in my mind:
comedy writers. I pause to take in the swirl of giddy tourists
and gruff New Yorkers . . . Do they know what is happening
right now? I'm a writer now. A professional writer, heading to
my first big-time, paying job, on America's only satirical comedy sketch program.

I take a moment to breathe in the stank of hot-dog water

and marvel at the towering Christmas tree, twinkling with bau-
bles, then glance up at Rockefeller Center, aka the Rock . . .
Wait, that's Alcatraz. Yes, it's both. Ominous. Inside this showstopper of a building, things get a bit darker: the lobby with its
nightmare murals featuring gods working menial jobs. *Poor
saps,* I thought as I shuffled by them. No sweat for me anymore. All I needed to make a living was my sharp brain and a
couple of dull pencils. I'd visited the show before, so I already
knew the pressurized atmosphere, the no-fun, we're-already-
fucked vibe of it. But here goes.

In my first group "pitch" session the very next night, I played
the role of "fresh meat" . . .

"Sketch ideas, anyone? How about you, new guy?"

Me? Already? Me *not* all ready. I sputtered, "Uhhhh . . . I
don't know, well, I flew in on People Express, so . . . what if
there was an airline called Greyhound Air and . . . they had
hay bales instead of seats, and . . . no toilet, so you had to hold
your pee the whole time, and instead of oxygen masks they had
carbon dioxide—'cause it's cheaper, and . . ."

A veteran writer (Al Franken) stops me with one simple
question: "Why?"

"Well, because . . . they're saving money, y'know? Also, so,
like, they can't even promise destinations; they just have
directions—the plane is headed in *a general direction* . . . like
'towards New York,' and . . ."

Again the venerated older writer (Al Franken) shoots back:
"Why?"

"So they can charge less, and be the cheapest airline . . ."

The veteran writer, someone I have idolized and known
since youth (Al Franken), seems kind of pissed at me. Is there
anger in his voice? Again he hits me with the "Whyyy?" Yes,
he's definitely angry at me.

"Well, it's a cheap airline, y'know . . . so they sell more tickets, 'cause . . . it's like, y'know, 'People's Express' . . . " Nervousness overtaking me—have I personally insulted someone? Is Al in the pocket of Big Airline? Is that blood trickling out my ear?

Now the venerated vet grows more heated in his query. "But *whyyy*? Why would anyone do that?"

"Why? I guess because it might be . . . *funny*?"

Now Franken is seething. "Whyyyyy?"

And in the face of that, I back down and end my career. "I don't know, it's a bad idea, I'll shut up for the next four years."

It's called hazing . . . Or maybe it's just Al's inimitable bulldozer manner (stick around; he saves my ass and we become friends . . . it takes a while, though). I watched it happen to other new writers in the coming years. It was a collateral effect of how on the edge everyone was all the time at that place, wondering about their worth to the show. *Does the show need me? Am I going to be fired next week? Was I already fired and no one bothered to tell me?!* Legitimate concerns on a ship in a storm with an inscrutable ghost captain and a nation turning its lonely eyes to you, every Saturday at eleven thirty.

Lost in New York

I sublet an apartment on Washington Square Park from an NYU professor. This was when you could buy shitty weed on the corner and there were lots of homeless people, not like now . . . I mean, just like now. Mostly I spent my time at work, but when I came home it was to someone else's life. It's fun to visit New York and get lost in the sea of humanity. But to get lost and stay lost, to not be able to find yourself or feel like you matter anywhere, at any time . . . It messed with my head. Many a young *SNL* performer and/or writer knows the feeling.

The show was getting funny again, with a cast who understood each other and even liked each other, which was a challenging trick, as the competitive aspects of screen time seemed to be encouraged by management, or lack thereof. Jon Lovitz was the "star" when I arrived; he didn't have many moves, but the ones he had were crowd-pleasers and he could be deeply silly, something I loved. Dana Carvey had started to hit homers and would become the biggest laugh-getter for the next three years, plus he's the sweetest, kindest guy going. Phil Hartman was built by NASA to make every bit he was in better. Jan Hooks was underappreciated and underused but was the funniest lady actor since Catherine O'Hara. Victoria Jackson would have been a riot on *The Tonight Show* in the fifties . . . the 1850s! Gooooood-night!! Kevin Nealon was one of the funniest understated comic voices—dry and subtle on a show that rewards loud—and yet he found his place. No one was competing with Kevin; his voice was unique in that group. In my second year, Mike Myers showed up, driven, and sure of his characters and talent. Nobody "handled" the show like Mike did; most people got handled by it. Also, Ben Stiller stopped by for a minute. If I'd had Ben's confidence and understanding of the business, maybe I would have moved on sooner, too. He tried, but right away he knew it wasn't the system he could work in. I had come on in season 13. By season 15, the show was feeling strong again, and all of us writers could feel it. We'd contributed to a new level of confidence . . . still not very confident, but a *modicum of confidence,* and that felt like something.

But let me go back.

Here's the thing I need you to know about my time feeling

out of place and resentful at *SNL:* I tried. I tried like hell to understand the show and serve it well. I was thankful for the opportunity; I knew I was born with a chip on my shoulder, I didn't expect to be handed anything, and I wanted to beat this thing. On Monday of my third week at *SNL,* I took out a legal pad and wrote:

- Use the Host!
- Write for the Ladies!
- Something topical! Read the news!
- One Set!—no films!!
- Loud and/or Recurring Characters!!

I figured out that if I could incorporate two of these *strictures* into a sketch, it would greatly improve my chance of getting something on the show. Sound like no fun? It was! Reverse-engineering comedy is an inspiration killer, but it's a good list if you ever get hired there, so tear this page out and stuff it in your pocket.

Uninspiring as it was, it immediately worked for me. In my third week, I wrote a sketch that made it to air: one of Lovitz's recurring characters, the Master Thespian, preparing to play Santa at Macy's (two ticks on the checklist right there). It led to me getting an earful from HRH himself.

I'm standing under the bleachers, where Lorne watches the "dress" show. The sketch began: it was set in the men's bathroom at Macy's, where Jon's loudmouth character is prepping "backstage" for his big role. It was going fairly well, and I was so jazzed at the whole thing even happening. I was actually helping to make the show! But I sensed an . . . agitation. He turned to me and snarled, "Where's the fucking echo?"

I responded in my dumbest Illinois drawl, "Whaaaa—"

"The echo! He's in a bathroom. There should be ECHO!" He was *really* pissed.

Meanwhile I'm thinking, *Echo? Who gives a shit about echo??* How about yelling at me, "Why are we doing this scene?! This is America's only satirical comedy show and we're making fun of the mannerisms of actors in the 1940s?!!" But, "echo" . . . I don't know what that means, even.

Finally it hit me: *Oh, right. Bathrooms sometimes have a slight echo in them . . . So see if we can arrange for the audio folks to stick some echo on the actors when they're in the bathroom.* I ran to the sound booth, its own separate little hidey-hole that I never once set foot in again in the coming three and a half years, and they promptly delivered us some echo for the on-air version of the sketch. The sketch made it to air! The echo they put in was very distracting, and in no way did it improve the piece! But look at it this way: I learned *nothing* from being yelled at about the "fucking echo." Well, I learned that if I stood next to Lorne I might get yelled at. I stopped doing that.

Sadly, as a writer I was a waste of bagels! I was trying too hard, but the more I failed, the more I tried. It's a sick cycle that afflicts many a fresh *SNL*er.

There was an after-party every week at some cool club with some celebs "dropping by." At one of those parties, early in my first season, our head writer, the beloved comedy writing legend James Downey, talked down the episode we'd just done. He counted maybe three good laughs, "and then 'Update,'" and he declared himself satisfied. I know no one had higher standards than Jim for what comedy can be, so I was bummed out that this was all that was expected. That this was good enough. I had yet to be brutalized by the schedule, which will pummel anyone's high hopes into shrugging surrender.

A month after I arrived, Conan O'Brien and Greg Daniels

joined the writing staff. They were direct from Harvard—actually, I think they'd worked on some attempt at an offbeat *60 Minutes* since graduating—but they still smelled Harvardy, all smart and like they belonged. Greg was quiet and came at ideas from left field. He was a good listener, and thank God, because there were too many talkers in the group already. Conan O'Brien was a ball of tension and silly riffing—he used to hyperactively mutter in a voice that was a glimpse into his interior monologue, funny, agitated. I am glad the world eventually got a chance to see what I saw at 2 A.M. on those Tuesday nights when we'd lost all connection to normal human behavior. In our sub-clique of writers, I was third or fourth in rotation. This would have bothered me a lot more if we weren't writing some great stuff. As a part of this crew, I contributed jokes to "The Superfans" (aka "Da Bears"), "The McLaughlin Group," and lots more.

Smigel was firing on all cylinders, and some of his best work didn't even make the show. He wrote one short film that was executed to perfection, and one of the best things never seen on *SNL*. It was a documentary-style short film, presented as if on Turner Classic Movies channel, supposedly using found footage of Charlie Chaplin from an early film that showed him "discovering" the character of the Little Tramp. As the piece progresses, we watch Dana, as Chaplin, stealing every aspect of the Tramp character from an extra in the background of the film, the extra played by Jon Lovitz. The narrator never notices the obvious ripping off of the character but keeps giving Chaplin credit for "a spark of inspiration!" It got not a single laugh in the dress rehearsal show. The audience was wrong on that one, dead wrong. It was the kind of singular smart-silly piece that would have been proudly played on *Mr. Show* and become a beloved classic. Watch an early Monty Python episode, when it was played for a live audience: it gets crickets—and from an audience of hippies! Scattered laughs, if that. Big, empty gaps with titterings sprinkled here and there. It's wonderful that the audience is there, but you mustn't listen to them; they don't know what's good.

I used to watch *SNL* in all its last-minute, hurry-up, out-of-breath production effort and think, *If only we could perfect these scenes a little bit.* Prep them. As Lorne famously says, "The show doesn't go on because it's ready; it goes on because it's eleven thirty." But what if you *could* put it on because it's ready? Wouldn't that be something cool?! You know, if people could learn their lines and take the time and effort to figure the best way to play the scenes, and if we didn't have the burden of pleasing tourists of all ages who waited in line and "just want to see that THING that I paid for." Well, no one paid for it—tickets were free—but you know what I mean, they just wanted us to PLAY THE HITS!

My week went like this: Monday morning, show up and watch other, senior writers snatch up the "top story" that seems to be forming for the week ahead. Desperation is in the air already. That evening, the host comes in for a meeting where the writers and cast pitch ideas to make them feel like *something* will be written that will be *kinda* funny. Most of the ideas are bullshit: you don't want to put your good stuff out there (not that you have hold of "good stuff" yet), because you want a fresh energy to greet your golden idea when it's read at Wednesday read-through. Then, off you go, pen and legal pad in hand, beads of sweat aborning. A smart writer like Robert didn't commit too quickly; he just collected possible sketch premises, or beats for sketches, or considered rewriting an old idea that fit this host . . . but only if it was a perfect fit. Old ideas struggle to get a second chance, but Smigel was very smart about this, and patient. Patience and smarts—two things I dream of having some fine day.

Tuesday, I would come in and the tension would build, a hunger to write something great or, leaving that lollipop dream aside, then just something that *had* to be in the show. Obviously if the sketch invoked the top news story of the week, that was a good start, but those stories and their most obvious takes would have already been claimed, usually by senior writers. We would write through Tuesday night and into Wednesday. The host would come around, and if you clicked—like with funny and smart folks such as Paul Simon or Sting—you could have some fun batting ideas about. Or possibly you would just sit and chat with someone and try not to feel awkward. Lorne might wander by, killing the laughter . . . Hey, maybe he was as nervous as we all were? I am only considering that possibility now, thirty-some years later. He knew he had to sit through all these sketches on Wednesday, so he had some skin in the game. I gave myself silent concussions just by sitting still, squeezing my brain muscles, trying to be funny in a way that would work on this show. Around 4 A.M. on Tuesday, you slump to the floor and grab a few winks, trying not to drool on the cushion borrowed from the couch.

Wednesday, wake up and write one last thing—maybe this last bit of inspiration was best of all? NO. Definitely not. Your brain is dull as a cotton ball right now. Read-through would begin in the afternoon. A room jam-packed with cast, and the huge crew that would have to mount this scattershot grab bag of brain farts. Sometimes there were more than fifty sketches! That's too many. And my little sketch, especially the super-weird one I wrote that very morning, an offbeat, unjustified, too-cute twist on a slight premise, had no possible shot. And you just know it. You know you're dead. And they read it and, yeah, it makes you sweat. After this you wait outside Lorne's office. I was never invited in, not once in three and a half years, and of course that is fine . . . I don't know, maybe I could have learned something about what they were looking for. It did bother me how many of Lorne's assistants were in there, piping up about their favorite comedy sketches and what would work in the show come Saturday. What made them experts? All the comedy they'd written? Burned out beyond burning, I would walk out of Rockefeller Center after dark and try to remember where I "lived."

Thursday and Friday, the production effort took over—building sketches, and some bit of rewriting, making choices. This was actually a chance to help, and I wanted badly to do that, to earn my keep. I may have pretended to be cooler than this pablum, but if you asked me if I could do anything to make the pablum happen, I'd stand up and salute, ready to go, happy to be used for anything.

Suddenly it's Saturday and things are getting fake-exciting! You're exhausted, the host is scared (unless it's Tom Hanks), and there's going to be a show whether anyone likes it or not. By this point I was done with it. Even the comedy I'd liked on Tuesday had stopped being funny to me by Saturday (except Dana Carvey doing "The McLaughlin Group"). On occasion I would go home before the actual live show started and watch from my apartment, sneering through tears.

Sunday would be a day to wander Central Park, numb, looking for scraps of comic premises for the next week. I would sometimes go to the old Improv comedy club on Forty-fourth Street and do a set, just to get some laughs: "Hey, I'm funny again!" for five minutes, but it meant a lot to me. It refilled my cup even just a little. And I often wandered around Central Park with my old friend from Chicago Jeff Garlin, and he'd put the whole thing in perspective. Jeff never thought *SNL,* or any-thing, was bigger than we were. He'd remind me that funny stuff is funny stuff and it can be simple and obvious. Until Adam Sandler came to *SNL* and reminded all of us that we could simply be goofballs to get laughs, I needed that perspec-tive, lots and lots of perspective. I'd breathe in one full breath and head back to "the Show" Monday morning to do it again. These were the days when I wished I had heroin! Just a taste!

Me with my first Emmy Award for Not Helping
Very Much at *SNL.*

My grades for the *SNL* experience: a solid C-minus, but with an A for effort (I know it didn't look like I was trying) and an F for citizenship. I owe Lorne tuition for keeping me on board all those years. Three full years of sketch-comedy col-lege, surrounded by valedictorians, and me trying, with every-thing I had, to grasp the tricks of the trade. The show might have been a hodgepodge, but greatness was to be had, and I noticed when it was. Jim Downey wrote the "First CityWide Change Bank" commercial parodies that lodged in my brain matter, a comedy spore that grew into a bunch of *Mr. Show* sketches years in the future. The "Change Bank" spots were two dry, testimonial-style commercials for a bank that *only makes change,* and those simple pieces made me rethink *where to look* for comedy material. Jim had made comedy from the sober, serious tone of these bank commercials. Later, "Rich Guys Negative Ads," at *Mr. Show,* and "Manson," at *The Ben Stiller Show,* are two pieces that I owe to this lesson learned. At *SNL,* Jack Handey was the favorite writer among the writers. His "Robot Repair" sketch is an example of comic perfection, and right up there with "The Audition," which is one of the best sketches from *Mr. Show.* Al Franken had mastered sketch and could turn an idea into a usable script with good form right before my eyes, and of course Smigel could do the same trick. I was lucky to be there and lucky to be kept around, and every summer I would put what I'd learned to some use on-stage in Chicago.

Ah, Chicago! The Wind up My Skirt

It would take about two weeks to come down from the pressurized atmosphere of *SNL.* I had a system that served me well in bouncing back: I would head back to Chicago to get onstage with my wildest ideas.

That first summer, after *SNL* had been cut short by a Writers Guild strike, Robert, Conan, and I left the picket lines and mounted our rejected *SNL* sketches at the Victory Gardens Theater under the name *Happy Happy Good Show.* Sound like fun? It was.

We did a scene about an improvisational puppet group, pok-

ing fun at Del Close and his acolytes. Conan and I played a
"two-man-performer"—two men who do the work of one
actor. Conan made facial expressions, I did the vocalizations.
Other bits included "In the Year 2000"—later a running bit on
Conan's talk show—and "The Superfans." Robert loves Chicago, almost more than I do, but then, he didn't have to grow
up there. We had fun celebrating/ridiculing the over-the-top
love of "da Bears" and Coach Mike Ditka, at this particularly
wild-eyed period of fandom. One sketch from *Happy Happy*,
entitled "Nude Beach," would make a rousing comeback on
the Matthew Broderick episode the following season, a great
sketch in my book (this book).

Robert Smigel and me on the picket lines for the
WGA, 1988. I barely got a job and already I'm
striking—the moxie!

In my second summer back in Chicago, I worked with my
friend and co-writer Tom Gianas to script that Eric Bogosian/
Bob Newhart mashup I'd always dreamed of—a solo show
with short pieces that were sometimes just monologues, sometimes acted out with the ol' fourth wall solidly in place. The
show was called "Half My Face Is a Clown," and the print ad

featured a photo of me with half of my face painted as a clown. The note of absurdity in that was a good representation of the show itself: it was absurd and down-to-earth in equal measure. In Chicago's theater-supporting goodness, I drew an audience—and I even got a good review. I did a monologue about getting temporarily held in a city jail, a suburban boy's descent into hell for two hours that he experiences as years in captivity. I recited poetic bombast celebrating Chicago: "City of the Big Shoulders! Hog Butcher for the World! Capo di tutti crapini! Where slush comes to melt! Making witches' tits seem warmer since 1942!" I even did some tumbling in a tight bodysuit, which demanded laughter—there could be no other human response. This show was my own strange back door into a spot on Second City's revered main stage. What happened was, Joyce Sloane let Tom and me put our little experience on at the ETC theater (the smaller theater in the back). Why she gave us this chance is beyond reason, but as I'd find out, she liked to shake things up once in a while. She was a real producer, with vision—she saw possibilities that were not obvious, and she probably liked to piss people off to keep them on their toes. So then, a few months after our triumph, she hired Tom to be the director of the next main-stage revue, a big opportunity. This caused all manner of heck as people asked, "What the hell? What's *he* ever done?!" Tom turned this intramural drama into a teapot-sized tempest by asking me to join the cast.

I couldn't say no to the call-up from ol' Second City, the stinky, cruddy, dark, and hallowed joint that had compelled me to dream of this life in the first place. I wanted the smell of old wigs and rancid beer to fill my nostrils. You haven't smelled wigs until you've smelled old wigs. I wanted rat poop in my stage shoes. I wanted the whole ego-elbow-throwing interne-cine battling of actors vying for a paying gig in a secondary market . . . and I got it. The comedy I'd get to make at Second City was solid, and the backstage drama was legendary. And, in the course of this little trick, I wrote the best thing I'd ever write for ol' *SNL,* at least if we're to believe some magazine's rating contest.

So I agreed to Tom's offer to help write the next Second City main-stage show *while* I was still writing at *SNL,* and then to open that SC show and perform in it, all summer, returning to *SNL* in the fall. I did not tell the management that I was going in for this double dip. I didn't want to bother anyone about it. So, for half of season 15 (1989–90), I was a ghost of a phantom of a shadow in the desperate halls of Rockefeller Center.

After Wednesday's read-through at Rockefeller Center, I'd fly to Chicago and arrive at the theater in time to do the improv set at Second City. I'd stay in Chicago Thursday and Friday, doing writing meetings with the cast during the day, join the improv set at night, then, on Saturday, fly back to New York and go right to the seventeenth floor in time to "help" put that week's episode on. Basically, I walked around till enough people saw me so that I had witnesses that I was "working" "there." It was fun to be getting away with something.

The truth is that Robert could easily cover for my small contributions to that week's show. That summer at Second City, more than anything before it, pointed me in the direction I needed to go. My own material. And at least the chance to perform, which squared the circle for me. I revered writing, but performing completed the journey. It was the payoff for the pain of writing! That summer, doing the Second City main-stage show that I helped write, I had the most fun a person onstage can have, watching the magical twirling ding-dong lunatic humanity of one Christopher Crosby Farley.

Second City: The Side Entrance

I still had another year to go at *SNL,* my best year, which I will get to, but first we need to discuss Mr. Farley.

"Second City is not the post office. You don't just put in your time and move up," Joyce Sloane told Tom Gianas, amidst the swirl of angry vibes we both endured when we said yes to Joyce's offer. We were cutting in line by joining the next big revue, him as director, me in the cast. We hadn't "paid our dues" in the Second City system—years of touring companies, taking classes, sniping and grousing and, oh yeah, spending hours upon hours improvising. There's not a lot of money on the line, so everyone gets paid in ego boosts, status bucks, visible and mostly invisible increments. It's a hothouse of hotheads!

"I hated you. It was really disruptive to all of us, and especially to me personally," said Mark Beltzman, a Second City stalwart who'd been paying his dues for years before I cut in line in front of him. A contingent of actors went to Joyce's office to register their disgust, and she told 'em (and I'm paraphrasing here), "Go on, then, if you don't like it. The streets have plenty of room for out-of-work actors: you can improvise soliloquies to the squirrels in the park till the Shakespeare statue arises to give you a standing O." What a lady.

This cast included Jill Talley, the funniest woman in Chicago, and one of the great comic performers in all American comedy in my lifetime. Jill had been in Robert's All You Can Eat crew and in *Happy Happy Good Show,* and later she was our go-to sure-thing superfunny guaranteed laugh-getter in *Mr. Show.* Jill is undeniable and, like Jan Hooks, an unsung comic actor of whom I sing here and now. Jill was on my side in this whole imbroglio, because we'd worked together in All

You Can Eat and also she just didn't give any shits. Tim Meadows was in this new cast, and we got along because Tim is nice, *and* funny—it's rare, but it can happen. Farley had gotten hazed himself, after being brought up to the main-stage show from out of nowhere, by none other than Del Close.

Del directed the revue that was still running, a loopy spectacular with an extended, nonsense-heavy scene called "Whale Boy," in which Chris played a boy . . . raised by whales? I can't quite remember. Chris moved like a fish across the stage, exuberantly leaping and exhibiting the most elegant, port de bras movements with his chubby, flowing arms. Farley could move like a ballerina. He could also fall just as gracefully, or as hard, or as in between—whatever got the biggest laugh. I'll never forget seeing him the first time, doing this scene, and how undeniable he was. Undeniably funny, undeniably likable, undeniably mesmerizing. Anyway, Del loved Chris, so Chris was in. Tom liked me, so I was in. Joyce liked Tom, so he was in. Once again, just like on that day seven years earlier, Del and Joyce were a one-two punch leading me forward in my insane, unstoppable quest for the holy grail—to be part of a cool and unique comedy show, preferably one that never grew bigger than cult status.

While I had not stood in line for the Second City dream, being backstage was no less a thrill to me. I was slop-struck at the hoarded props, costumery, and hats, and the rank odor of some thirty years of funny people hanging out and thinking of funny things to do. In fact, it was a bigger thrill than *SNL*'s pro-style corporate-comedy vibe. This was where the greats had begun their quests: Bill Murray and Harold Ramis and Fred Willard and Catherine O'Hara and Joe Flaherty and Gilda Radner and the list really goes on and on. It smelled and felt *right* to me. I was back in the back of the class, the basement.

Dave Pasquesi was the keeper of the artistic flame, and a

renowned purist in the Del school of improv. Dave was the one person who could improvise a scene that was show-worthy. Tim O'Malley was well trained in this work, and a great Chicago-guy presence, relatable and solid. Holly Wortell had a funny, smart, cultured presence and could play onstage with anyone. That said, Dave and Tim were the ones with bunched panties about my inexplicable arrival. I got elbowed in the ribs during a blackout onstage, and one time Pasquesi scolded me for playing an extremely dumb character ("Play to your intelligence" is an improv maxim, one that I don't agree with), but I soldiered on.

The harshest blows were the glares as I would walk around the theater in those first few weeks—that and the silk scarves that all actors wear, knotted up and thrown at my head as I walked past. You know what? Silk doesn't hurt! Not even when you roll it into a tight ball! So, joke's on you. I withstood the resentment and we put up a show. It was a good show—not great. Tom Gianas would mount exceptional revues without me or Farley, and with less headwind, in the years to come. But our show featured the best sketch I'd written up to that point, Chris as Matt Foley, the motivational speaker.

The Shining

So, this happened.

One night, during the improv set, Jill Talley and Chris Farley and I were slapping each other around, to the delight of the drunk audience who stayed late (the improv set at Second City is free and starts after the scripted revue). There were some good laughs, and everybody was watching Farley because . . . how could you not? Suddenly, in the midst of it all, I had a weird sensation, and a tingling in my crotch, and a ghost pumpkin appeared in the air before me and said, "You know

what—you might be better onstage if this were a drama."
Okay, well, I'm making up the ghost pumpkin, but I did have
this stray and grandiose thought—that my presence, while
comic enough to wrangle some laughs, was probably a bit too
complicated for the fun simplicity that stage comedy embraces.
It was a stray, existential flash of insight—sometimes called
"the shining," and usually suggestive of budding psychosis or
full-fledged dementia. Still, I finished improvising the scene,
Farley fell down at some point, everyone laughed, the lights
dimmed, and I let that little heart wind/soul whisper/brain fart
drift back into the ether . . . sort of. It left a mark. Drama? Me?
Who knows? I liked comedy too much to test the waters.

In one improv set, Chris played a high school coach hectoring the student body about not doing drugs. "Look at you
kids! You got nothing going on! You're losers, the lot of ya!"
He pushed his glasses up and swaggered around, visibly sweating for the pleasure of the audience. It was a hilarious character, and he had done versions of it his whole life. I imagine it
was an echo of every sports coach, gym teacher, and camp
counselor he'd ever had, and saying the same things they'd told
him: "Look at you, you're headed to nowhere, you clown! You
loser!" Everybody always had a lecture for Chris about how he
was messing up his life. Chris would let his interior monologue
out throughout his day: wherever you were, whatever you
were talking about, he'd interrupt it with put-downs of himself. He'd say "I'm a retard" or "Fatty fall down," and then
he'd fall down, wherever you happened to be—walking down
the street in public, in the middle of the day, even if he landed
right in a dirty, wet puddle and had to spend the rest of the day
in wet pants. Anything for a laugh. ANYTHING. And there
were a ton of laughs. Right up to the end. And the end was no
mystery, right from the start.

The night after seeing Chris improvise that angry coach's hectoring speech, I sat down on my mattress, which was on the floor, because I didn't waste money in those days on bed frames. I was only in town for two months before *SNL* started up again, and I wasn't buying furniture. I took out a legal pad and wrote a scene for that voice. A sad fella with no life but lots of spirit, who uses his own abject misery as the prime driver for excellence. When I grew up in Naperville, there was a group of hippie types who hung out by the bridge over the sluggish, brown DuPage River—and I pictured that very spot for a desperate middle-aged loser to park his van and contemplate his empty, broken life. A colorful mental picture, and Chris painted the scene well when he acted the shit out of it the next day at rehearsal, and then every single time it was done onstage, seven times a week.

The sketch was done the way I'd written it, except for the million flourishes of performance that Chris did, varied every time he performed it, every move adding character, tension, surprise, laughs.

My daughter, when she was eight or so, asked me, "What's the best time you ever had doing your job?" I answered, "Doing a scene with Chris Farley seven times a week at Second City." Chris was on a mission *every night:* to crack up the other performers, everyone onstage, and the audience would follow. I hate it when performers "break"—usually it is a cheap ploy by the performer to be all chummy with the audience and cajole an easy laugh. But Chris made me break. He kept going with the exaggerated character mannerisms, adjusting his glasses, flopping his sweaty hair around, yanking his belt up, wobbling side to side, then getting right in your face, sputtering and licking his lips, a lovable mad dog. Many nights he picked up Tim Meadows and swung him around, just as he did with David

Del Close and Chris Farley backstage at Second City (rats not pictured).

Spade on *SNL,* and for the same reason—to push Tim to laughter. When he spat, "Dad, you'd do me a big favor if you'd just shut your yapper!" at me, from two inches away, it was the greatest show ever on earth. No one will ever beat it, and no video can do it justice. I've never seen a piece that absolutely swept an audience up so completely. By the time those few minutes were over, every person in that audience was thoroughly in love with Chris Farley.

Lorne dropped in to see the show later in the summer and, given that he's no dummy, soon Chris and Tim would be joining the cast at *SNL.* And maybe, just maybe, he saw me onstage, heard that I wrote that killer scene, and thought, *Okay, I didn't completely get it wrong with this Odenkirk fella.*

The Corniest Story Ever Told

The worst part of watching Chris's downfall play out over the next few years was the inevitability of the whole damn thing. It drove me nuts. His rise to fame, blazing moments, assured destruction—it played out just as everyone said it would. Said it to his face. Even back at Second City, I'd watch Chris stumble off into the night after killing it onstage and my mind would write "taken from us too soon!" and all that. Someone would say, "Chris, you're gonna kill yourself if you keep this up!" and it was the billionth time he'd heard it. It didn't help that, usually, the person predicting his terrible doom was someone Chris knew was envious of his talent and skyrocketing career.

Chris tried. He did fight back. But he also, not so secretly, embraced and even maybe found purpose in fulfilling the hackneyed arc of it all.

One time Chris was drunk. Nothing special there. It was an afternoon, late in our run, a Sunday thing . . . could have been Monday, I'm not sure why. I was at Second City with my girlfriend at the time, Claire, so it was some kind of social event that would have brought everyone to the theater on a weekend. A memorial service. Alumni were always dying of kidney-related issues, but what matters to this telling is that Chris was getting loud and random—still being funny, but his loud, drunken antics were grating on people and the whole thing was escalating. When Claire and I arrived, Chris had opened his jacket to show us his secret stash of two full bottles of white wine in the inner pockets. He finished both, quickly, and soon after that he began tossing furniture through the air. I saw Second City regulars share a "not this again" look. They were afraid of his behavior, but even more, they were tired of it. It was new to me! I offered to walk home with him. It was not even a block to his place at the time. His apartment looked like a basement after a flood: clothes strewn about, takeout food packages remaining long past health code limits. He was still in a woolly mood, and Claire, who had walked with us, wisely decided to wait outside his apartment while Farls and I went inside so I could be cleaned and gutted. As she told me later, "I couldn't tell if he was angry or just being funny." Both, of course. Once inside his apartment, Chris started upending the furniture again—man, he could throw a couch! Outside the room, listening to the rumble, Claire seriously considered calling the police. I wasn't sure how to defuse it, so I just kept ducking and talking to him. Then, suddenly, Chris just stopped, got real emotional and timid, looked into my eyes, pleadingly, and asked me, "Odie . . . do you think Belushi's in heaven?"

Ah—the eternal question. Is John Belushi in heaven . . . playing chess with Abraham Lincoln? I was stumped. There were a lot of presumptions in there, but I was thankful that he was suddenly calm, and hoping it would maintain.

It took me a moment. "No, Chris, *nobody* is in heaven, because there is no heaven."

I didn't say that. I didn't want to burst his bubble. As Matthew 18:3 instructs us, Chris was truly "like a child." (And look how well that turned out for him! Nice job, Matty—ya really blew it.)

"I don't know, Chris. I guess so." I tried to reassure him: "Yeah. I mean, probably. Now, put down the recliner."

Honestly, looking in Chris's face when he asked that question was heartbreaking. The cartoon heaven Chris was clinging to would not be helpful in finding a healthier way to live.

But it's also true that Chris tried. A few years later, at a random party in Hollywood, I saw him among a crush of bodies. He was with Spade, and they were just passing through . . . I couldn't believe when he turned down drinks like a champ. He said, "No, thanks," and he meant it. It was a rare moment when I thought Chris might conquer his demons and get a chance to make the most of his life. It was a moment, nothing more.

Chris Farley and me backstage at Second City during a show.

The last time I saw Chris was clearly going to be just that. He was in a limo parked in an alley in Aspen, Colorado, with a neon sign on the hood that was flashing LAST CHANCE TO SAY GOODBYE.

Chris was in Aspen to do cocaine and attend the *SNL* twenty-umpteenth-anniversary thing. He'd told his limo driver to pull up behind the bar where David and I were hosting a "*Mr. Show* Is Still Happening" party. Someone tapped me on the shoulder—"Farley's out back and he wants to say hi." I went out there—not sure why he wouldn't just come in, probably so he wouldn't be bothered by the regulars.

Then I saw the limo sitting there. Chris opened the window. A bad scene inside. Crammed into the seats were four strangers beside Chris. One of them I recognized as the skeevy guy who'd offered David Cross cocaine a few hours earlier. Chris looked like a big zit, about to pop. Red, bloated, stubble-faced, and sweating profusely.

We chatted, and the whole time I'm thinking, *Goodbye, my*

friend. Chris picked up on what I was sending back; he'd been getting this look of forlorn pity all weekend, I'm sure. Should I have grabbed him by the lapels and shouted, "You're throwing it away, man! Kick these shitty people out of your limo and get to rehab tonight!" I considered it. But I also knew that he'd heard all of it, so many times. What good would it do to tell him again that he needed help?

I watched the limo pull away and a few weeks later we all had a funeral.

What a dumb story.

Shit.

Look at Me Go!—My Last Season at *SNL*

I got ahead of myself there.

After my summer at Second City, there was one more year of *SNL* for me.

The confidence I regained every summer in Chicago reliably put the wind in my sails that main-stage summer, perhaps even more because that stage was a childhood dream come true. Once everyone calmed down and we were performing the show, and it was getting laughs, it was the closest to what I'd yearned for, the closest to pure joy in showbiz, since I started dreaming this thing. A buncha funny people goofing off, professionally, and nobody lost in the mix. It made me less intimidated by the big New York show, and with new voices coming in to *SNL* who needed some help, I was able to put my hard-earned knowledge of SNL's "needs" to some use.

Farley, Sandler, Rock, Schneider, and Spade made me feel like I had something to offer, and I was happy to help them put together some of their new ideas. Sandler, most of all, made me see the show, and comedy, in a new and better way, because Adam was having a good time. The intimidation factor of

SNL, of the big time, of more experienced people around him, did *not* faze Adam. He would happily pitch the thinnest of notions, and he had a blast doing it, and his good energy was infectious. I needed some of that. It was the opposite of this brainy math-problem pursuit of the "craft" of sketch writing, and a great reminder that, especially in comedy, performance matters more than writing or ideas. Loony behavior trumps clever constructions. . . . Of course, if you have both, well, then you got something truly great.

That year I helped Chris Rock write and produce his Nat X talk-show bits, wrote a funny commercial for "British toothpaste" (loaded with sugar—which Lorne, the biggest Anglophile of all time, hated *sooo* much), and got yelled at by Jeremy Irons, who, when reading the monologue we'd written for him—I think it was me and Schneider—got really peeved: "I mean, I can sing, I can *dahnce,* I can spin plates, I can recite *Shake*speare, and you have me doing *THIS*?!" He wasn't wrong; it was weak. I wrote something about the soldiers returning from Operation Desert Storm and each receiving a not very personal television tribute, and the best scene I wrote that got on was George Steinbrenner as a mini-mart owner who can't fire anyone and has *wayyy* too many employees. In this, my third and a half year, I was as good as I was going to get for "the Show," and the falling short didn't bother me nearly as much anymore.

I made plans to move to L.A. and start from the ground up, with a healthy sense that it wasn't me and it wasn't the show— *SNL* and I just weren't meant for each other. For at least two seasons I thought I could make it work by sweat or stroke of luck, that I might hit some kind of stride—but I could finally admit that wasn't in the cards, and I didn't feel bad about it, either.

I didn't feel like I needed to bother Lorne, but Robert said I should tell him I was outta there. It was a short call, and he did not scoff at my desire to perform; he clearly likes the spotlight, too. Gee, I felt bad that I'd wasted his time, been such a gnat in his bonnet. Leave the man's bonnet alone! From the start, I had wanted to be part of a team that made the show its own. But that show is bigger than any team. It's justifiably a juggernaut, and it's hard to wrangle it into any writer's personal voice. Only Michael O'Donoghue and Adam McKay seemed to me to have done some version of this: been a "star writer" whose work is distinctive and takes the show in a unique direction.

Basically, I had to realize that I wanted what every comedy writer wants: my own damn show.

Chris Farley was there that season, and that was something remarkable. The first breakout moment for Chris was the "Chippendales Audition" sketch on the Patrick Swayze–hosted episode in season 16. It was a huge bummer to me to see that scene get on the air and get such attention. I know it confirmed Chris's worst instincts about being funny, which was how he proved his worth—that getting laughed *at* was as good as getting a laugh. Writers I knew and respected defended this sketch because it had a funnyish idea buried in it: the Chippendales judges prefer Swayze's dancing over Chris's but can't put a finger on why. But that idea is not what produced the gales of cackling (and gasps) from the live audience. Chris flopping his overstuffed body around did that. I feel like I can see it on his face in the moment when he rips his shirt off. Shame and laughter are synthesized in the worst way.

Fuck that sketch.

Lorne allowed Chris to do the "Motivational Speaker" scene the following year, after I'd moved to L.A. It's common for performers to bring characters to *SNL* from their beginning stages—the Groundlings or wherever that may be. But this was more than a character; the sketch was done verbatim from what we did at Second City, except for Chris destroying the table, which Robert Smigel added for a big final moment. The sketch worked just as it did back at Second City: everyone watching was won over forever. I am happy it's a reference point, often *the* reference point, for his work on *SNL*. The audience is definitely laughing *with* him on that one.

I watched it slaughter from my sunny L.A. home. A great feeling, but I didn't for a second think I'd left New York too soon. In fact, I'd arrived in L.A. just in time.

I owe *SNL* so much. I had quietly, excruciatingly learned the components of a good sketch and developed a sense of structure that gave me confidence and led to all my best sketch work still to come. Lorne had subsidized my education in sketch writing, and now he would see NONE of the benefits. Poor fella. I took my diploma and ran.

Chapter 5

L.A., Comedy, Year Zero

————

I left *SNL* certain that I had a couple years of pain and re-building ahead. Figuring out L.A. in every capacity—the biz, the secret routes around town—it was a city that made the Chicago boy in me very nervous. Would I be forced to eat sprout sandwiches and write friendly jests for dreaded awards shows? Would they insist that I surf? NO! I draw the line at surfing! I was afraid of the John Denverishness and "good vibes" that I associated with Los Angeles, all that horrid soft-serve culture from my seventies childhood. Leaving *SNL* is hard to do: it's a job, it pays, but more than that, you spend your time ridiculing everything that comes out of L.A.! Now I would be forced to make pop culture. "Blecch!" as *Mad* mag-azine put it.

I really had no idea what I would do once I landed in L.A., but I'd saved a bag of loot working at *SNL,* so I had a cushion. I decided to do a stopover in Austin, Texas, to visit my Monty Python super-pal Steve Meisner, and we stayed up late watch-ing videotapes of a new show on the also new Fox network. Steve had recorded the entire first season of *Get a Life,* which I would describe as a sitcom turned inside out. *Get a Life* had just enough sweetness and heart to it to keep it from being de-constructionist absurdist art, but it was more commentary than not. If you knew the sitcom conventions of the past thirty years, the show was making fun of them, broadly and rudely. I loved it.

In my final season at *SNL,* I had watched *Get a Life* on Sunday nights; it would be my last laugh before heading back to the grind for the week. It made *SNL* feel almost uncool, like there might be a place to reinvent comedy outside of 30 Rock. But I knew it wasn't exactly setting the ratings house on fire. *The Simpsons* had begun a year before, and it was rightfully seen as the most important new American comedy show; the door at that show had been opened to me a year before, but I was wary of it. Animation seemed like a lot of work—no time to focus on my own material. I was right about that—animation allows for numerous rounds of rethinking and rewriting and the *Simpsons* writers I knew put in long days with no time for doing their own projects on the side. My whole life is side projects! I wouldn't have survived the focus the show demanded, but I was in awe of what they were creating.

Anyway, after bingeing the first season of *Get a Life* till 2 A.M., Steve claims I jumped up and announced, with great certainty, "I'm going to work for THIS show!" He remembers being annoyed at my disturbingly unfounded confidence, like I was having a psychotic break.

The next morning I woke up on the couch to find a phone message from my agent, a young go-getter named Ari Emanuel.

Ari said, in his curt, shouting-out-the-window-of-a-passing-car manner, "Hey, Bobby! There's a show called *Get a Life*—do you know it?"

"Yeah, Ari, I watched it all ni—"

"They want to offer you a job on it! Do you want to write for it?"

"Y—"

He'd hung up. He just needed to hear the first letter of that word. Ari was in a hurry, and still is. He's done all right for himself—as of this writing, Ari represents most of the elements in the periodic table.

I then called my friend Steve and asked him to please take a break from his day job and give me a ride to the airport—I was needed ASAP to write for that show I'd screamed about the night before. He didn't really believe me, but he was probably a little scared of my alternate-reality pronouncements and wanted me out of the house. I called him later that night after my interview to tell him I'd gotten the job. That's some weird Norman Vincent Peale visualization shit, and I don't blame him for being unnerved and put off.

So I had a job before I landed in L.A. And a damn good one, too, on a show that I loved. At the age of twenty-eight, I was still finding myself. I still am, and I have given up feeling bad about that. The show itself, *Get a Life,* was actually in the process of losing its purpose, and I wish it hadn't gotten wobbly right when I got there, but it did. I still had a great time.

The first season of *Get a Life* is simply magic. The main character, Chris, is a bold man-child who lives with his parents and steps out into the world with a big smile and the brain of a small, capricious insect. Only Chris Elliott could have made the character as likable as he did—it was a version of the character he'd played on segments of *Late Night with David Letterman.* Bob Elliott, Chris's real-life father and one half of Bob and Ray, played the dad, so I would get to meet one of my comedy heroes. Only very briefly, but still . . . good for me.

In the first, and much better, season of the show, the absurd scenarios are built around friendly premises and sweet/stupid moments: Chris gets the keys to "the big city," Chris finally receives the model kit for a two-man submarine that he sent away for when he was ten, Chris gets the lead in the community play—this, by my estimation, is the best episode of all: "Zoo Animals on Wheels." These story ideas were a comedy writer's dream—the place your brain goes at 2 A.M. when you're tired and making each other laugh. Adam Resnick and Chris Elliott had written the initial pilot while at *Letterman. Dennis the Menace* was their touchstone—an early-sixties sitcom where the kid provoked plot with his troublesome machinations. David Mirkin, an established sitcom writer, shepherded the project through network battles and had his work cut out for him getting a second season to happen as it struggled to find enough comedy writers to watch it to jack up those Nielsen ratings numbers.

How lucky was I to be arriving in L.A. just as ol' Rupert Murdoch was creating the mess he called the Fox network, America's fourth network! It would never work—who needs FOUR options of television programming—it's too much! The best thing about Fox at the time was they had no idea what they were doing. Awkward beginnings are when good things can still happen. Once a network knows what works, well . . . chances are no longer taken. Something beautiful dies with success: the freedom to flail. But for now, and for the next few years, Fox would flail, and I would benefit. I've learned that, just like Del, "I belong in struggling organizations."

Meta Life

During the abbreviated second season (13 episodes) of *Get a Life,* I was living the L.A. comedy-writer dream. In the morning I'd take the meandering drive over Laurel Canyon (I bet Jim Morrison vomited in those bushes once!), then get waved through the security gate on a real "film lot," the classic CBS

Radford, where they filmed *The Mary Tyler Moore Show,* and I'd park where my name, correctly spelled, was painted on a cement parking block. A parking spot named after me? Hollywood magic. Across the ravine from my parking spot was a small, legendary swamp where *Gilligan's Island* had been shot out. I'd head into the "office," where, for the next few hours, I pretended to be a real sitcom writer on a not-so-real sitcom, and I would eat snacks. Eating snacks is part of being a real sitcom writer—that and asking "When's lunch?"

I laughed a lot in that writers' room. Just not necessarily at the comedy plots that were being bandied about and too quickly put up on cards to be turned into script. It was a strong group of comic minds. Adam Resnick, one of the funniest men alive. The distinctive genius screenwriter Charlie Kaufman. Jace Richdale and Steve Pepoon, both solid comedy writers, and David Mirkin led the room. David had a real L.A.-in-the-seventies vibe, not a bad thing in itself, and he had an impressive résumé. He also drove an Italian sports car that cost more than the house I grew up in—and throw in my college tuition as well. He had long hair, wore jeans every day, and had a mustache. A mustache! In 1991! All he needed was a hot tub and the picture would have been complete. However old-fashioned he looked, he very much wanted to make something groundbreaking. The problem was that it wasn't the same ground that Adam and Chris had wanted to break. David often name-checked *The Young Ones* as an inspiration for what the show could be. *The Young Ones* was an early-eighties BBC comedy that had a confrontational vibe, where *Get a Life,* especially in its first season, had an innocence to it. I'd watched and appreciated the first season, but now it was getting more absurd, and even kind of mean-spirited.

One great thing was that I got to meet Bob Elliott and thank him for the wonderful work of his career. When the show was canceled, I had had fun but hadn't learned much about actual sitcom writing, because *Get a Life* was really a mock sitcom. Ironic distance infused everything about the show. The characters, the plot twists . . . we wallowed in meta-ness. So: I was in L.A., but I hadn't sold out! I was keeping genuine expression at arm's length—something I tried to maintain for my whole career but failed to do. After a while you just can't keep not being genuine; you run out of gas.

L.A. was okay by me. I liked having a lawn and a car, I liked that the city quieted down every evening (except when it was in the midst of a full-scale riot). L.A. was a lot less intimidating than New York. My girlfriend came from Chicago to live with me. Claire was an actress, and after almost a decade in Chicago, she was willing to give L.A. a shot. We had met as extras on a bad movie. I did the job of extra—excuse me: "background artist"—two or three times, just to get the vibe of a real film set, and this was a particularly crap movie that starred Jim Belushi, but it was in Chicago in the eighties, so what do you want? Claire and I made it through those cold Chicago early days together, and had been on and off, mostly on, when I was in New York. Over the next two years in Los Angeles, as she worked to get her acting career going—one of the hardest things to do—my busyness and success would strain our relationship. When I got done writing for the day at *Get a Life,* I would prepare for my weekly show in a theater in Santa Monica.

It's shocking but true: there *are* theaters in L.A.! If you want to get better as a performer, to get bolder, they are there, empty, waiting for you to sweat it out and find yourself, safely, with no one watching. So I started doing my one-man show *Show-Acting Guy!* at a theater in Santa Monica every Saturday night.

Me and Tom Gianas and the great George Takei, shooting a demo of my one-man show *Show-Acting Guy!* It never saw the light of day and therefore, I can assure you, is a masterpiece.

I told jokes and did monologues with acting attached, alone onstage, until a friend from the early days in Chicago butted in. Andy Dick and I had shared some really fringe stages back in Chicago. Andy had a delightful zaniness that paired well with my yelling at him. We'd invent improv setups backstage and serve 'em up hot, right off the brainpan, and some of those bits became solid scenes that we did for the next few years. In one, Andy played my "student" who, for his final test, will take part in my "Master Improvery" exercise. First I'd take suggestions from the audience—random suggestions, lots of them, for locations, film styles, relationships, professions, ANYTHING. Next I'd invite Andy to improvise a scene, alone, and I would feed him these prompts. Random as they were, going faster and faster: "Living room! Hitchcock! Father/daughter! Dr. Seuss! Iceland!" It was chaos. Andy would try to incorporate the suggestions, but he would end up crying and then yelling at me, completely out of his mind, enraged. I'd watch stoically, then hug him and announce, "You just graduated—congratulations!" It was fun for us, and the audience didn't leave the building. Janeane Garofalo was one of the audience members who loved how Andy and I wasted time onstage. She brought her new friend Judd Apatow to see us, and from that connection we all ended up doing *The Ben Stiller Show* together. Good stuff starts in dumb places.

So, have I finally mentioned Janeane Garofalo?

It's about time.

Janeane was the spark of the big bang, of a comedy reinvention that still resonates. Off-the-cuff, "real," impromptu, personal, disarming, sloppy, meandering, intimate—everything that we now prize in a good podcast. She did it first. She made it cool. Most of all, she brought everyone together. Everyone who would make comedy new and funny again.

David Cross. Margaret Cho. Patton Oswalt. Kathy Griffin. Brian Posehn. Greg Behrendt. Dana Gould. Judd Apatow. Ben Stiller. And the list goes on—right up to whatever's on Netflix this week, the week you are reading this. She'd never claim to have started the movement of "alternative comedy"; she'd never claim to start anything. Janeane epitomizes the Groucho Marx comment "I refuse to join any club that would have me as a member." She refuses to be the touchstone for this new form of comedy, or claim to be the first to do it, or take any blame at all for what would become most of the comedy you see today. But I assure you, she was the spark.

I had met Janeane a year before moving to L.A., when she was rooming with Jeff Garlin and another road comic on Genesee Avenue, across from Fairfax High School. I liked her right away. Who didn't? We all liked her, and she liked us. She was funny, smart, quick, a big reader of books, and a big fan of everyone else, a cheerleader in Doc Martens, though she didn't jump around much: those things are heavy. Like a lot of comedy writers, I don't laugh aloud at most comedy shows, even when I like what's happening. Claire noticed this among all of the comics in the "scene": "The comics wouldn't laugh out loud for each other. They would acknowledge a good joke with merely a nod." She also noticed that "the guys were relentlessly tough on the women comics." Were we? Shit. I bet we were. But in my rosy memory I just remember laughing at these funny women and wishing I had half their talent for storytelling, although I was glad to lead a less chaotic personal life. Janeane, though, she laughed—loudly and warmly and generously—at all of our efforts onstage. Often the biggest laugh in the room, sometimes the *only* laugh. I'd take it any day.

Slowly, an audience began to coalesce around all this more personal, idiosyncratic, semi-serious stuff we were all doing. Incrementally, painfully, people came to realize there could be something more to comedy—and the awareness has continued to grow to this day.

After the numbing sameness of the eighties boom, it was shocking to find audiences were willing to show up to these out-of-the-way "comedy nights" looking to be surprised by our unpredictability and exploration. I guess Janeane had an inkling this audience might be out there, or maybe it was just a shot in the dark.

This was a tight group of performers. We could, and did, often fit in one room. Sometimes it was a rooftop where we congregated, sometimes a large table at Jerry's Famous Deli, usually somebody's apartment, Dave Rath's (Rath was a funny guy who, for some reason, wanted to be a manager of comics—it takes all kinds), Cross's, or Margaret Cho's. We became such a tight gang that Karen Kilgariff suggested we have a name, specifically "The Wolverines." Do wolverines laugh at each other's jokes? Wolverines have a reputation for tearing into meat—we did that, but as I recall it, we were a new kind of wolverine: supportive and friendly.

Janeane's act was wholly improvised, political, and personal. The opposite of the comedy of the preceding twenty years, and one might note that she wasn't a guy, either. She threw a wrench into every trope. A deep self-loathing brought out the best in her: "I was a straight C student, a middle-of-the-roader in every aspect of my life. A quitter. Just a quitter." How could I not love her attitude? That's the attitude that fueled a million grunge-rock songs and painful revelations; in this case it fueled a whole new wave of comedy.

Janeane started one of the first alternative nights in the corner of Big & Tall Books, on Beverly Boulevard across from the classic old Hollywood joint El Coyote. Doing stand-up at a bookstore was a new thing, never done before that I'd seen. And why not? Books attract smart people! Set up a mic and small speaker, talk funny at people—the books don't mind. The venue is everything, and suddenly everyone was riffing on their most recent, most personal thoughts and traumas— nothing about airplane food, unless someone had had a traumatic childhood encounter with it. The scene grew slowly but picked up speed until, after about a year and a half, there was an "alternative" stage you could perform on nearly every night of the week. Bookstores, coffee shops, dying restaurants, already dead theaters.

But one show ruled them all, and it was a show that had "rules" to it, which I would usually resent, but these were good, helpful rules that led to a distinctive show. It was called *The UnCabaret,* Sunday nights in the basement of a supper club called Luna Park.

If you weren't there, then you missed it, and no amount of

me telling you about it will make it as great and powerful as it was. But what Janeane and *The UnCab* started has evolved into the sprawling, confessional, and intermittently funny podcasts that proliferate today. We, too, were "intermittently funny" and the audience liked it.

Beth Lapides and Greg Miller booked this show, and their rule was: new material every week, no club acts. Also, get personal. "Honest and not remotely funny" was prized over "packaged and killer" material. Almost everyone brought a notepad onstage so they could remember what they'd just thought of a few minutes before getting up there. The room itself was the best, designed by a genius at audience stimulation. It was in a basement beneath a restaurant, packed tight as a jockstrap on a porn star (as they say in the Vatican); it had the ideal low ceiling, with a barely raised stage, and lights that made it impossible to see the audience's eyes from the stage. You can't see them, but they can see right into your eyes, and your soul. The house was packed with . . . wait, who were these people? Where did they come from? Scenesters. Cool L.A. people. Elites! I love 'em. They knew what was up, or they had gotten lost on their way to the bathroom from the restaurant upstairs. They were a little drunk, too. I didn't get to know them by name, but they sure got to know us, because they were *focused,* not wanting to miss a thing, sensing they were at the start of something. As Todd Glass put it, "They watched us like they were at the opera."

Kathy Griffin's stories were shocking and funny. In fact, I almost couldn't believe them at all. But over time it became apparent that crazy shit happened to her on a daily basis. In a way, she was doing the purest form of this—her personal life on display, and very funny to hear about from the safety of your seat. I stayed way in back as she talked about relationships gone awry at lightning speed and shocking conflagrations. Greg Behrendt explored his yearning for coolness and swagger, in conflict with his girlie insides. Dana Gould and Patton Oswalt were both doing acts that were, especially in Dana's case, alarmingly personal, and yet both could work the regular comedy clubs with similar material—that was really surprising and didn't quite carry over to the rest of us, although Kathy eventually found a club to work her material on Tuesday nights—but that's because *the audience* was starting to change, nothing to do with the performers. Margaret Cho was also built for the self-revealing comedy that this new audience ate up. I was probably the least personal act on the stage. I wasn't about to do therapy onstage. (My therapist could barely get me to discuss personal issues—I didn't want to burden her.) I did an end run around the personal sharing . . . starting with some small moment or memory and quickly blowing it up into broader comic silliness. The performances at *The UnCabaret* would be nothing out of place in a comedy special circa 2021, but back in 1992, this was totally new, outlandish, edgy shit. Richard Lewis was the only comic who had worked this area in the Boom era before us.

Okay, there was a lot of navel-gazing, some too-dry moments, it wasn't wall-to-wall yuks. But these were funny people, and they were always aiming for laughs, and they got 'em, too. And in the end, it wasn't that mysterious, really! David Cross described "alternative comedy" simply as "comedy *without the cadence.*" Speaking of one David Cross . . .

One summer day (this is L.A., so it could've been one of those gorgeous February days, sunny but also cool; please, I invite you to hate L.A.), I was sitting down to eat a large sandwich on my couch. I remember it being quite large because I made the sandwich when I was already hungry, so I put everything into it. Cheetos, ham, turkey, mayo, A1 steak sauce, ramen noodles, my hand . . . I was about to bite into this mountain of deliciousness, Judge Judy was on television, about to scold a jerk, when there came a rapping at my screen door. The front door was open, so I could see who it was behind the screen: Janeane Garofalo herself! She had walked over to my place—she lived on Curson and I was on Martel, four blocks away.

"Hi Janeane!" I said. I was happy to see her, but not happy enough to get off my ass and open the goddamn door, but like I said, I had that sandwich in hand and one of us was going to eat the other, so . . .

"Hey, Bob. A friend of mine from Boston is here with me . . ." There was a spindly fellow standing behind her, wearing shorts and holding a basketball. I took this information in, unmoved, and she went on. "His name is David Cross. He likes to play basketball, and I told him sometimes you do, too. He was wondering if you wanted to play."

"I'm eatin' a sandwich."

They stood there, outside the screen door, Janeane Garofalo and my future and best comedy partner of all time, then walked away. The screen door never opened. I blame the sandwich.

All for One: *The Ben Stiller Show*

So the "alternative comedy scene" was feeding my heart, and I was paying the bills with a series of TV jobs, even some awards shows! Why not? A couple bucks and free lunch, and not too much of a time suck. As *Get a Life* crashed like an Italian sports car on Mulholland, I got yet another go at sketch comedy.

When *SNL* is having good seasons, it seems built on a few

good team-ups: the relationships come first, then the comedy. I had a shot at this with my next big break, *The Ben Stiller Show,* and it was the most fun I'd had making TV, and it's still a high point for me, mostly because I *wasn't* in charge.

I'd first met Judd Apatow at Sandler's apartment in North Hollywood. It was, like everything in Adam's orbit, a great time. Things could get fratty around the Sandman, and that part made me uncomfortable, but I certainly saw the attraction of the sheer fun Adam has being who he is.

Janeane dragged Judd to see my show with Andy Dick, then she dragged us all up the street to see David Cross at the Improv. (I nodded politely at his so-called "act.") Basically, Janeane cast *The Ben Stiller Show* with her comedy crawl on that night. She had incredible power at that time, and she used it well.

A brief glimpse into that special night when I first took in this "David Cross" and his "comic stylings." The Improv in Santa Monica was a typical shithole comedy club: there was nearly no crowd there—maybe fifteen people, but let's be generous and picture thirty. This would have been a Saturday night, late, maybe 1 A.M. or so. David was introduced, at his own request, as follows: "Next up to the stage is a young impersonator who just won the Southern Belle Rye Whiskey College Comedy Competition for his amazing impersonations . . . Here's David Cross!" Then David, in shorts and a ratty T-shirt, took the stage with an upbeat energy that never flagged. He had something in his hand, a metal device of some kind (in fact it was just a drink strainer), and as he approached the mic, he held the device to his throat like a cancer survivor might do with an "electrolarynx" and, maintaining his impossibly cheery go-get-'em comedy club spirit, spoke in a voice that sounded like a talking electric razor: "Allll righhht—everybody having a good time?!" The audience laughed uncomfortably, but this young laryngeal cancer survivor kept the party spirit a-croaking. "Alll riiighht, we're gonna have fun tonight!" His unstoppably happy attitude fucking killed me. He proceeded to do "impersonations" ("Jack Nicholson as your dentist! I think it would go something like this . . ."), every "voice" the same identical robotic, gravelly ham radio signal. Of course, David loved that a good chunk of the audience was uncomfortable with the idea of laughing at/with a cancer survivor. David loved to prank people . . . and this particular prank was really funny and sad, in a Chaplinesque way. I still didn't really give David the time of day when I saw him around the offices of *The Ben Stiller Show*. I was too lost in my own head. I eventually found my way out, and David was a key reason.

Fox, "the desperate network," had given Ben and Judd the time slot opposite *60 Minutes* to make a sketch show to appeal to anyone who was not watching *60 Minutes*. It was an impossible time slot for any show, might as well throw something crazy at it.

I'd read Ben and Judd's pilot script, and it was the kind of detailed parody mashup that Ben excelled at. Eddie Munster in *Cape Fear*—pop-culture reference points smashed together and whipped and served dry. Closer to *SCTV* than Monty Python, but also its own unique thing. Ben and Judd assured me I could write my own stuff, which turned out to be entirely true. I asked about the title: "Shouldn't it be something more wide open? People might think this is a talk show." They obviously didn't agree. In the end, the show was a wonderfully executed opportunity by some wonderful opportunists—all of us—and was an amazing stepping-stone for our careers. Thank you, Fox.

Judd fought the network, Ben did the directing and stuck his neck on the chopping block, and the rest of us just enjoyed ourselves. My job, which I embraced in a death grip, was to be the most indulgent, cockiest writer on the staff, and try to get better as a performer.

What responsibility accompanied the privilege of having our own show? What was Judd in his office arguing with the network about for hours at a time? At the time, I did not care; I was having too much fun doing whatever the hell I wanted. But recently, Judd enlightened me . . .

"The hardest part about the show was figuring out what to do in between the sketches. Ben was a real visionary about wanting to shoot comedic short films. He never had any interest in having a studio audience for anything. His influence was *SNL* but also *SCTV,* Albert Brooks, and Monty Python."

Ah, yes, "what to do between the sketches," the bane of every sketch show. The network wanted to know what brought it all together. How about "nothing"? Would "nothing" do? Can our show just be an extremely well-produced pop-culture pie fight? I guess if you're going to have a pie fight with someone else's money, they have a right to bother you about the pies and their planned trajectories. My recollection is that we took at least three expensive tries at "linking material" to tie the sketches together with a "hip and cool vibe." The job that Terry Gilliam's animations did so well for Python. In one attempt, Ben has romantic problems, and Janeane and Andy and I are the pals he talks to about relationship-based blah-blah, and this somehow . . . becomes sketches? In another, Ben, Janeane, Andy, and I hang out in this TV clubhouse of sorts and our witty repartee somehow . . . becomes sketches? Finally, the network settled for Judd calling his celebrity connections in to banter with Ben, Janeane, Andy, and me. At least the Fox network would have some celebs to promote the show with. Turns out there were more than three attempts at this cohesive material . . .

Judd enlightened me: "The first version of the show, the one we pitched, had Ben as the teacher at a film school, and the films would be the ones made by his fictional students and guest lecturers. That got tossed quickly." I like that one! I wish we'd done it! Somehow the desire to add narrative to a sketch show is a strong one. In the "clubhouse" attempt, Judd reminded me, "there was a minor storyline there which ended with a policeman played by John O'Donohue storming in and beating Ben after an alarm is accidentally set off. That didn't work, either, so we went MTV style: handheld chats with the cast and celebrity guests like Garry Shandling, Dennis Miller, Flea, and Sarah Jessica Parker." The best quality to this approach was that it was easy to ignore: it didn't step on the sketches, which were amazingly well produced.

What Judd was arguing about with the network was nothing that could be argued away, as Judd explained, "The head of the Fox network loved Ben. Peter Chernin. But after we were picked up, he got a promotion and we never heard from him again. His replacement did not like the pilot. I remember he disliked the 'Cape Munster' sketch, which made me realize he didn't understand the style at all. This led to me ignoring almost all of his notes." Sure, that might have provoked some disagreement.

There was one more lesson, one I'd been learning my whole career: get your stuff in front of the right audience. That's difficult to engineer, but Judd knew the *Stiller* show was doomed in the place we were at. "We were up against *60 Minutes* at seven thirty on Sundays. We were so sure it wouldn't last that all of our first commercials were Ben playing an agent character telling people, like Ian Ziering from *Beverly Hills, 90210*, that they shouldn't come on the show because it will be a disaster and Mike Wallace will crush it."

What about me? This is still my "bio"—was I helpful? Surely Judd had fond memories of me and my wonderfulness? Judd did not: "I was semi-terrified of you, because your sketches were so great and you also were really vicious if you didn't like a sketch we planned to shoot. My first job as a staff writer was as the head writer with Ben, and I was always playing catch-up. I didn't know what I was doing and worked very hard to keep that hidden from everyone who worked on the show. I had some decent instincts about editing and what was funny, but my main instinct was to shoot everything you wrote. That always served us well."

I was guilty as charged—of being viciously opinionated. This pursuit of sketch was deeply personal for me, and I look back on it now a little confused and embarrassed.

There's one more thing Judd added to this golden, faded memory. "One odd piece of trivia: Ben and I were so green that we didn't hold auditions for the cast. We just looked at each other and said, 'Who's funny? Ben, Andy, and Janeane. Okay, we're done.' We didn't meet with anyone. And the town was packed with talent. It never occurred to us to do a search. We knew we had the right people by some primal instinct."

In the end, I think we made some good stuff, some very good—but also for a very targeted audience. If Ben hadn't been such a committed actor and great director, it would have been nothing but a strange indulgence. I liked the show when it veered into more generally shared pop-culture riffs, and especially liked that they basically shot anything I wrote. The writing staff, full of nubile comic brains who would go on to make cutting-edge comedy in the coming decades, took the show in wildly varied directions. Dino Stamatopoulos and Brent For-

George Burns's office was one floor down from mine during *The Ben Stiller Show.* I went down there with my pal Mike Rowe and asked him to "turn down the vaudeville."

rester were geniuses who snuck originality past the parody—Dino's "Skank" being a prime example: a sitcom with a crabby sock puppet as the star, surrounded by real people. He was making fun of *ALF* and other cloddishly written, cloyingly emotional, cheeseball sitcoms. Jeff Kahn invented mashup parodies ("The Grungies"/"Woody Allen's Bride of Frankenstein") that made the most of the show's particular point of view and are still standouts of the whole project. *Mad* magazine and *SCTV* worked the same angle, regurgitating film and television tropes, but we did it more exactly. Far more exactly. Ben was determined to become a director above anything else, and his favorite part of the show was working with the cameras and the director of photography and nailing the looks. We had a crane shot for a *Die Hard* parody in a supermarket, and that's insane. Do you know how much a crane shot costs? More than most sketch shows would ever have in their budgets. I didn't know what a DP was (DP as in Director of Photography, as in, the guy who knows lighting and such), or what they did, but Ben was up on all the film lingo—he loved it. We were all driven to make it, but Ben was on another level.

Maybe, just maybe, this show was the most personal sketch show anyone's ever done. Ben, the son of a famous comedy team, Stiller and Meara (contemporaries of Bob and Ray, ex–Second City–ites, and future George's dad on *Seinfeld*), grew up around showbiz. Possibly he'd met Eddie Munster (the actor's name is Butch Patrick) or dreamed of being an actor on shows when he was the same age as the tiny werewolf boy. This might have been the source of Ben's intense focus on movies and television and fame. There's a little of that in all of us satirists: making fun of people and culture, pushing it away while secretly wishing we could be included.

As for me, I wrote like a writer just released from *SNL*. I figured out there was a way to do the "mashup" thing and make it smart, my best piece being "Manson," where Charles Manson (whose gibberish was familiar from his television interviews) lives with a farm family as their Lassie, the harmless dog hero of fifties TV. We nailed that one, the look is perfect, the unsettling silliness, the strange "logic" of it.

When it was at its best, *The Ben Stiller Show* was a bunch of funny friends making each other laugh. Check out the *Cops* parodies we did, which left us room to improvise, as well as "Information 411," "America's Most Suspicious," and "Three Men and an Old Man." These hold up, but better than the comedy we made was the fun we had making it. I would get up early in the morning, drive my car a few blocks over, and pick up Andy Dick, one of the funniest people I've ever met, then drive three blocks in the other direction and get Janeane, quadrupling the IQ in the car in a heartbeat. We'd drive out to

Pacific Palisades, or somewhere where the production could afford a location (somewhere far away), and shoot all day. The fumes of youth and naïveté lifted our spirits, and no one's addictions had overwhelmed them yet. Nothing was better than this experience we were having—we barely noticed the world on fire around us during the Rodney King riots. Claire remembers, "The whole city was on fire, with looting and shooting on Melrose, just two blocks from our apartment, but Bob and the cast and crew were oblivious up in the hills of Griffith Park, taping their show. They even shot during the second day of the riots. It wasn't the first time I thought comedy writers are pretty out of touch." True enough.

Judd argued us to thirteen episodes, as our subject matter and comic takes went further off the rails. The final, unfinished thirteenth episode was pure insanity, with Andy as a Willy Wonka character, and beyond that it made no sense. We won an Emmy! How about that? We won for Writing for a Variety Series, and yes, we beat *SNL* in that category. I'll admit it was a personal, vindictive triumph for us to beat the great, gilded contraption of *SNL*, with its eighteen writers, thirty-two cast members, and ten-jillion-dollar sets. I spoke to Robert Smigel, who had stayed at *SNL* writing sketches and his "TV Funhouse" cartoon pieces, and he tried to keep my expectations low. "There's no way you guys are going to win" was how he put it, I think. But I thought we had a shot, because the nominated episode of *Stiller* was very strong and not too weird. Lots of funny ideas squeezed tightly into twenty-two minutes. Next to that, *SNL*'s loping ramble would fall short. Any which way, we won. Ben gave me the envelope announcing us winners because I had written the bulk of that particular episode, and *SNL* was canceled the next week. No, wait, *we* were canceled. We'd been canceled months before the awards show even happened.

Brent Forrester, later the writer of great episodes of *The Simpsons* and *The Office*, had this to say about the too-cool-for-school gang that made the *Stiller* show: "You, Ben, Judd, Janeane, David Cross were all young tastemakers, with extremely strong opinions about comedy and a sense of what was wrong and old and lame about network comedy—that, combined with the fact that we kinda knew we were going to get canceled, gave the show a certain freedom. Because Judd just simply refused to compromise. None of you guys would compromise at all."

Ah: no compromise. I remember those days . . .

The confidence that the show gave me was key to moving forward and trying to make something great. The fact that I met David Cross on the show was the most important thing. But after the Stiller show was tucked into bed with golden statuettes, I planned to never do sketch again. I'd move into narrative and character like a grown-up man—as long as I can keep my friends together and work with people who make me laugh.

After *The Ben Stiller Show* ended, I did everything I could do to keep my friends together. "Everything I could do" means that I wrote a television show for Janeane, Andy, and me to star in. It was called *Life on Mars,* and HBO backed a pilot for it. Set in a coffee shop in L.A., it had us all playing versions of ourselves and having adventures based on some version of our lives/hopes/addictions. "Mumblecore," but funnier. In the pilot, I am a TV writer, and a famous, edgy, legendary poet (William Burroughs–ish junkie bohemian) comes to town for a reading and needs a couch to crash on. I offer mine, and he propositions me in the middle of the night; I wake up and . . . my hero hits on me. My character is mentally and spiritually toyed with. It's the comedy of embarrassment, unpleasantness, awkwardness, and fear. Picture *Girls,* but more guys than girls. Also, don't picture Andy Dick, because he chose instead to get paid a lot of money and do a reboot of *Get Smart* that was simply, objectively, awful.

It was an attempt to stretch myself, to discover a new side to myself. The problem was, at this stage of my life, I was still determinedly one-sided!

Bernie Brillstein, the King in My Corner

Besides my inexplicable confidence, *SNL* left me with some really good connections. In particular, future superagent and world crusher Ari Emanuel, for my agent, and a manager at the Brillstein agency.

After I'd been in L.A. a few months, I decided to leave my manager but got called in to the head of the management company, a legendary showbiz personality named Bernie Brillstein. *Sure,* I figured, *I'll stop by this guy's office, he'll talk past me and promise me stuff I have no interest in, and then after a few minutes, when he senses I don't care about anything he cares about, we will carry on not knowing each other.*

But I liked Bernie, right from the start.

I loved Bernie.

Weird, because Bernie was "old showbiz" through and through, and I have chewed your ear off about staid, corny old comedy . . . But it's not that at all! Really! Bernie started in the William Morris mailroom in olden times. He'd worked for a short while with Elvis himself, and, get this, he was part of the brain trust—a key part—that foisted *Hee Haw* on the saps of America in the dreaded seventies. This wonderful bastard had made that stupid show happen! And yet I liked him so much right off the bat.

But Bernie had also been a big part of *SNL*'s early days, and all that it spun out into: the Blues Brothers film as well as *The*

Muppet Show and Jim Henson's early days. Bernie loved show business, he loved creative types, he loved lunches and valet parking (he told me this, proudly), and he loved being ahead of the curve and building careers. That's where I fit into his grand scheme. His scheme, it turns out, wasn't so grand. I think that was his failing. He liked helping cool new voices find their place just as much as he liked making big, stupid money—when he *should* have liked that big, stupid money MORE! But, like everybody who is in this business for the right reasons, he couldn't help himself. He was broken that way. I felt it immediately, and we had a great time over the next decade-plus.

When I walked into Bernie's office that first day, he was on the phone, yelling at someone and smoking a long, thin Kool cigarette (look it up), I think because he thought that this some-how made the nicotine less dangerous to his overstressed body, it being "kool." He was wrong, of course. He hung up and looked at me.

"I hear you're leaving us, kid!"

He called me kid. He called many people kid, so I wasn't insulted, but liked the chumminess. The fact that he had any interest in me—why? I wasn't bringing in the big bucks. Bernie was a gambler, but he wasn't a fool. His chosen game in Vegas was craps, best odds in the casino (still terrible), but if you bet on the right mercurial oddball . . . He liked danger, is my point. I don't know anything about craps, but I was danger . . . seeing as how I only wanted to work on the fringes.

For a brief moment I helped out at the brief moment that was *The Dana Carvey Show.* Robert Smigel was producing and invited me to come to New York and write for a few weeks. The first time I was in an office with the show's writers, nearly all future superstars, everyone in the room was laughing to beat the band over an idea for the pilot episode's cold open. Dana would do his Clinton impersonation, talking about being empathetic and "feeling your pain," as Clinton was wont to do, and then he would open his shirt to reveal a set of teats, which he'd then use to feed some puppies, because he was truly that nurturing. Get it? *Holy cow, I hate that idea,* I thought as everyone was bent over laughing. I would usually speak up, but I figured that, over time, people would regulate their blood sugar and it would be seen for what it was—appalling and not funny. Besides not making me laugh, it simply didn't sound like Dana Carvey–flavored comedy to me. It was absurdist and unsettling, two things Dana is not. And that, from my point of view, was the core problem with that earnest experiment: the actual show never felt like "Dana Carvey." Which is a shame, because he is as funny and likable a performer as God bothered to manufacture, and it was a splendiferously talented group of writers and actors. But I took note of how, not unlike at the *Stiller* show, there was a lack of a "shared sensibility" among the creatives, and to top that off, the whole meringue was plopped in front of the wrong audience. The show was scheduled for the hot prime slot after *Home Improvement,* a very popular, right-down-the-middle laugh-track fest. Maybe if the better pieces from the show had been put on late night somewhere, or off on a cable channel where you had to seek it out. . . . Fringe comedy lives on the fringes for a reason, and it's where I would aim for, never the middle.

The Kids in the Hall were doing everything pretty much right in my book. Their show hung together, was distinctive, really likable, and you got to know them even while they were playing stridently strange characters. Plus they had a number of homes for the show, all in off-brand time slots and locales— right where it belonged. This made me envious and mad. Not at the guys—I liked them all—but at Canada in general. Somehow they were able to bring Canadian niceness to the brainwarping comic mayhem. How much maple syrup do I have to drink to become that nonthreatening? There isn't enough in the world.

Even Bill Hicks Can Die

On February 26, 1994, at the age of thirty-two, Bill Hicks, the abrasively funny stand-up comedian, died. I did not know him personally, but he and I had exchanged a nod and a grunt backstage at Paul Provenza's talk show *The Green Room*. The actual green room of *The Green Room* was small both actually and metaphorically—the tight circle of comedy performers doing new stuff. I had the feeling Bill knew me, and I certainly had heard of him; he was already a legend as an angry purist. He felt about stand-up the way I felt about sketch, and with him being only a year older than me, it was a kick in the pants when he shuffled off his mortal coil.

"Wait, so there's a clock on this nonsense?" Someday I, too, would become just another ghost who wouldn't be getting an "overall deal" or a pitch meeting or another chance.

It shook me. I started making hard choices. Claire and I broke up; we'd gotten engaged but were both struggling to find satisfaction in our relationship, and as time went by it felt like the stakes were rising. She points out that my "super focus" did not help build a relationship, and here I was, knowing I was about to get even more focused.

One day in the summer of 1993, my old *SNL* pal Conan O'Brien and I were shooting hoops at Fairfax High and talking about who in the world might take over for David Letterman. Letterman had ditched NBC in a huff when they picked this

Leno guy to talk to celebrities on *The Tonight Show* after Johnny Carson had had his fill of it. I think some words have been written about that mess-around already. NBC tapped Lorne to produce Letterman's replacement, and he'd tapped Conan and Robert Smigel to do the nuts and bolts of making the show. In a few days there was going to be an audition of club comics and possible host fellas (No Girls Allowed!) at the Improv club on Melrose. Conan and Robert had shared the list of names with me, the usual suspects at the time. I remember Jon Stewart and Allan Havey being near the top of the list. Conan and I were shooting hoops as we mulled over who might make a great, exciting new host. It was fun to be included in the conversation.

"Would you want to host?" Conan asked me.

Later, after he got the job, I recalled this moment and thought that Conan was asking me just to ask himself if *he* would/could host. It's an audacious ask for a comedy writer to want to be plugged in to hosting one of the only network talk shows, and taking Letterman's place was a very big deal at the time. But Conan told me recently that he truly wasn't considering himself for the job. What went on there, between him and Robert Smigel and NBC, is a story I cannot wait to read in his autobiography. (Get to it, Conan!) But he tells me now that he was just shooting the shit. Anyway, I took his query seriously and mulled it over. At that point I'd been on TV but only a little. I'd been on the *Stiller* show and done some guest appearances. I'd had tons of stage time (but needed tons more). But taking David Letterman's seat? Letterman was the sharpest tool in the shed—they would need someone with much, much more experience, presence, and confidence. Still, I imagined myself telling jokes about the day's news at the top of the show; that could be fun. Then I pictured doing "desk bits"; sure, those could be funny. Then I pictured myself talking to an actor or musician I admired. Cool. Then I pictured myself talking to an actor or musician whose work I didn't know (the great majority of them).

"No. No, I wouldn't want that job," I told him.

I had no idea he liked the idea of being a TV chatterboxer. About a week later, it was arranged for Conan to do a demo-tape hosting using the *Tonight Show* set. I was shocked that he'd be getting a screen test, and astounded when Lorne backed him. The only thing more mind-blowing was the amazing job Conan did hosting the show, and he didn't seem to mind at all talking to "celebrities," even chatted with me a few times over the years. It was a rare leapfrog over everyone that worked out perfectly.

Ari Emanuel was my first agent. I think he worked at a place called something-something-something. It doesn't matter, because the agency doesn't matter—the *agent* matters! (Same

Ari Emanuel and me, intentionally out of focus.

goes for managers.) Ari and I spent a lot of time on the phone, hashing things out. *Who's buying what? What will I write next? What will sell? What is it all for?* Ari is now a "master of the universe," and I slowed him down every day for a good fifteen minutes. You're welcome. It took a while to become clear that I had no intention, ever, of making it big, and my next chance at my own show would prove that definitively.

I did use Ari as a template for the character I played on *The Larry Sanders Show.* Garry Shandling had been kind enough to hang out with the *Ben Stiller Show* cast for one of our episodes, so he knew me from that. I auditioned, which should have killed the opportunity for me, but Garry took me aside at the audition and walked me through the character. It wasn't hard to steal Ari's fast-talking, headlines-only, freight-train energy. I'd had an earful from him for years at this point (and enjoyed every minute of it).

Working around Garry on the *Sanders* show was inspiring and intimidating. He was maniacally focused, utterly consumed in the pursuit of perfection. But is there such a thing as perfection in what we do? There is not. Everyone has to come to their own terms with that conundrum; Garry never quit wanting to achieve total mastery. He was the final arbiter of every detail of *The Larry Sanders Show,* and every detail was always being scrutinized. The dialogue was examined under a microscope, then reexamined, then thrown out.

It was a lot of fun for me, though. For the first time, I got to know the pleasure of being "just an actor." I needed to know my lines and say them in the right order when the director blurted, "Action!" The fun of not having any real responsibility outside of "pretending" was new to me, and it's a great benefit of an acting gig, excusing yourself from reality.

Garry Shandling was a complicated guy—I think that's been

established by other books and documentaries by now. He could be so upbeat and encouraging to me, and to so many others. But to himself: always searching, uncertain. Garry wanted the world onscreen to be real, with complex, difficult-to-love characters—and FUNNY, too. Perfectly funny. He was playing an egotistical host of a late-night talk show, not someone the audience could easily feel empathy for. He'd set for himself quite a challenge, and he succeeded in everything he was after, I only wish he'd had more fun doing it. He suffered for his art.

There was no show like *The Larry Sanders Show* before it on American TV. Only in Britain did they experiment with not-very-likable characters in a dry, vérité manner. HBO really supported it. *Sanders* was the first time I ever saw a show stay on the air because of how intensely people supported it, not how many viewers it pulled. At the time, the highest ratings on the channel, by far, were for the movies, not the original programming.

For the people who actually watched it, *Sanders* was a new level of excellence and smarts in American comedy. It was shot "like a feature," which is to say it was lit naturalistically, which was appropriate to a show full of dark places and gray areas of human behavior. All of us young punks watched Garry so as to learn from the master. We watched him scrutinize every camera choice, every acting choice, and especially every word in the script. This was on set, when we were about to shoot a scene, so I'll bet these lines had been through two or three rewrites by then. He would gather a couple of writers around at the start of each scene, and together they would beat the snot out of each line, asking if there wasn't some improvement that could be made. I heard the pitches for fresh lines, and I watched lines tossed overboard with abandon. Jokes, to comedy writers of

Garry's intensity, have a very short half-life. I never spoke up, but I did feel that things were traded out for fresher but weaker lines, at times. Garry wanted something so perfect and undeniable that it felt like he was bound to be disappointed in the end. It's hard to know when to let go if you're trying to raise the bar every single second.

I had no trouble doing this kind of acting, playing someone more "real" than a sketch-comedy character. It suited me fine. In fact, I loved going toe-to-toe with Rip Torn, a legendary thespian, an Actors Studio/Lee Strasberg type. Rip didn't intimidate me; he inspired, especially if you got him talking about his early days as a young actor. Some people *loooove* this acting gig, I noticed. The drive and confidence of his character, Artie, mirrored Rip's own. Janeane and I had an abbreviated relationship in real life, and even though it was a mess and had JUST ended, we had no trouble playing a relationship on *Sanders*. That's as Method as it ever needs to get. We parted friends and both knew we almost screwed up a good friendship with that romantical unpleasantness.

As hard as Garry was on himself, he was equally forgiving and encouraging to young talent. Garry had a basketball half-court at his beautiful home in Mandeville Canyon, with a majestic view of the ocean. For a couple of years I became a part of his Sunday basketball group, a random collection of cool people that included comedy geniuses, management fellas, and one country music artist. Garry got way into Buddhism and meditation, and I hope it helped him have some interludes of solace. We all wondered when he'd make something new, especially a television series . . . and he was usually kicking something around. I think Garry may simply have been crushed by his own standards, wanting to do something better, more groundbreaking, more true and funny than the best thing that had, so far, ever been on TV. This kind of idealism is the triumph of writer's block, as any writer knows.

Finally, I met David Cross, I mean *really* met him—looked him in the eye and wrote some comedy sketches with him—and the mystery of what the hell I thought I was doing in this business of show was SOLVED!

David had been lugging his shit around the country doing stand-up and skipping town when the creditors got too close. In fact, he'd moved around his whole life, and did comedy wherever he went, so it's amazing how many times we missed knowing each other. He had even spent some time in Chicago when I was there, both of us kicking around the same nowhere club rooms, never seeing or hearing of the other. Atlanta was the place he called home. Boston was where he'd made his comedy connections, doing stand-up in that active but also bro-ey scene, and he did a lot of sketch with a group called Cross Comedy that featured future *Mr. Show* cast member John Ennis. Cross Comedy had been seen by Al Franken a few years before, to be considered for writing/acting possibilities at *SNL,* but the group was passed over, no doubt because of David's confrontational approach. He was always messing with the audience. Manipulating the relationship to make the audience edgy, uncertain, primed to either laugh or make a run for the exit. He unsettled audiences into laughter. He liked making people question where the comedy of the stage ended and the stupidity of the real world began.

"A big part of David's vision for the show was to suck the audience in—making them think one thing and then have something else happen" was how John Ennis described David's Cross Comedy instincts, which was never my approach, but if it made *him* happy, sure. To me, the best thing about a David Cross was not the confrontational aspect, but, rather, the funny funny funniness of the man.

Once I stopped slamming the door in his face, I started noticing how funny he was, and we very easily started cooking up comedy conceits and whimsies.

David had gotten a gig writing quips for a big-time comedian who was performing at the Montreal Just for Laughs festival. He invited me to crash in his hotel room and we would snark around and see the best comedy the world had to offer. That year, the world's best comedy showcase included some asshole from England who had built an act around farting into a microphone. Ah, the British, so dignified. David and I performed every night we were there, elbowing our way onto stages in front of exuberant, open-minded crowds. It was a blast, and all our bits, worked out that day or just before going on, killed. Of course, we had to comment on the *fartiste,* so David played a guy who tells stories punctuated with distinctive farts. I am in the audience, as arranged beforehand, with a speaker under my chair, and I start farting in appreciation of David's hilarious act, eventually drowning out *his* farts with *my* farts. He's upset, and I'm extremely apologetic: "If you weren't so funny, I wouldn't be farting so much!" Eventually . . . I don't remember what happened. A lot of farting. The audience loved it. Maybe that Brit was onto something.

We also did a bit called "Naked Phrase Guess," based on an old improv game/performance bit. In the setup, David tells everyone he's an expert improviser and I am a beginner, then he tells the audience we're going to have some fun. He'll improvise a scene with me, and while we are finding our way through the scene, I also have to try to guess a common phrase that the audience will have chosen before we start the scene.

David then tells me, "So, Bob, you have to go backstage, where you can't hear the audience shouting phrases . . . Oh, and you should take your clothes off, too. All of 'em."

"Wait, you want me to get naked?"

"Yep. That's why it's called 'Naked Phrase Guess'!"

What do I know? I'm a beginner! I take his word for it, go backstage, take off all my clothes, hold a sock over my junk (I have large socks), and we do this scene. I guess at the phrase, and the audience cheers, but David doesn't let on that I nailed it and the scene devolves into confusion, and we bow. Big applause. My ability to get naked is directly related to my being "in character." I could never get naked myself AS myself. This compartmentalization of my selfhood bodes well for a future in dramatic acting, but I just knew I would do anything as long as it was not me who was doing it, but some character I was playing.

Montreal birthed our friendship and professional partnership, and it's just as good now as it was back in those first days. We dig each other. We're very different people—I probably hold David back more than he'd like, slowing us down, but he's funnier than I am, so we both win. . . . Wait, no, I win. Tough beans for him. Most important, working together, we always land on what is funniest about an idea, and about the approach to the idea, and then how to wrassle the idea into submission and tickle the laughs out of it.

The funniest, and pretty much only, running argument we've ever had was when he insisted that I was part of the baby boom generation and he was a child of Generation X. We are two years apart in age! It's ludicrous. But he *needed* me to accept that I was substantially older and at least slightly less relevant or "with it" (his words) than he was. David needed me to be the straight man, the Joe Friday to his Tommy Chong, and I was happy to not agree to that. We were and are the same side of the same cookie (laced with arsenic) and love the same mix of silly-smart comedy equally and look out for each other's thoughtless indulgences. We support and appreciate each other's strengths perfectly. It remains so to this day. A documented miracle.

When we returned to Los Angeles from our honeymoon in Montreal (we still haven't had sex, but we almost kissed once—in *Run Ronnie Run!*), we quickly got focused on working together more. Dave Rath, the funniest manager who ever managed funny people (he repped Janeane, among many others of our circle), had been hornswoggled into booking out a giant, empty, dead nightclub space on Hollywood Boulevard. This was back when Hollywood Boulevard was real sad, all the bright lights broken. Rath came to me and asked if I wanted to host the first night of what would be a round-robin of Thursday night shows, each week a different host/curator. I said sure, I had some sketches lying around, I always do, and that was that. It only took a year and a half for us to survive the development process on the greatest little sketch show in a whorehouse not in Texas. *Mr. Show with Bob and David*: this is where it starts, with nobody watching . . . and it ends there, too. In between, tons of laughs and suffering—don't forget about the suffering, that's what makes it great.

Post-Montreal, David and I finally sat down face-to-face at my bachelor hovel on Sierra Bonita and within five minutes we had our quest written in stone: "Let's make a sketch show where one sketch mutates into the next, with a theme— a 'runner'—threaded through it." We might soon have added, "And no commercials to break it up, and a mix of absurdity and real-world, smart satire unseen since Monty Python and the early days of *SNL*." That's a lot to ask for. But that's the

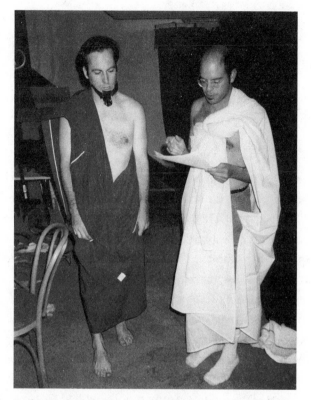

Backstage with David Cross for the "13th Apostle" sketch. Note the beard made from duct tape—like they did it in Shakespeare's time.

math of *Mr. Show*—Python through an American lens, a bit more rough and direct. Actually putting the show together and finding a home for it was a risky effort, one I would have doubted if I could have, but it was impossible to doubt something so damn funny. Within a month we'd written sketches like "Change for a Dollar," "Marshall, the 13th Apostle," and even the epic "The Joke: The Musical," which Jack Black would raise to Broadway-level sing-songery. It was meant to be, and I realized that David was the smartest, funniest, most pissed-off guy since ME. I know why I worked with him—pure funny—but why'd he tie his fortunes to me?

Let's find out, shall we? Let's ask this particular horse himself: "Would you agree that your childhood formed you into a defiantly independent person? I will note that even the comedy group you had been a part of had your name, and only your name, in the title . . ."

David shot back, "How rude! But yes, for sure the situation I was forced into by my dad taking off suddenly and leaving us in an alien place with no money and a mountain of debt definitely shaped me. That and always being the new kid (we moved every year—sometimes twice within a year) at school or the apartment complex. I was told by my mom after my dad took off (I had just turned ten a couple of months prior) that 'Now you are going to have to be the man of the house,' and I kind of resented that, but knew that it was true from that point forward. We were all latchkey kids, and my youngest sister was just five at the time, so it was up to me to watch over everyone and be responsible (which I think was why I became *so very* irresponsible later in life), as my mom now had to go to work. BUT I say it was all worth it, as the place she got her first job (selling copier ink and toner out of a mobile home) gave us the Globo-Chem slogan 'Take It From Me, I Love You,' which was on their pens. And you can note that Cross Comedy, the sketch group I put together in Boston, had my name on it, but I, too, will note that I didn't name it; Robin Hordon, the club manager at Catch, named it. I said sure, and the rest is forgotten history."

"Hmm," I nodded, unsatisfied, then proceeded to probe further into his "defiant" individuality, asking, "Probably this irascible self-reliance of yours is one reason you like stand-up so much?"

David's email response laid bare this brittle corner of his peevish, cranky persona: "I think that makes some sense as to why, in part, I love stand-up so much. In fact, I never crave it more or feel a primal need to do stand-up more than when I am in the middle of working on a production that I'm either collaborating on or have not much say in. Meaning, even though I could be having the time of my life, if I'm saying other people's words or thoughts or philosophies, then sometimes I will feel the urge to get up onstage and do *my* jokes and ideas, etc. I'm stating the obvious, but my stand-up is all me doing whatever the fuck I want and saying whatever I want. That includes the N-word, the C-word, the F-word, the P-word (poo-poo), the L-word (on Showtime), the A-Team (syndicated), the G-Spot (the adult channel), and 'Jews.'"

I had one last question for this esteemed Hebraic farceur: "So when we started working together, was there ever a hesitation to get wrapped up in a team effort, especially with someone as critical (and unjustifiably confident) as li'l ol' me? I'm especially talking about the early days. . . . As I recall it, we were both pretty all-in pretty fast. It was an easy choice for me because you are so fucking funny."

Avoiding my compliment, Cross obfuscated, "I would not say there was a hesitation really but more of a cautious excitement. We both were taken aback and a little excited that we meshed together and produced really funny sketches so well, so quickly and so easily. It was almost jarring! In part because we're quite different. It was about the direction we could each take each other's idea that worked so well. I could bring a half-baked but overblown idea to you and you could strip it down to the core and say, '*This*—this is what the idea is. Lose all that other stuff.' And I could take one of your ideas (which would almost always be written in a more 'classic' sketch style) and suggest a completely different place for it to go, and by layering each of our styles onto the sketch, they became something else entirely. The 'Terra Delu/Heaven's Chimney/Wacky Religions' run is a good example (probably not the best example, but I don't have the time to look back at all the others just now). All this is to say that it was unique and thrilling to meet someone where that happens. And it's a very rare thing and I think we both realized that, and also, up to that point I had never worked with someone so driven and exact. I was the opposite. In fact, and I've said this before, but so much of what I've produced came about because someone else had the idea and plotted the course to get it done. From Cross Comedy (I think it was Marc Maron who suggested I do what eventually became that show) to *Mr. Show* to *Shut Up You Fucking Baby!* to *The Increasingly Poor Decisions of Todd Margaret,* those were all the result of someone else suggesting or pushing me to do the thing that resulted in all of that work. So not only were we making great stuff, but your drive got us our own TV show! And one thing that I think I subconsciously fought at first was what you were teaching me. The idea of taking a completed sketch that I spent a couple of days working on and getting rid of all of it except for one line of dialogue and throwing everything else away and going back to my computer for two more days and creating an entirely new sketch around that one line was absurd to me. (Because I used to be lazy—another way in which you changed me; now, unfortunately, like you, I am a bit of a workaholic.) I resented how hard and long you were expecting me, the guy who liked to start drinking at four and going to see bands and 'living life man!,' to work. But you expected that from everyone you worked with, because that's how *you* worked, because that's how much work was needed to be done to get it right. And of course you were right: I just resented having to be responsible. The mitigating factor in all of this was simply, I was having the time of my life."

Literarily, a Miracle! The Early Sketches

"Marshall, the 13th Apostle" was about the newly discovered terribleness of "prosperity gospel," in the form of a heretofore unheard-of apostle of Jesus H. Christ who'd written a book entitled *Power, Profit, and Passion!* and who asked the messiah, "Jesus, I used to be like you: dirty, smelly, thinking I was the son of God!" and made Jesus's offer of eternal life even sweeter by adding an "unleavened bread LEAVENATOR!" David played Marshall, and I played Jesus as a mild simp, whom he runs over easily with his flimflammery. "Change for a Dollar" was a filmed sketch we wrote to show how we intended to jump between live and filmed performance in our show, even within a sketch. Nothing this silly had been on American TV since they reran Python, I was certain, and proud of it. But could we get it on TV?

After *The Dana Carvey Show*'s attempt to conquer prime time and *The Ben Stiller Show*'s run at the hot spot of Sunday nights, I wanted to aim for the fringe of the fringe . . . *wayyy* over yonder. HBO was the place. It was respected, it did risky new stuff, and only the elite (cool folks) were paying attention. It was nothing like the behemoth that it has become since then. Which meant that expectations were low—oh, and no commercials got in our way! So, David and I agreed, it had to be HBO or . . . no one. We were aiming at an impossibly small target.

David and I invested our own funds to make short filmed sketches that linked up with the live stuff. Some of the pieces we did were later redone for the actual show, including the aforementioned future fan favorite "Change for a Dollar," in which I go into a convenience store (McGinty's 4 Day Market) and ask for change for a dollar. The request has to go up the chain of command of this little store until it reaches the president of the United States, with a lot of anguished hemming and hawing at each step. Clarified silliness. Indulgent performance. Like nothing on TV at the time. We shot these pieces with no production value, edited them on the computers of friends, and demoed our future TV show multiple times over the next year and a half. We were immediately a hot ticket in the world of hipster comedy, but take note: we did something really smart and risky (I mean besides spending our own money producing). We put each show up *only one time*. If you were a network exec/agent/heat seeker, you HAD to attend the show when we did it. We never repeated material, so you would have missed it completely. In a town like L.A., where the sun sets and everybody can't wait to go home and go to sleep early— seriously, compared with New York, you cannot get people *out*—this was key. Giving interested parties no option other than to get their asses to the theater was crucial.

Every two months or so for the next year and a half, we would do a live show, with filmed pieces interconnecting with the live performance stuff, showing everyone exactly what we wanted to do on the TV. After six months and three shows, we were eighteen thousand in the hole (thanks, *SNL* paycheck!). The first three shows were on Hollywood Boulevard, in the back of this forgotten nightclub. This was Hollywood, 1994; Weezer's Blue Album had just come out and energy was building around a new generation of angry, snot-nosed smart-assery. Around this time, Janeane and Ben had a touch of mainstream acceptance with the film *Reality Bites,* and there'd been a rumor that Janeane was even being considered for the cover of

Time magazine. (This was back when that was a big deal. Remember that? Trust me.) Were we the next wave of comedy or just an offshoot?

In the end, we were both.

We made our way forward employing THE THREE STEPS TO SUCCESS IN SHOWBIZ:

1. Persistence
2. Begging
3. Waiting—then start again at the top

Keep in mind, NO ONE wanted a sketch show! Sketch shows are full of ideas! Yech! People don't watch television for ideas; they watch for the commercials. Not only did we want to do a sketch show, we had all kinds of other rules about it that would alienate a network. It's almost like we wanted to fail. Guys, listen to me, this was surely a fool's errand.

Anyway, the first two live shows were called *The Three Goofballs,* and in each one David and I teamed up with a third member. In the first show, Jeremy Kramer, an elder statesman of the comedy moment, had that short-lived role. In the opening of the show, there are three boxes onstage—energetic showbiz music plays, like at the beginning of a Lakers game. I pop out of one box, David pops out of the second, and the third remains closed. We rush over and open the box to find our friend, our third goofball, bereft of life, suffocated for the sake of our big opener. We take a moment for "thoughts and prayers," then decide, "He'd want us to carry on with the show!" At this point, Jeremy's ghost interrupts us and yells, "No, I wouldn't want you to carry on . . . I would want you to mourn me! I died here!!" Somehow that became the first scene, and on we go.

The third show was called *The Cross/Odenkirk Problem,* and by now Carolyn Strauss, an HBO exec, was showing up and encouraging us. In our fourth show, going into debt even deeper (what did we care? No kids, no houses, no nothin'), we started getting more serious. We shifted the show to a nicer (still cruddy) venue—the Upfront Comedy Showcase, in Santa Monica—and renamed it the *Grand National Championships.* (I imagined people reading in *TV Guide* and thinking, "Championships . . . of *what*?! Dammit, now I *gotta* check it out!") Somewhere in here we had our first and best big meeting with HBO bigwig Chris Albrecht, Carolyn's boss. Chris was a comedy aficionado from way back, having made *The Larry Sanders Show* happen and even backing *The Ben Stiller Show,* so he was familiar with my oeuvre and bad attitude. David and I finally landed on what we thought was a generic, respectful name for a TV show: *Mr. Show,* something that would give us *maximum latitude.*

It's what every young comedy writer wants. A show that is completely new and different every week. NO STRUCTURE AT ALL, no intro, no theme song, no RULES. Just ideas! Brilliant, funny, caustic, angry, delightful ideas flowing past like a rushing river, and then, abruptly, the show ends. No goodbye, no apology, no explanations. Of course, this kind of show would be cold, impersonal, exhausting, and a total failure. Thank God we got some good advice from one of the brains behind *Hee Haw.*

Bernie Brillstein sat us down and said, "Boys, you gotta put your name in there. And you gotta come out at the start of the show and say hello." He was asking for the show to have a modicum of structure and personality to it. We didn't have to hold the audience's hand, but if we could just bother ourselves to wave hello to them at the start . . .

Bernie, the old pro, was totally right; he fought us on it and we relented.

So we had it—this wonderful, big-break pitch meeting for our dream show with the execs at HBO. We came in and unspooled our excited pitch. Chris Albrecht listened to our blather, nodded, and suggested that this thing might be a go. Bernie looked at both of us with a *that's enough* nod. We shut our stupid mouths. Chris leaned over to David and me and said, "Whatever you do, make it something you would never see on regular TV."

We agreed but weren't sure what we were agreeing to.

Chris dialed it in for us: "It doesn't matter if people *actually* watch the show, just so long as they *think they should* watch it." He talked about *The Larry Sanders Show*'s numbers—not great, but how that didn't really matter; it generated attention and excitement and commentary. So . . . he was saying, "Fuck the ratings—make something worth talking about."

We would, happily, fuck the ratings.

Chapter 6

Valhalla, I Am Coming!
At Long Last, Mr. Show

———

It was a major sea change, in music and comedy . . .
and it was weird to see it, because at the time you
knew it while you were in the audience. It was like
"We're seein' something here . . . This is special."

—JACK BLACK

Now I get to answer the question everyone wants an answer to.
What happens when you get everything you've ever asked for?
Do you get happy all of a sudden? Is it everything it's cracked
up to be? Yes to both. Chris had expressed that we should try
to keep the "nightclub" vibe the show had in its rough, discovery phase. No slick TV-studio environment. David and I did
not concur, but we also didn't argue. In the end, Troy Miller,
whom we will meet below, saved money and found a failing
restaurant/nightclub/cavern that would satisfy Chris with the
"vibe" and make us suffer. But we'd have three sets, a live audience, and a big TV screen to show the audience our filmed
pieces. It was essentially a goddamn barn from the early 1900s
where we shot those first four episodes. It was rumored to have
once been part of an old-time film studio, but so is every single
building in this part of town. It most definitely began life hous-

ing livestock, smack-dab on Sweetzer, just off Hollywood Boulevard. Did the famous movie horse Trigger drop a deuce there
once? Quite possible. It still had a lively herd of crickets living
inside it. Loud crickets, so we'd better get big enough laughs or
they would have been there to provide "commentary." Right
before the first live taping started, I walked around kicking
baseboards to silence the demons.

After a year-plus of live shows, we had reliable material for
those first four shows. David remembers our earliest bits: "I
believe it would be one of the following: 'Third Wheel Legend,'
'The 13th Apostle,' 'Racist in the Year 3000,' and 'Spank.'"
"Spank" was David's performance artist who wants to make a
statement by shitting on the American flag but finds himself
too constipated to do so. He, of course, blames the flag itself,
and it turns out (in our sketch) he is right—the flag, devised by
those devious founding fathers of ours, is just the right combo
of colors and style to induce constipation in future performance artists. Around this time, some dangerous artist had
done a similar statement piece dubbed *Piss Christ,* where he
mixed urine and religious symbology in such a potent combi-
nation that the Catholic Church shook their heads, locked
their doors, emptied their bank accounts, and threw in the
towel. Like many *Mr. Show* sketches, this one started firmly in
the real world. We riffed on something that had happened already, or quite often predicted something that was coming in
the near future. The show did nothing "on time"—we were
almost always ahead of ourselves.

David recalls the first big laughs we got as "something we
improvised in Laura Milligan's kitchen at a party where you
did Ernie, the pitchman, doing the 'Talk to the pan' infomer-
cial." Ah, yes, pure insanity. This was me as a British pitchman
screaming at a female co-host to "touch the pan!" and then

whacking her on the head with the pan, spinning her around, and pretending to hear the pan talk to me . . . Anyway, the core joke was that pitchmen are insane and when they really get going they make your head spin. That's how they get ya.

So we had the comedy goods, but we needed one more element to deliver on our grand vision. That element was a man named Troy Miller. Troy had been kicking around the fringes of the comedy scene, making short films as a director and producer, and he was the one and only producer and director for our impossible vision. In fact, he turned the cool million that HBO bequeathed us into four half-hour episodes. Wow. A magician, this Troy fella was. We would have a chance to show our stuff, then show it again three more times, to fall down and then save ourselves with one more bit. There was a lot of luck alongside the years of preparation and intense focus that made *Mr. Show* happen, but meeting Troy Miller was probably the biggest piece of luck in the luck bag.

David and I wrote like the hyperactive idiots straight out of the film *Reefer Madness*—amped, giggling, dancing real fast, driving jalopies with the music turned up. We knew we couldn't compete with *SNL* on the super-topical, shared-reference thing, but we also knew we probably weren't up to (or maybe that interested in) reaching Monty Python's stream-of-consciousness mélange. We weren't all British and highfalutin. We were thick-headed Americans, and our show would be more grounded, and we'd swear A LOT! Because we could!

At the end of episode 1 of *Mr. Show,* I pull a live baby chick out of my pants, where it's been incubating throughout the whole program, which becomes an advertisement for special pants that incubate your chicks for you. Perhaps this was a metaphor for the show we had just birthed? Perhaps. But I can say with confidence that it was some *deep* nonsense, and "not like anything you could see on regular TV." That's what the man asked for.

Troy Miller made it possible for us to deliver something professional, but also to take a run at big pop culture with satires like "Coupon: The Movie." A trailer for a film "based on" America's favorite coupon at the time (for white tube socks), this bit feels big and professional, which is necessary to hit its mark. Troy shot the piece entirely in one day, in a generic rented suburban house way outside of L.A. "Jeepers Creepers: Semi-Star," a musical about a reluctant messiah played by Jack Black, was also a famous single-day shoot—why don't they film all features this fast? We were tripping over each other, and the sun had to be boosted in post, as it had barely been peeking over the curvature of the earth as we made the final shots of the day. Dino Stamatopoulos wrote this extravaganza, a riff on *Godspell* and *Jesus Christ Superstar.* Eban Schletter did the music. But Troy was the indisputable hero, overseeing an impossible effort—which included every scrapper from our group of L.A. comedy friends making up the cast of thousands: Laura Milligan, Doug Benson, Sarah Silverman, and even a real, certified actress, Jeanne Tripplehorn. Jack Black was still unknown by the big time, and he ripped the songs to shreds. "Megaphone Crooners," another scene in which David and I play singers of the 1920s (you know, that Jolson crap), would have been nothing but piffle if Troy Miller hadn't been clever enough to shoot it on a Super 8 camera, then transfer that footage, in black-and-white, to video. We knew NO production tricks, Troy knew ALL of them, and invented a few new ones.

Our first season was pretty random—shows sprawled and ideas got away from us. We were so thrilled at having this huge, borderless canvas that we just splattered comedy in every direction. But after the past year and a half of live gigs, we had confidence enough to sell it. The audience bought into our razzle. Speaking of the audience, we were stretching to fill the seats for two shows ("rehearsal" show and "air" show). We hired an audience service, and the first episode had a large contingent of Latinx teenagers who seemed to be coupled up, as though a busload of kids on their way to their prom were diverted into a hipster comedy show. They looked at us skeptically, but I think our confidence and willingness to look stupid won them over. They lauged! They drowned out those blasted crickets real good.

There are a few gems in the first season, most notably "Good News," a report from a Christian news outlet where I play the slow-talking host and David is Burton Quim, a representative of Overcome, which helps gay sinners like him to straighten up, again and again. "Burton will tell us about his most recent lapse, and the lapse he has planned for August, which should take him to Rio de Janeiro!" I say, ending on a positive note. This kind of scene, about something happening in the ol' zeitgeist but not strictly "topical," would be our bread-and-butter, if bread-and-butter were comedy sketches on a TV show.

The twice name-checked "Change for a Dollar" was a defining bit in that it was something *SNL* could never do, since at the time *SNL* was unfriendly to pre-taped bits. This one had to be pre-taped for many reasons, most notably that David and I interchangeably played each idiot in the chain of command. Blowing up the world of the bit, something that begins live and then returns to that rinky-dink live set at the end, was a thrill and made us seem cooler than cool at the time.

"Popemobile Chase" was another attempt to riff on the biggest story of the day, but in a way that no other comedy show could do. The O.J. car chase is transposed to a situation where the pope has clearly murdered some dude, leaving behind his papal staff, ring, and hat, and then instigated a police chase in the popemobile. He is obviously the suspect, and the subsequent trial is an exploration of TV trials and random jokes. An "Experts Lounge" at the courthouse is a room full of experts all waiting like young actors at a cattle-call audition, hopeful to be chosen for the case at hand. The sketch meanders. Indulgent. David and I would find, after a while, that the freedom we had was dangerous, and indulgence wasn't always so great. The best thing was to write a really tight, funny sketch that played by the rules but also surprised, and had almost a classic-comedy quality. Those became our holy grail. Python had already done the sprawling thing better than anyone ever could.

HBO maintained a hands-off, low-expectations supportiveness that verged on not giving a shit, which was just dandy for us (except when it came to promotions). We had no money. Ever. That was okay, we had Troy. We were happy to go without dressing rooms, often stripping to our undies in the street, and "stealing" locations. "Watch out for the cops" was often announced as we geared up for a day of shooting—followed by our patented excuse should the boys in blue come down on us: "Just say that we're college students making a film. DO NOT say 'Fuck tha police'!" I was thirty, so I might have had to casually drop the qualifier "grad school." We got bounced from a location once or twice, but no one was ever arrested—the heat had their hands full in L.A. around that time, so a big thank-you to both the Bloods and the Crips in equal measure.

A review by David Wild in *Rolling Stone* dubbed us "an American Monty Python." That was awesome. Come on. We coulda quit right there. We almost did. Because outside of that review, and a general excitement in the cognoscenti of L.A.'s fringe, no one cared about us.

Chris Albrecht and Carolyn Strauss at HBO were alone in

their love for our fervent insanity. So what saved us? Some anonymous fourteen-year-old who asked his auntie for tapes of "something called *Mr. Show*." His auntie, being an HBO exec in New York, responded like all HBO execs at the time (and for the run of the show), asking him, "What's that?" After this golden child informed her that it was a funny, crazy sketch show that was on the network she worked for, she went and did a little digging, and was surprised to discover that we actually existed right under her nose. The boy got his videotapes of our first season, and she proceeded to forget we ever existed. But Chris took her request and spun it into a fable of youthful exuberance for our product (youth being cable buyers of tomorrow). He proposed that maybe our show could put HBO on the radar of teenagers, and this "angle" did the trick, barely, and we got a second order for six more *Mr. Show*s. Thank you, Anonymous Boy!

We had no idea this perfect genius nephew was out there waving his magical E.T. finger in our direction, reanimating our dreams. We figured our one good review and general feeling of artistic success and sense of righteousness would win out sooner, not later. After season one, David and I took our loot and went to Amsterdam to finally, one time only, do a drug.

If You're Gonna Write a Comedy Scene, You're Gonna Have Some Rat Feces in There

In our second season we moved to real offices in the KTLA lot at Sunset and Bronson, and we shot in a real studio building, not an abandoned horse dormitory. We also began to add writers, but at all times we worked to keep the "show head," the sense that all this material, hopefully with a wide range of comic style, still belonged together on the same show.

I ran the writers' room in an opposite manner to every room I'd been in before this one. Instead of beating ideas up, especially weak ones, this gang would build them up—especially weak ones. You'd pitch a bad idea, or bring in a weak first draft, it would lie there, and I would ask, "It's kinda funny— what was the funniest moment in there for you?" and we could find that funny moment and build it out. In a first draft script about "The Devastator," a roller coaster that goes underwater for two minutes per ride, killing most passengers, there was a line from one survivor who was eager to ride it again—our re- write built from his idiotic exuberance. Our writing process, "make it work," transformed many a half-assed notion into hard laughs. But, even better, writers didn't pitch crap that they didn't want to talk about, only stuff they had a genuine good feeling about.

The writing staff was all guys, and yes, that was a mistake.

We had so many funny women around us, and *on* the show. Jill Talley, first of all, but also Karen Kilgariff, Mary Lynn Rajskub, Sarah Silverman, Brett Paesel, et al. The show was behind the times in this way, and it's a shame that I can do nothing about it now.

The writers we did accrue were top-notch funny people, and not a one came from "Harvard's School of Clever Fellows" in Cambridge, Massachusetts. Paul F. Tompkins was and is a great storytelling stand-up comedian, the best of our time, I think. Paul and Jay Johnston had done some sketch shows under the moniker "The Skates." It was crazy stuff, with Jay bringing an organic, likable looniness that not many others could pull off. I remember one line where Jay is a hostage and he's tied to a chair and getting flustered and he spits out, "What's with all the questions?! Queries?! *Queests?!!*" That last word is not a word, and all the more wonderful for not being something. Paul wrote "Megaphone Crooners" for *Mr. Show*. I had a hand in it, having just watched a documentary on PBS about that old-time shout-singer Al Jolson in which everyone who knew him talked about what an awful, cruel, angry person he was, then they would praise his talents for singing and dancing, then they would cut to a clip of him stomping around like a man killing ants and "singing," which sounded to me more like yowling in a cave. Our piece was almost as funny as the documentary.

Brian Posehn was a distinctive part of the L.A. alternative scene and had been in our shows from their first trial runs. Brian is a heavy metal–loving sour apple who hates anything mainstream more than you. His childish antics helped us stay grounded and immature, which I love in comedy. Bill Odenkirk (yes, he's my brother) somehow inherited my father's wisecracking joke-smithery without the alcohol-fueled antics. Bill tossed funny lines and twists into many a scene with ease, and wrote strikingly pure sketches like "The Fad Three," a short film about a Beatles-esque group of young men in Liverpool in the early sixties who become world-famous for *getting their picture taken* and nothing else. Like a lot of *Mr. Show* scenes, it is about something without aiming dead center, and yet, in its subterfuge, it goes far deeper than a direct parody ever could. Dino Stamatopoulos became a very important writer over the next three years. Dino and I went all the way back to Chicago days, when he would perform in a duo with Andy Dick. He loved classic structure as much as I did. Dino and Andy had a bit, done on the *Stiller* show, where they performed "Who's on First?" but the straight man of the team gets physically violent in his frustrated responses. Dino could write grand sagas like "Jeepers Creepers Slacker Guy," but he also wrote some of the cleanest, most economical comedy pieces, like "Hunger

Strike" and maybe the finest sketch of the show's run, "The Audition."

Finally, Brent Forrester and Eric Hoffman were two writers who came aboard for shorter runs but were prized as part of the staff. Brent wrote another "best ever" sketch called "The Pre-Taped Call In Show," where David slowly, on camera, tears his hair out as the host of a television show that is pre-taped a week before air but still invites phone calls, which are inevitably off-topic, because the show you are watching is the show from one week ago and the topic you should call in to discuss is the one announced for the following week. Monty Python had "Déjà Vu," this was *Mr. Show*'s even more tightly written homage. Eric Hoffman wrote "Bugged Drug Deal," a quite silly concoction where I play a cop who uses sarcasm and belittlement to obscure the fact that David, a drug dealer, is, just as he suspects, trapped in an obvious setup.

So, yeah, to celebrate our triumphant, unseen first season, David and I headed to Amsterdam, where, together, we shared a big hash-infused slice of brownie pie. I had a nibble, David had the rest. The next day at noon, David was still eye-squintingly high. Take note—they're family-sized! This is the only time we imbibed "drugs" together, and we certainly didn't write our show while high, as nearly every fan ever suggested. I find that insulting; I'm no Seth Rogen, although David probably could pull it off. This li'l escapade got us a scene where David plays a guy attempting to smuggle a little hash back into America by hiding it in a baggie and putting the baggie inside a shampoo bottle so the drug dogs won't smell it. When he gets to the customs desk, he is so nervous that he keeps saying the word "shampoo." "Where were you in Europe?" asks the customs officer. "I was in Italy, and I shampooed up to Holland," says the dope fiend, and it gets more shampooey from there.

After that scene, I did my rendition of a TV detective who hosted a TV show of the time; my version was named F.F. Woodycooks. Like the nutty guy who made this *real* show (I cannot stress it enough: this outlandish character was only a jot of loony larger than the cartoon-sized real person), I host a show where crimes are reenacted and softheaded advice on "avoiding crooks" is doled out. It was a challenge to get Troy Miller, the director, to understand just how relentlessly dumb we wanted to go with the violence. We had to end up looping footage of Jay Johnston rhythmically punching David in the face to get the desired effect. It was an insane joy to push the comedy this far. I'm proud that we didn't hold back, and the piece holds up even if you have no idea who we are referencing. Pure comic heroin.

SNL had missed the boat years before on Jill Talley. Thank God; otherwise we couldn't have had her, and she never didn't kill it. Jill's a South Side Chicago gal and she is, as they used to say, "funny as a guy." She held her own opposite Chris Farley at Second City, and she brought along her husband, Tom Kenny (later to be SpongeBob SquarePants). Tom brought precision, incredible range, and that most rare of qualities among our troupe of peevish misanthropes: likability. We needed that likability, as the rest of us were a buncha *pills*. In episode 205, Jill is the standout when she plays a character who runs through the episode, a foulmouthed grown-up in pigtails and a dirty ballerina costume, who goes by the name Superstar and begins and ends an episode all about the cheap and common journey of stardom at all costs.

The second season was really the start of the comic ass-kicking that *Mr. Show* would bring to American sketch and alternative comedy, with highlights like "Rap! The Musical" (a Broadway musical *about* rap music but with no rap music in it!), "The New KKK" (no longer racist, they're just against slackers and are mostly about various hobbies, including stamp collecting), and "Mom and Pop Porn Shop" (exactly what you think it is, a doddering old couple running a porn shop with pride and folksy common wisdom: "Don't blame the dildos!"). Lots of great stuff, and we worked so hard to get the transitions right, to move organically from one scene to another. We approached this effort with hope and faith and lots of elbow grease, taking hours upon hours talking about the most clever move to get us from one scene to the next. In the mom-and-pop porn shop scene, as it winds down, they hear a loud bass beat coming from the upstairs neighbor, Pops takes a broom and pounds back, shouting, "Keep it down, there are people trying to masturbate down here!!" The camera rises up, crosses the floorboards, and we see David and me as the soul-singing duo Three Times One Minus One and we launch into our hit single "Ewww, Girl, Ewww" (of which these are the whole of the lyrics). This couldn't be a smoother transition, and all that is great, but we never got the Terry Gilliam palate-cleansing breath of absurd air to space out our often overly thick comic premises. Too bad. Onward.

Episode 4 of that season is a golden one. We have a corporate-retreat open, and David admits to our investors in the audience that we cannot assure perfect standards in our comedy: "If you're gonna write a comedy scene, you're gonna have some rat feces in there . . ." After that, a hidden camera shares with our audience that the show is written by child labor in Pakistan or somewhere. We have some fun with that notion, which includes a glimpse of Paul F. Tompkins as an ethnically obscure slave driver who keeps shouting "Al Wazir!" as he whips the comedy-writing youth—"Al Wazir" being the name of the chicken takeout restaurant that our staff favored through all four seasons of the show. I commandeer the screen as Van Hammersly, a billiard trick-shot artist who "uses" his skills to teach history. It sounds like it doesn't make any sense, and I assure you, it doesn't. This was something I was improvising at a party one night and everyone agreed it needed to be documented so that future generations would know I was Syd Barrett–level unhinged. At some point in the proceedings, David Cross interrupts as Grass Valley Greg, a tech wizard (he invented the delete key!) who has too much money and is using his newfound nerd-power to torture the people around him. This was based on a hearsay story I'd heard about Paul Allen, the Microsoft co-founder, throwing "events" and forcing captive audiences to listen to him play guitar. Who knows if he did, but it was really fun to see David in that baseball cap with the ponytail attached, being an indulgent hippie asshole. At the end of the episode we present "New San Francisco," wherein that great city is turned into a Disneyfied theme park. This little masterpiece of music, coordinated performance, and corporate blandification could only be performed with lots of preparation and rehearsal, something other shows just didn't have time for. Deep satire like this also stays relevant for decades to come, sadly.

We were on a roll. Our cult was growing, as cults will do— slowly but intensely. We had great respect in the comedy world and were included in the Kool Kids Klub of awards considerations (promotional BS, though it was the biggest charity event of the time): "Comic Relief 8," where we did our famous "Naked Phrase Guess" bit, with me getting fully naked in Radio City Music Hall and playing out the scene just as we had years earlier in Montreal. I almost showed my dick, but then at the last second I decided I'd make the world wait forever on that big letdown. David and I got to fly on a private jet to New

York, and I can tell you that private jets are the only way to fly . . . UNLESS Robert Wuhl is talking THE ENTIRE TIME. Like, literally never once shutting up. But the best thing was simply knowing what we were doing and getting to do it, for two more years.

The writing and production moved to more professional digs, at Hollywood Center Studios, the old Desilu lot (thanks, Lucy and Desi and everybody in between), and by now we had abandoned trying to make the show look like it was in a nightclub. It was a TV show. We weren't fooling anyone. Our production standards went up—again, the only direction they could possibly go—and we expanded our writing staff with two bright young things named Scott Aukerman and BJ Porter. In episode 402, they wrote their greatest bit, "The Dalai Lama," telling of how a typical American dipshit teenager is discovered to be the next reincarnated lama. I play the dumb, lucky goof, and David plays my best pal, who comes to visit me in my sweet Tibetan digs years later. Together we get wrapped up in a competition between the monks in my spiritual retreat and the fat kids from the fat kids' camp across the lake. Scott and BJ were particularly great at riffing on pop-culture stuff from their (recent) childhoods.

It was a great comedy-writing room. There was *almost* no notion that we couldn't find the funny in, spin it out and turn it another way to make you laugh even harder. The assumption with every pitch pitched was that there was something really great and hilarious buried in there. This was mostly true. When Brian Posehn wrote a HORRIBLY UNFUNNY six-page scene about a heavy-metal band that visits a kid who tried to commit suicide after hearing their song "Try Suicide," it died hard at the read-through table but then, after we Rumpelstiltskinned it, turned out the single biggest laugh I've ever heard from an audience in my life. The reaction to the "Titannica" scene (episode 310), when I threw back the bedsheets on David Cross's character and revealed his gnarled puppet body, was a tidal wave of laughter that had an almost physical wallop, far from the nonreaction the original pitch had summoned from a group of tired, lunch-hungry writers when it was proposed a few weeks before.

The script Brian brought to the writers' room left us all as silent as a bowl of pears in a painting by the "great" Cézanne, only Brian Posehn was no Cézanne and nobody was paying to see silence. Brian was the only one who laughed—nay, *scoffed!*—at us, his fellow writers, for suffering through this cement-flavored hunkajunk. To add insult to injury, he was lying down when he sneered at us. He had the habit of stealing the entire couch, his lanky frame cluttering every available cushion with bony limbs and derision. "I know I took advantage of the couch in the writers' room and embarrassingly now would fall asleep during long writers' meetings," this somnolent and sorry excuse for a Shakespeare recalls, "partly because they were long and also partly because I didn't care. I was way too comfortable and almost lazy in the room. . . . I leaned into the lazy-stoner, slacker, Gen X, club-comic thing." Thanks for that, cool guy.

After reading his inscrutable rune of comedy, I asked the stumper of all time: "So . . . how could this be funny?" The writers could barely get it up to hem and haw in response. As Brian tells it, "Man, I wish I still had that first draft somewhere so I could clear up exactly what was my idea and what came from the collaboration to fix it. I just remember mine was more mean-spirited, ugly, and laugh-free."

After sweating, we all agreed this exchange between the acid-burned youth and a leather-brained band member was funnyish . . .

"I tried suicide right after hearing your song 'Try Suicide'!"

"Yeah, we know, your parents sued us."

"Yeah, but you guys won. That's so *awesome*!"

This one upbeat exchange in the midst of a horrid scenario made everyone smile. I suggested, "What if the kid had a puppety body, y'know, so he looks like . . . *a wet cigar*?" Suddenly, snarling, begrudging smiles returned. A rewrite was off to the races, and that puppet body slaughtered at the live show a few weeks later. It was a total surprise for the audience when I threw the sheet off, revealing the tiny brown limbs waving around in the "cool air." The arms were operated by David, and a cramped Jay Johnston worked the legs from underneath the bed.

The best episodes had the most variety in them and were a version of what Del Close was in hot pursuit of: a TV version of his improvisational game "The Harold." We weren't improvised—in fact, we were written with care and deep focus—but I think Del would have approved despite our hard work. I like to think he may have seen an episode at some point, but I doubt he did. He probably thought paying for HBO would be feeding the beast. Episode 309, entitled "Bush Is a Pussy," a title I hate and find totally unrepresentative of the episode or our general political outlook (like good liberals, we mostly feasted on our own), is one example of an episode that had the kind of light-touch thematic through line we longed for. It features Jay Johnston as the embodiment of "Mediocrity," a pallid ghoul who roams through the filmed sketch, "The Great Philouza," a mini-epic riff on the film *Amadeus*, but ours is about marching-band music composers. David's character is middling, and so Mediocrity haunts him, laughing derisively as he competes with our John Philip Sousa stand-in (myself as John Baptiste Philouza). The whole episode begins with me, as me, being replaced by my understudy, Tom Kenny, as a terrible, awful, no-good, very bad, faux Robin Williams named Kedzie Matthews, the epitome of mediocre smoke-and-mirrors "comedy" of the time. There's a scene about a magazine called *Value* that ranks humans according to their worth (how much money they have), which puts a lot of mediocrities into prime spots in the history of humankind. The episode also has an all-time fan-favorite scene, in "Mafia Mathematicians," which was built out of the chatty arguments that Quentin Tarantino and Scorsese like to fill their films with. In this case, Mafia tough guys are arguing ad nauseam about what the highest number is, landing on twenty-four because the boss (myself doing my best peeved De Niro, and a damn good one, too) insists they quit with the nonsense right there. This causes problems almost immediately, but the boss wants twenty-four to be the highest number, so they have to make it so. At gunpoint, a Nazi apologist argues, "To say we killed twenty-four Jews . . . is an exaggeration." As the episode concludes, we see Kedzie onstage doing his fake-improvised word-association garbage act, and Mediocrity is loving it. We tried for this kind of cohesiveness and hit it once or twice.

Seasons 3 and 4 are us hitting our stride. David and I were no longer drunk on the freedom HBO gave us, and becoming skeptical of sprawling nonsense, and more in love with the more challenging work of classic sketches with tight internal logic and satisfying endings. To me, these include "Hunger Strike" (a selfless hunger striker is giving his final political speech and can only talk about the food he is craving), "Young People and Their Companions," "Lie Detector," "Weeklong Romance," "The Burgundy Loaf," "Pre-Taped Call In Show," and "Lifeboat." "Toenapper" is another doozy you can do with your high school sketch club (they still have those, right?). "Toenapper," written by Bill Odenkirk, tells the tale of a kidnapper who kidnaps a kid (so far, so good), then chops off the kid's toe to prove that he actually has said beloved child, and leaves the severed toe in a jar in the park for the cops to find. Only, hold up, a snafu: he accidentally left the kidnapped kid in the park and kept the chopped-off toe. Oh, and it gets worse. Instead of chopping off the kid's toe, he mistakenly chopped off his own. What a mess! Playing this sketch, which was done live in the studio with two sets going at once, was the greatest joy a comedy boy can have. Hard laughs throughout, with an entirely fresh idea and a little story to go along with it. They don't write 'em like that anymore.

The best sketch, the one to rule them all, was Dino Stamatopoulos's "The Audition." David plays a happy, eager actor who comes to audition for a big role with a prepared monologue from a play that begins with the lines "Can I use this chair? For the audition . . . ?" to which the casting people respond, "Sure, go ahead," which makes him snap back, "NO! This is my monologue! Please, don't interrupt." In the course of doing his monologue, he repeatedly asks to use the chair, and they can't help but respond every time, and he has to begin again. This took a lot of rehearsal on David's part, as he had to recite the same monologue each time, full of pleading requests and pauses . . . and he nails it.

I'm gonna ask Dino where the idea came from. *Hey, Dino, where'd you get that crazy idea?* Dino says, "When I was in Chicago I wrote this play called *Trent* that was okay, but it didn't get a lot of people into the theater, but then, after the show was over, it was just me and a few friends sitting around and we had a whole theater to ourselves and so we went up and just did fake auditions. One after the other. Funny people, and . . . it just came out . . . I just started doing that: I think I just said, 'Can I use this chair?' And then I thought it'd be funny if that was the monologue, and it just completely wrote itself in one take. It's rare. Every once in a while a sketch just writes itself." Thanks, Dino!

We had a few short films that seemed to have originality and oomph, and rose above parody and our one-nickel production challenges. "I'll Marry Your Stupid Ass," about two determinedly straight guys who are so mad at each other that they challenge each other to *marriage* and end up staying together purely out of barroom rage, for a lifetime. Rage and love— equally powerful! David directed a wonderfully delicate bit called "Goodbye" in our final episode ever. The awkwardness of two fellas saying hearty goodbyes and then running into each other, again and again, elicited some kind of real, relatable emotion from the actors (me and Jay) but also from the audience. I maintain our show was the first sketch show to garner empathetic reactions from the audience: there was more than one heartfelt "Awwww" drawn from the live crowd in playing out a sympathetic character's tragic moment.

As for my personal favorite sketch, I'd have to say that "The Story of Everest" rules them all. Jay and I had been brain-wrestling in the writers' room and I asked him where he got his hoarding instincts. His house was loaded with shit. He explained it was hereditary; in fact, he remembered that there was an outdoor Weber grill *inside* his family's kitchen back in Chicago. One day his uncle came into the kitchen and told a story and, in the course of it all, leaned on the grill, tipping it over and sending ash flying everywhere. Everyone pitched in to clean up, and once things were spotless, the uncle proceeded to tell a fresh guest about the disaster they'd just endured, and in the course of relating the story, he leaned, again, on the grill and, again, filled every nook and cranny of the kitchen with fresh ash. We turned this into a story about a mountain climber who is full of himself, having just returned from climbing Mount Everest. In relating the story of his conquest to his parents, he stumbles and knocks his mother's thimble collection all over the room. They clean it up, his chipper brother arrives, and in sharing the story of how he knocked his mom's thimble collection over a few moments ago, he knocks the wall of thimbles over again . . . and again. He never gets around to telling the story of conquering Everest, and his family loses interest in his mountain-climbing triumph and is much more interested in his inability to maintain his balance in the living room. Ain't that the way of it? Jay's falls are perfect. Wild comic explosions that surprise the audience every time—watch it once and then play it back: he NEVER forecasts a fall. Cleese-level perfection.

The sketch killed, and built up perfectly for maximum laughs. Again, this was a live sketch, and the audience had to sit patiently while we reset the wall of thimbles. Our crack prop team worked hard and fast, but still it took forever between takes. David and I made jokes, ridiculed each other and the audience, and people were patient about it until we did it one too many times. The fifth or sixth time Jay falls, the audience didn't laugh *at all*. Even the crickets shut up and shook their heads in shame. The audience suddenly realized they may have fallen into a purgatory where a comedy scene keeps repeating itself to no purpose. We cut that take out of the final sketch; it was one too many beats where the "plot," such as it was, didn't move one iota. So, yeah, we took things too far once in a while, but the TV audience didn't have to suffer for it.

The lesson of *Mr. Show* is this: Give the artists what they want (freedom) and the audience wins! "Monster Parties: Fact or Fiction?" (episode 407) is a monumentally stupid deep dive into parody/novelty songs about Halloween (obviously very much focused on that "Monster Mash" nugget from the sixties). The night we spent in the Hollywood Forever Cemetery shooting the "monster party" was one of those memories of getting away with murder that will comfort my soul between here and death. These kinds of experiences are one of the better reasons to go into show business. It's the same feeling I had some years later in the Albuquerque desert with Bryan Cranston and Aaron Paul and a colossal crew, out in the middle of nowhere, sand blowing in our face, shivering to beat the band, kneeling over a freshly dug grave as Saul Goodman with a very real-looking toy gun aimed at my head. I digress; the "Monster Parties" bit is a masterwork. Dino Stamatopoulos once again led the way and wrote that shitty ditty. In it, Scott Adsit plays a folklore expert and, for a brief moment, is seen pleasuring himself to video of David's character telling his story of confronting real monsters. Becky Thyre has maybe the funniest line in the sketch when she declares to David's character, "You are now officially hypnotized . . . in the state of Rhode Island." Everybody in that piece is funny throughout.

My little brain and medium-sized heart are laid out on full display in the course of these four seasons of TV. It's a thoughtful, twisty, silly, swear-filled rant that crams all my judgments and joys into one neat boxed set. "Lifeboat" (episode 401) is my *Huckleberry Finn*: a low-class collection of "folks" are gathered to argue their clammiest personal intrigues before a nationwide audience but are forced to hold their petty bitchfest on a lifeboat lost at sea, their lives in the balance. The characters are unable to extract themselves from their petty infighting long enough to grasp their imminent demise, and one of them offers his reasoning as "because life is precious, and God, and the Bible." A sentence that explains nothing in itself and everything at once, and the only thing missing is a cheap, made-in-China MAGA hat, but that would have just seemed too outrageous even to us.

David Cross and I worked like one brain in making *Mr. Show.* If he provided the spark, I'd provide some structure, and we'd switch off those roles in writing, rewriting, rehearsal, performance, and editing. David pitched more jokes overall. Simply, David made things funnier. The amazing thing is that both of us feel complete ownership of the show and nearly every piece in it. It's amazing how we always landed on the best joke/angle of approach, one that satisfied both of us. As a performer, he crushed me. No one is more fun to watch. He pulls giant laughs in "Pre-Taped Call In Show," "The Audition," and "Hunger Strike," and that's the reel that should get him into heaven, otherwise I don't want to be there, either.

As far as sketches that sprang purely from David's brain, he lays claim to: " 'Prenatal Pageant,' 'Mayostard,' 'Spank,' 'Dream of a Lifetime,' '13th Apostle,' 'Last Indian,' and 'Downsizing' were my ideas, but by the time they went through the Odenkirk/*Mr. Show* filter ultimately had more depth to them. As for 'Downsizing,' that was my (not very successful) attempt to do a Monty Python–type sketch. Something just silly and absurd and fun to do. It was blatantly inspired by the sketch where Cleese is interviewing Chapman for a job and increasingly frustrates him with nonsense (you taking the Cleese role and I the Chapman role).

"One of the coolest, brain-expanding aspects about *Mr. Show* was the idea of writing for someone else. I had never really done that before. It had never occurred to me with any other sketch writing I had done," the impish genius added.

We never chased the audience, and we never caught them, either. The show was built for cultish love, and it succeeded. We wanted only the "out-crowd," the few, the proud, the misanthropes. Our greatest impact was in inspiring young performers and writers to like sketch a little more, and mislead them into following their passions.

"Why do you think we became enamored of 'classic' sketches over random stuff, over that time?" I needled David recently. He, par for the course, denied my premise:

"I can't separate any of that experience that way, or never thought to; it was just as hard to write *anything* and make it great . . . especially when we were doing *Tenacious D* and we had no break—zero, none. There was one point where we worked thirty-nine days in a row, no weekends or anything. But we were having so much fun. I haven't laughed that much in my life since then, cumulatively."

"What drove us, when it was so hard and we both had plenty of other options?" I pestered my friend.

"Well, wait a second, Bob, don't forget . . . Why would you trade this thing, where we get to do whatever the fuck we want with some of the most talented people we've ever met, for something else? Both of us had friends who were more 'successful' than us, critically, financially, and they weren't as happy as we were."

"True," I granted him, "but looking back, it's sometimes consternating to me that we cared so deeply about the intricacies of sketch while knowing almost no one was watching. But I guess the audience isn't made up of only comedy writers."

"Well, a lot of our audience ended up becoming comedy writers."

Over Uneasy

Two weeks before our fourth season premiere, an HBO exec called us and said, "Hey, this is not bad news, guys, it's . . . not." Of course, this was bad news. "It's *interesting*, let's just say . . . Anyway, we are going to switch your time slot. You guys are going to be on Mondays at midnight now."

"But we've always been on Fridays—who watches TV on Monday at midnight?" asked either David or I.

"I know, I know. Well, every night of the week we will have something special at midnight! You guys are getting Monday. To kick off the week."

"But Monday is a bad, bad day. It's a mistake—nobody even wants to have Monday *day,* much less Monday *night,*" said David and I, in unison.

"Yeah . . . I know, but Monday has to happen whether people like it or not. So you are officially being buried there—I mean, uh, *killed,* not buried . . . Did I say 'killed'? I meant *disappeared.* We are officially disappearing your show on Mondays at midnight. G'bye."

I looked over at David and saw him getting fitted for a plane ticket. He looked at me and saw a giant carp wearing human clothes, sucking air. The fourth season, our best from top to bottom, was two weeks from airing, but right then we knew we were finished. My son, Nate, was born a week after we taped the final show, so I was on the verge of my greatest role—"Anxious Dad"—and David heard New York might be lucky enough to get a Trump hotel with a Trump toilet in it that he could shit in for the rest of his life, so it certainly felt like a moment.

I remember sitting at my desk, looking across the office at him, and wondering, *How hard should we fight for more?* We could have, but also, we'd done it. Planted our flag. Did we really need to wait around for everyone to salute it? In truth, I was just trying to show that it could be done, and in my mind (and I think David felt the same), there it was, take it or leave it. We did our part. I knew that over time, the work we'd done would still be funny and people would see it, or not. What I didn't know was how prescient our outlandish notions were.

"The Mr. Show Water Cooler" *is* Fox News, with sweaty propaganda passed off as homey reg'lar folk shit-shootin'. The soccer team Real Madrid actually did recruit a seven-year-old (see "The Recruiters," episode 205), and the notion behind "America Blows Up the Moon" (episode 306), well, that was something NASA actually looked into doing, for some reason. Oh, and "Rap! The Musical"—come on, we should get a cut of *Hamilton*!

In the end, the show's biggest contribution to the general culture was to provoke and prod other, younger screwballz (pronounced like "screwballs") like us.

Tim Heidecker: "We knew this guy in Philly named Cotton Candy, who is a real guy. He was our age, a little older, and what Cotton Candy would do for a living is bootleg tapes. He'd go to shows; he would be the guy with the video camera bootlegging, like, Smashing Pumpkins or Nirvana, and he would sell them on the internet and through the mail, I guess. But he had all these great tapes, the stuff that ends up on YouTube now, but there was no YouTube. Cotton Candy had the *Mr. Show* tape. There was a tape. Just the whole run of the show on a VHS tape. And that was just—we just ate that up. That was mind-blowing. Life-changing."

Once we were done shooting, HBO actively tried to hide the show from an audience. The show was off the air and unavailable on VHS or DVD (well, they hadn't invented DVDs yet; a few months later, though . . .). This situation was confounding and made no business sense. It was like shooting yourself in the foot and then shooting yourself in the other foot, just . . . because you were an idiot. There were people who would happily have paid real American dollars for a set of their favorite obscure TV show. Who was in charge over there at HBO? David and I pooled our pennies and paid a professional dubbing house to make sets of every single episode on VHS tapes, and we mailed these sets to the coolest video stores in the coolest cities in America. This was a money-losing proposition, and it was also illegal, as we did not own our work, so we took care to attach a warning on every tape: "YOU CANNOT BE CHARGED FOR THIS VIDEO! However, if you want to do the video store a favor and rent another movie (We recommend 'Homer and Eddie') then we think the video store will be nice enough to lend you this episode of our show for free—just return it along with 'Homer and Eddie.' Between our comedy show, and 'Homer and Eddie' you are guaranteed to laugh at least once." Over the years I have run into many people who were "loaned" these top-quality copies, and hopefully a few of them found *Homer and Eddie* half as funny as David did . . . It's one of his favorite films of all time, primarily for the cinematography. You've never seen funnier cinematography.

It wasn't until years later that a DVD set of the show was finally released, and when it premiered in the top five DVD purchases on Amazon and stayed there for weeks, an HBO exec remarked, "Can you believe it? Who knew?" We were pleasantly surprised, too, but did you have to put it *like that*?

In 1994, David Cross saw a mock-rock duo at a seedy bar near Little Tokyo: two ample gentlemen with acoustic guitars, perfect pitch, and a deep love of the tropes of rock music. Together they delivered a grand vision of rock's future built upon its past, imagined greatness, posturing, utterly resplendent and powerful and a kick in the collective balls. I am speaking, of course, of Tenacious D (as in "tenacious defense," as pursued by L.A. Lakers coach Pat Riley).

David invited "the D" to perform at one of our earliest

Mr. Show test shows, at that crap club on Hollywood Boulevard. I got to see a young Jack Black. It was not unlike seeing Farley for the first time: he was an undeniable force for entertainment good onstage, an absolute joy across the board. Unlike Farley, he had more confidence in his talents and himself—good for him. Demons wilt at genuine self-confidence.

Tenacious D were awesome, and for the next few years Jack and Kyle Gass (Kyle is said to have the elusive power of "perfect pitch") would perform on the "alternative scene." It worked, despite the clash of styles—here they were with their rock tribute, then followed up with someone else's quirky comic ramblings about having sex with their therapist. The fact that this worked is a tribute to the audience of connoisseurs, small but open-minded. In the first performance I ever saw of the D, they did their song "Tribute," which is a tribute to "Stairway to Heaven" and also a tribute to itself, so it contained the essence of their very existence.

Any performer/writer who sees another talent for the first time spends all their brain power doing the math: *How talented is this person versus ME? What have they got that I haven't got, and how can I take it from them or CRUSH them, or simply have them killed?* People like Jack and Farley, their talent is disarming and you're forced to sit back and enjoy—and consider quitting showbiz. I always wondered where Jack got it from . . . so I asked him about it. "I don't think I ever met anyone who had the confidence that you seemed to exhibit about your journey—and it was justified—but also, even people who are madly talented and gifted don't have that confidence. Most people are just scared and clawing their way, especially when they're starting out."

Jack explained, "You know who helped me at the right moment? Fuckin' Anne Bancroft."

To which I replied, "No shit?!"

And he went on. "In my later years I went to a great school, a private high school, and her son, the great Max Brooks, his parents were there, and we did a production of *The Miracle Worker* that Anne Bancroft was in the original movie of, and so she came to the show, even though Max wasn't in the show, but she knew that we were doing this play, she knew the author, and she came and gave us a little pep talk before the show. And then, after the show, I went home and she'd left a message for me—she'd called my house and we weren't there, and I'm glad we weren't there, because she left a message on the Code-a-Phone. A tape that I played hundreds of times. She said, "Jaaaack . . . born to do it . . . you were born to do it." That just meant so much to me.

But the real miracle, I opined, was that "you believed her."

Jack agreed. "Yes. She was great, she was my mom's favorite actor in *The Turning Point.*"

I got to make a series of short films with the D. David and I co-produced it, but I took on the burden of the day-to-day. Each *Tenacious D* episode consisted of two twelve-and-a-half-minute stories, insane plots that transformed into songs—this was before Adult Swim and long after the Three Stooges, so no one was making twelve-minute episodes, or had, for decades. I thought it fit their punchy energy to keep the plots short. I wrote most of the stories, but they were all built on the songs and repartee created by Jack and Kyle in their live show. The plots stole specific references from their lyrics, sometimes in humorously tortured ways. One of my favorites is about Jack and Kyle's car breaking down in the desert near a commune and the song "Jesus Ranch" suddenly coming to life in very specific ways. The main guru of the place, played by the smart, subtle, and always funny Jim Turner, is named La-Ga-Gwing, after the nonsense jabber that J.B. sings in the chorus. This story was a literal lifting of the song's inventions. In between the filmed stories, the boys would talk to the camera in a classic Burns and Allen manner. It was a really fun presentation—but possibly a little too crude and homemade for HBO, which seemed to lean "classy" (hey, it's a "premium" service). Tom Gianas, my old friend from Second City days, was the perfect director for the *Tenacious D* shorts; they had a garage-rock vibe, a grubby, low-rent sixteen-millimeter look that made them ten times more lovable, and they were already quite lovable. There were a few rankles, with me leading the way through script writing and production. Once, Kyle Gass pulled a Norma Desmond and threw one of my scripts to the floor. "I'm not readin' this shit!" he said. He was pissed because I rewrote the whole thing over the weekend. I thought he was kidding, but he wasn't. Thankfully, he changed his mind and it got big laughs. But maybe I wasn't cut out for producing other people's material; I could be pushy and quite sure of myself. I was still a control freak, as I'd been on *Mr. Show*. Hey, it had worked well for me, I thought. It was the legacy of my difficult father in some ways; I knew that, and it bothered me, but I wasn't sure how much I could grow out of it. I was about to try, though, and this experience with the D was one of the reasons.

The show, a delight and an artistic success to me, went away because I asked for more credit for hauling the "executive producer" load around, pretty much single-handedly. My power grab created a kerfuffle that dampened enthusiasm, you could say. After all, this thing was so purely the spirit of Jack and Kyle, I can see how they felt like it was an overreach. As for me, I was exhausted, juggling my own projects, a new baby at home, and Kyle tossing scripts on the floor. I felt I deserved a spotlight. I remember Kyle arguing that I should be satisfied that "we always mention your name when we're onstage or talking about the show!" Sure . . . that was nice. But I was pretty exhausted, too. My son was a baby (having just been born, it was inevitable), and I had some movies to ruin, so . . . Anyway, the lesson from this episode is CREDITS DON'T MATTER AMONG FRIENDS!

Ah well, onward, deeper into showbiz!

Postscript: I remained on good terms with the D despite this difficult interlude. I think they could tell I wasn't trying to be malicious, grabby, selfish, and, beyond that, Jack and his team knew that he was headed for far bigger things than our little shorties on HBO, and I gave them a good excuse to move on. I'm proud they wanted me to contribute short comic reductions for their various gold-plated albums—most notably the track "Flutes and Trombones," on *Rize of the Fenix.*

Film-Flam: The *Run Ronnie Run!* Tragedy

David and I and some *Mr. Show* writers—Brian Posehn, Scott Aukerman, and BJ Porter—wrote ourselves a sketch-comedy movie. Every couple of years, one of these cinematic kitchen sinks slips through the cracks: *The Groove Tube* (1974)— which I saw at a drive-in theater and remember nothing of (I do recall the porn that came after—a sumptuously production-designed and quite spirited takeoff on *Alice in Wonderland*); then there was *The Kentucky Fried Movie* (1977), which "did the trick," I guess; and, of course, the great ones, Python's *The Meaning of Life* (1983), maybe their least great work, but still pretty great. The script we wrote, and that we *should have* made, had, among other bits, a parody of a Woodstocky music festival where a Phish-type jam band played only one song for three days, until people start dropping dead from boredom. David played an abrasive Bill Graham type—cutting every corner he could find. This one could have been a crowd-pleaser. The smartest/dumbest piece in the script was a 1950s black-and-white sci-fi film wherein visiting aliens who've come to Earth in peace instead cause mayhem and chaos, provoking a military overreaction because guess what, the aliens' heads are shaped like penises! Note: in our story, Europeans are fine with the penis-headed aliens and don't get what all the fuss is about. I'm sure not all the bits would have worked equally well, but I'm also sure that some of them would have worked great and made for a movie that played and stuck around. We shoulda made *that* movie. Shoulda, woulda, coulda—ah, regrets, the purpose of autobiography.

Look, I'm not a *total* idiot, I'm an incomplete one. Still, I was easily conscripted into a new approach, something that would complicate our initial plan to *simply make a sketch movie* and doomed the entire enterprise, and if there's one lesson *Star Trek* has taught us all, it's simply this: never doom the enterprise. We should have just done what we did the entire time we made our little TV show, which was: try to please an audience of two, me and David, and everybody else in the world could follow along or go hang.

The writers met in our old *Mr. Show* offices at Hollywood Center Studios, and we all worked to keep the vibe of our show intact for our grand feature, including starting with our own "Let's all visit the snack bar!" animation, which includes the personified candy box visiting the bathroom, where dancing toilets are happy to receive them. This is the sole piece of writing from our sketch movie script that carried over into our new draft. Michael De Luca was the only film executive crazy enough (young enough) to get our sensibility. He offered to make our feature. Almost immediately we started getting pressure to abandon the sketch approach and consider "narrative"—a STORY, dammit, like a real movie has. As David recalls, it was "a New Line note that we got repeatedly and consistently throughout the drafts and subsequent readings." I stepped right in it. Wanting to be cooperative, but also thinking they were onto something, I helped sway David and the other writers to dump the sketch-movie script we'd written and go for the Sandler template: idiot man-child goes on balderdash journey and learns slightly more than nothing. We were "a buncha smartsies," and we outsmarted ourselves: surely we could do this lowest-common-denominator type of story, and maybe sneak in some cleverness? Did we already have such a character in our grasp? One who goes on a quest, and hilarity ensues? We did, indeed! From the first season of the show: Ronnie Dobbs, a rags-to-riches-to-rags white-trash scoundrel who gains fame from being arrested multiple times on a *Cops*-style TV show. I would play the same character I played in the television version of the sketch, a British television producer named Terry Twillstein who sees the magic inside the crude, unseemly antics of David as Ronnie. Jill Talley would be Ronnie's trailer-park wife, and David Koechner would be his drunk-buddy. It was a rise-to-infamy tale perfect for our time, with lots of crude jokes and some sidetracks that played almost like sketches within the narrative film. Sound great? Let's agree that it sounds all right, and leave it at that. The script we produced has more funny lines than the *Fast and the Furious* films have automobiles, but funny lines won't save yer film. (Fast cars *will*—take note!) Making the movie was fun, *really* fun. And magical . . . until it turned into the worst experience I've ever had in show business.

The writing was a hoot. Brian Posehn, Scott Aukerman,

BJ Porter, and David and I, sittin' in a tree, laughing our collective asses off. We would shoot for two months in Atlanta, so David could take us to the best barbecue in the country and showcase his love-hate relationship with Dixieland: "I was born there, lived there a year, moved around in Florida for four years after that, moved up north (two places in Connecticut, three places in New York) for four years after that, and moved back down when I was nine," he tells me. All I know is, wherever we go in America, making this movie or on tour, he can say, "I used to live near here." Troy Miller was directing and also executive-producing, so the team was back together. However, unlike with the TV show, David and I would not be producers on the project; we'd been asked not to take that credit, as there were already too many producers—a common problem in Los Angeles, alongside rats and Scientology pamphlets.

Just as in every filming experience ever, every scene was turning out better than it seemed on the page; an experienced filmmaker knows that this tells you nothing at all. But we were thrilled as the performers brung it big-time. I especially loved watching David as Ronnie get chased through a skeevy house, barking dogs, clutter, and sketchy folk scattered throughout, each room a sadder scene than the last, including a grizzled, bony old man sitting in a bathtub of green water, until the cops finally find their prize squirreled away under a Piggly Wiggly sign in the dirt yard—a one-shot masterpiece. And David Koechner as Clay, Ronnie's buddy who keeps getting the short end of the stick and always takes the blame: "It's okay, Ronnie, I was a little drunk, too . . ." And a bunch of great moments with Ronnie Dobbs talking to his Asian nephew, who is in a wheelchair—a loving homage to the Jackie Chan tear-yanking scenes in *Rumble in the Bronx*.

Oh! We nearly killed some people, too! We almost killed

them with *a cannon*. An actual cannon that had been built to shoot bowling balls. We'd written a scene where Ronnie runs into a bowling alley and turns a bowling ball return mechanism up to the highest setting, simply to create chaos. We wanted bowling balls to come shooting out the back of the alley and into the parking lot. The local special effects team that built the mechanism was two jokers working out of their garage. Using what little they knew of physics, they built a cannon to launch a fourteen-pound ball out the back door, but instead it sailed clear across a thirty-five-yard parking lot, over a fence, past the grass embankment, and onto a very busy two-lane highway. 'Twas a beautiful southern night in September and we all watched slack-jawed at the horror unfolding before our eyes. The ball didn't even bounce until it hit the very active roadway. The headline "Family of Four Killed by Bowling Ball Sent from Hollywood" was easily conjured, as was the image of us reading it from our jail cells in the Doraville Correctional Facility in between beatings. Luckily, there was a break in traffic and no one got hurt. Just us. And our careers.

Okay, fine, the film had lots of fun sequences in it and, thanks to Troy's astounding resourcefulness, some big production-value moments. The best scene in it is the Hollywood cult scene, near the end. Ronnie's character has become rich and gone Hollywood, including joining a cultish group that meets on the lawn outside his big mansion. Jeff Goldblum was kind enough to lend us his celebrity status and his awesome comedy delivery as part of a group of New Agey airheads gathered around their leader, Tom Kenny. He is asking each member what his heart wants most of all, and when he comes to Jeff he gets the dry "I want . . . my money back." The cult leader prompts him to take it further. "And, uh, I want angels to give it to me, and, oh, uh, pixies to count it out for me, and a gnome or a hobbit or an elf . . . but no matter what happens with any of that, I *do* want my money back."

A word about Mandy Patinkin's guest appearance in the film. Such an amazing singer, his angelic tenor lifting to the heavens the lyrics "Can't a man not drink his beer in silence? Can't a man not crudely lie and scream? Can't a man not control his bitch with violence? Y'all are brutalizin' me." A prettier presentation of terrible instincts there has never been.

Okay, the film has its moments, actually quite a lot of moments, but things just don't ever find a rhythm, there's no momentum to it. Do they still teach "momentum" in film school? Cutting David and me out of the editing process doomed what was always a questionable effort. This hinky script cobbled together by chicken-drunk dingbats needed all the help it could get every step of the way! Most films do. But instead, once filming ended, David and I were both told to "scram" and not come back. Insult to injury, we were told to scram by our friend and co-conspirator in all the hijinks of the past six years, Troy. It was such an unbelievable switcheroo that I simply didn't believe it. For the next six months, through all of postproduction, I would pace my living room with my baby son, both of us crying (and drinking "bottles") and me constantly glancing over at the phone, waiting, knowing it would ring any second and Troy would be on the line to say, "Get down here, this thing's a mess." It never happened. The phone never rang; it just sat there, silent and angry. I suffered a long, excruciatingly slo-mo explosion of all hopes and dreams and any career momentum I might have had. The worst thing about it: the old saw *If I'm going to fail, at least let me do it by my own hand.* I am certain that David and I could have made *Run Ronnie Run!* more focused, and that means quite a lot to a comedy film. When a tone is set, one that works even intermittently, a joke or two or even an entire scene that fails can be disregarded by the audience. Editing choices can remake a film. I'm certain David and I could not have made it all winning, but it would have been better, and at least we could have walked away knowing we'd done our best. Our one fan at the studio, Michael De Luca, had packed up and left before we finished shooting, so we had no one to look out for us in this process.

I can guess at why Troy shut us so completely out of the process, and I think it's two things. One being that I had not been kind enough in the course of making *Mr. Show* all those years. When it came to matters of taste, editing choices especially, David and I were the only voices that mattered, and he probably resented that. Second, the journey of making movies is one of fear, followed by moments of confidence, then fear again, a sick spiral if you're doing it right. Those first cuts are really exciting and you feel like you are absolutely killing it. It's easy to fool yourself that the film is awesome, out of pure excitement. Possibly, Troy simply thought the movie was just great the way it was. This is hard to believe if you actually sit down and watch it, so my money is on the first explanation.

Lesson: KARMA IS A BITCH! BE NICE TO PEOPLE! YOU CAN BE RIGHT WITHOUT BEING A DICK ABOUT IT!

I've only seen the film twice. New Line, wise to what they had, relegated it to DVD status. Meanwhile, David Spade had made a far less ambitious exploration of white-trashiness, entitled *The Grand and Fantabulous Adventures of Joseph P. Durt* or something similar—a simple and likable character study of an oft-misunderstood archetype. His film did make it into theaters, and pleased enough people to warrant a highly considered revisitation years later. Wonderful, for him.

Bitterness is everywhere in L.A. It's what burns off the marine layer by ten thirty every morning. You've got to find ways to combat it, but sometimes you just have to acknowledge it, smile at it, and turn it into a podcast. Too bad for me, podcasts weren't invented yet. So I did what anyone at a low point in their career in the biz has done since time began: cocaine. Lots and lots of cocaine. I rubbed it on my eyelids. I powdered my ass with it every morning. I found that it kills athlete's foot pretty quick, but it works best if you put it in your nose.

Chapter 7

Development Heck

———

When Nathan (the baby from the previous story) was twelve, and his sister, Erin, ten, I was invited to pop in at the then unknown cable TV drama *Breaking Bad* for a turn as the sleazy but lovable (go figure) lawyer Saul Goodman. This was the next big break in my career, which means there's a ten-year gap that I have to account for. I worked the entire time. Like a coal miner but with TV shows, still I was covered in coal dust for most of it—my choice. Interesting projects, always with the best intentions, the highest hopes. Except for the commercials. I did those for money. Still tried to make them funny, though.

Quite a few projects only made the initial stages; none made it to air. This is what people call "development hell." I'm going to downgrade it to "heck" for your sensitive eyes . . . Nah, I'm downgrading it because, while I sweated a fair amount in those ten years, I also had a great life. I lived in L.A., so the weather was good. But also I had married a great, smart, beautiful woman named Naomi Yomtov, and we quickly had two delightful kids (right from the start, they were "delightful"—it's on their birth certificates), and so all of that was good. Plus, as I said, I worked. The whole time. I was even onscreen a fair amount—small jobs, mostly, but some great and interesting ones. The *Curb Your Enthusiasm* I appeared in was fun to do, and people still quote parts of that nasty dialogue to me. The best thing about acting gigs was getting a break from writing, which is way more challenging and, in equal measure, rewarding.

Bernie Brillstein and me, waiting to get shut down again. I loved every minute of it.

Through much of it, I had Bernie Brillstein by my side, always telling me to "count on yourself, kid." I followed my inspirations, I threw wild pitches, always working on the edges of my own "wheelhouse." I asked a lot of the industry, but in return I tried to be an easy no. When the network or studio would call to pass on a project, my response was "Thank you." I didn't push or beg, or offer to change anything to make it more suitable for them. I'd offered them my vision and that was that. I also thought a lot about *Run Ronnie Run!* and how that project crashed, possibly because I had spent years insisting I was the sole and final arbiter of funny. I thought I'd try to get more into this thing the kids call "collaboration," and let other people be right once in a while, not push back as hard. Let other people do the thinking—hey, this could be sweet!

Somehow, I still had a lot of street cred. *Mr. Show* resonated. The good laughs we got and the cool, underground factor, endured. Thank God! It was the reason I sold so many offbeat projects in this decade of head-pounding.

Cads kill me. Men who go through life making wisecracks, being overtly rude, taking advantage, being self-obsessed disasters. They're just funny to me, though I enjoy such antics from a safe distance. Because of this hobbyhorse, one of my favorite funny films is *Breathless,* by Jean-Luc Godard. I don't think it's meant to be a riotous comedy, but it makes me howl. Jean-Paul Belmondo as the dickish cool guy "Michel" is a big laugh to me. So . . . one day I got the idea "What would it be like if the future was really shitty?"—with crappy, disposable cardboard cell phones, flying cars for the very rich, lots of pollution, and just as many relationship problems as ever? *The Near Future* (2000), a film for HBO, told the story of Luke, a real shifty fellow—my version of Godard's kool klown (it also owed a debt to his film *Alphaville*), a guy who wisecracks and lies his way through a barely there existence. Breckin Meyer played this schemer with a heart of shit, somehow charming women and not minding all the enemies he is making along the way— until . . . a stranger comes to kill him.

Katharine Towne was perfect as the beautiful ingenue: she had a sharpness, she radiated smarts, and we knew she was wise to Luke's foolery. Mike Hagerty, a Second City legend, played the postal worker sent to take Luke out, with a gun that is too complicated and futuristic for him to use. I was ridiculing the whole notion of progress, this was my *Blade Runner,* co-written with Chip Pope and Howard Kremer, two writers who'd done a great show called *Austin Stories* on MTV a few years earlier. What we created is a helluva watch. Hard to say why I couldn't put it over; we had some great ideas and characters and a lot of mood. This was one that got away. This one, though, it still feels worthy. I was so far out of my wheelhouse with this mix of sci-fi, noir, comedy, and drama that I couldn't feign the confidence enough to fool the network. YOU'VE GOT TO BE ABLE TO FEIGN CONFIDENCE. Maybe if I could have put up a better front.

After that, Chip and Howard and I did one of the funniest pilots ever with *Highway to Oblivion* (2001). *E! True Hollywood Story* was a very popular series at the time, telling the story of celebrity wreckage using archival footage, testimonials, and hokey reenactments. We stole that pastiche format to tell the story of a celebrity hanger-on. Howard Kremer played Erskine Brubaker, a goofy, slightly dangerous guy who comes to Hollywood with the flimsiest of plans to crash on the couches of various celebs. In the pilot, Dave Foley of *The Kids in the Hall* is Erskine's patsy. Dave is hilarious, as always, and gets walked on by the pushy Erskine. Until, Erskine lets Dave's beloved cat out and the cat gets run over by a delivery boy, played by Derek Waters (later of *Drunk History* fame). Erskine and a friend secretly bury the cat, then—after Dave discovers that his cat is gone—they all decide to dig it up so he can mourn it properly, and the whole crew is arrested for pet-grave robbery. Foley's celebrity status gets him off the hook, and Erskine is forced to move on to another victim. Shooting these overdramatized reenactments, faking security-cam footage, and doing dry testimonials to camera (long before *The Office*), there were so many opportunities for comedy. You know what there wasn't? A decent female character. The female co-lead we'd written was written horribly by the worst part of me. This doomed an otherwise very funny and inventive show. I'm not a "bro," I don't have any frat boy in me, but you'd never know from this script, where the main female character was a stripper who was being conned and didn't seem to mind it.

Here's another doozy: *The Super Nerds* (2000), a TV movie about two characters who work in a comic book store. Written with and starring Patton Oswalt and Brian Posehn! That's a nerd A-team right there. But nerd culture was just beginning to rise up, still considered very niche, and the show was just good, not great. But great fun to make.

David Cross, Brian Posehn, and much of our *Mr. Show* cast reassembled for a very fun tour of live shows. We cobbled together a tale from that early sketch movie we'd written, entitled *Mr. Show Live: Hooray for America!* (2002). In the story, a TV actor with no discernible ethical compass is recruited to run for president by a conglomerate of power-mad companies. The candidate decides that, instead of spending his vast campaign fundage for ads, he will just send a check to every American voter if he is elected. He buys votes outright. He gets elected, of course. David plays the actor who gets picked by the corporation to be the zany, say-anything presidential candidate. We thought we were putting on a broad satire; we were, of course, performing a documentary, a few years before the events in the documentary actually happened. Another scene in this show featured Brian Posehn as a death-row inmate who is too mentally incapacitated to be put to death. The state (I'm pretty sure it was Texas) spends an ungodly amount of money to perform dangerous, newfangled surgeries and therapies on him to raise his IQ to where he can be justifiably executed. Later, something close to this actually happened in real life. Wow. This is why comedy is hard—the real world keeps surpassing us!

The alternative comedy scene kept growing and getting more adventurous, and *the audience* was the reason. They were getting it, and liking it. New York followed L.A. and alternative comedy nights popped up there. When I was in NYC, I would perform at Luna Lounge with Janeane, Marc Maron,

David, Jon Benjamin, and new voices as the scene built. In Los Angeles, the coolest club was Largo's original location, on Fairfax, just across from Canter's. It was tightly packed, comfortable, and extremely well curated by the best booker there ever will be, Mark Flanagan. People like Flanagan ("Flanny") are the people who make cool shit happen by giving new voices a place to grow. You could really get the energy going at Largo. It's where I saw one of my favorite comics, Zach Galifianakis, for the first time, and where I met Fred Armisen and watched him do precise, hilarious characters with the subtlest degree of caricature. Not for a second did I think Fred would make it to *SNL;* he was too interesting and smart and subtle. But Lorne's taste came through on that one. Fred was, for me, the reason to keep watching that show for the next decade.

I had it in mind to work with Fred myself, and to try doing *Mr. Show* for a wider audience, on network, no swearing, keeping all the silly/smarts. The Fox network was doing great now, so was less willing to try something crazy, but we got in under the wire with Gail Berman, an exec still willing to experiment. Stealing a format from a great Brit sketch show called *The Fast Show,* I planned a pre-taped sketch show that would open with a news team and lots of topical jokes that could be updated on the day the show ran on the network, with the sketches shot on other nights and banked. The show was called *Next!* (2002), because, like they did on *The Fast Show,* we would be cutting sketches up and then revisiting them throughout an episode, to keep the pace up. We made a very funny and smart two episodes, with a great cast that included Jill Talley, Jay Johnston, Susan Yeagley, Jerry Minor, Rasika Mathur, and . . . *way too many* other people. I had guests upon guests, including Brian Posehn and Patton Oswalt and Zach Galifianakis, and even Ray Romano and Andy Dick—everyone I could jam in there. We got good laughs from the live audience (some of the bits are on YouTube), but once it was put together, it just came across as a giant ball of comedy, hurtling and smashing into a million pieces, overloading the test audience with faces and ideas.

The most "network-friendly" project I made at this time was *The Big Wide World of Carl Laemke* (2003). In it, I played a dad making observations about Middle American midlife livin'. This was back when America had a middle instead of just two sides. Greg Mottola (*Superbad*) directed, Zac Efron played my eldest son, and Leighton Meester was the neighbor in love with him. Zac later told me that getting this audition had kept him in the game, that he and his mom had a conversation on the way to the audition about taking a break from the biz if it didn't work out. I liked him, my casting director *loved* him, and we had a great time making that show. It was just a learning experience for him, though, as no one saw it.

These were shows that went to pilot, but there were many others that only made it to the script stage. Many, many others. This period in my life was creative rope-a-dope, and Bernie Brillstein was my Angelo Dundee. Bernie was in my corner, encouraging me, and he was always the last to let go. In fact, I would be the one talking *him* down when the network said no. "Bernie, it's okay; they're right, it wasn't panning out. We did our best. Here, I got a new thing . . ." I always had a new thing, and I think Bernie loved that about me. Also, Bernie had had a long career and a front-row seat to so many fringe ideas that blew up big (*SNL*, the Muppets), so he knew that the fringe is where truly big stuff is invented. Also, he simply loved the fight, the showbiz gossip, pitch meetings, bitching, and badgering the network for a response, for movement, on a project. Then, he loved being indignant, wronged, screaming "Fuck 'em! What do they know?! The show is great!"

The internet finally showed up and I made a show with

Derek Waters (*Drunk History*) and Simon Helberg (*The Big Bang Theory*). Naomi was first to suggest these two pals work together, as they were actually friends and had a funny repartee. Derek would goad Simon, who was funny but more controlled than Derek's casual vibe. The *Derek and Simon* (2007) short films for HBO were about two friends who cockblock each other, reliably. A cast of young amazings including Zach Galifianakis, Jake Johnson, Ashley Johnson, and Eric Edelstein joined us. It was hip and smart and, best of all, not trying too hard. In my favorite episode of the lot, Ashley Johnson played Simon's date, who's never heard of the Holocaust (she went to a college where she had made up her own curriculum, and had left WWII out of it). Simon takes her to the Holocaust Museum on a first date and she is simply devastated. "We have to get the word out—people need to know about this!" she says, completely gutted. We made a few episodes of the show; HBO and others were trying to figure out how to make stuff that belonged on this new web-world thingy. But before we could really get going, the "Big Bang" came along and everyone moved on. One more failure I have to alert you to before we get into worldwide success and golden days. Because, you fool, failure is where it's at! It tells you more about anyone's talent and drive and self than anything that works. Pay attention—it all works out in the end.

I made David Cross do a sitcom. Really, I did. A normal sitcom, with an audience and a TV living room and two kooky roommates. I thought: What if we got the set to *Everybody Loves Raymond* and cooked up a cockeyed scenario that let David do stand-up, rant and rave, and be funny in all the many ways he is funny. *David's Situation* (2008) was the final project Bernie and I pursued together. It smooshed together *The Young Ones, Everybody Loves Raymond, It's Garry Shandling's Show,* and even *All in the Family.* It was for HBO, and they had the actual *Everybody Loves Raymond* set in mothballs, so we simply repainted a little and changed the tchotchkes. David played "David Cross," retired from showbiz, now employed as a writer of simpering travel essays for in-flight magazines. Sharing this prefab suburban house in a flyover state with him is a crewcutted right-wing nut (Eric Hoffman) and a tie-dyed left-wing nut (Matt Besser). David is caught in the middle, because here's the thing: David might lean liberal, but in truth he is a freethinking contrarian. He hates everybody and wants no part of a club that would have him as a member.

In the pilot episode, David's home is being rented out to a TV show to "catch predators." David has the role of "bait": impersonating a clueless, nubile piece of fresh meat, complete with lollipop and whirligig beanie. When an old friend pops over for a visit, the banter between them is misconstrued as predatory, and the cops BUST IN and David's pal gets arrested. Zach Galifianakis played the clueless buddy, a free-spirited hippie who wants fame so badly that he's thrilled to have made it on TV by any means necessary. Then we get to see his music video, a song about infamy being as good as fame (and ain't that so?)—and, while that's no longer a revelatory observation, it was back then, before "Don the Con" showed the world how it's done. At some point, David even wandered off the set and did five minutes of improvised stand-up for the live audience, then wandered back into "the show." A planned, unscripted moment!

The audience, largely made up of *Mr. Show* fans, was energetic, tuned in, tuned up—*too* excited even. I directed but appeared onscreen for a half a beat as a guy on a plane reading one of David's columns and *humph*ing at it. They went nuts. We should have appeared on the show together. And maybe it was all too high-concept. But it was fun.

Weirdly, having the network at the taping to see how hard it killed actually kind of hurt us. The taped version, edited together, was a letdown compared with the in-person experience. Like watching a party you weren't invited to. In the end it came off as more of a prank than an actual suggestion for a running TV show.

Bernie was in a recuperation hospital from which he wouldn't be recuperating. I came by his room and screened the pilot episode for him and explained that the brain trust—me, David, and HBO—all agreed that we weren't moving ahead with it. He was disappointed. There were a lot of laughs in there, this amazing energy that happens whenever David and I put our heads together—a lot to like. But I said, "We all agree that we just didn't have it figured out. Anyway, don't worry, I already have another idea." I did, too.

He looked at me, took a beat to think, and said, "You're tough."

Did he mean I was resilient? Or that I was tough *to get a message to*? That message being: *Quit. Already.* Maybe both. Dumb and unstoppable—a real one-two punch.

Bernie passed away in August of 2008, after a life of good food, laughs, shouting into the phone, and too many flavorful cigarettes. I know he had a great time in show business, and I was glad to be a part of his story.

Marriage Material

Naomi and I have been married for twenty-three years. Our secret to staying in love? Every Sunday, without fail, I give her twelve roses. And, just so she doesn't get a swelled head, a note that says, "Here, my dear, is one rose for each of your faults."

If I've become a more rounded person (and how could I not; I was shallow as a communion wafer for most of my run), it's due to Naomi and her example in my life. She works with a gusto that outgustos mine, but she is always looking for side roads to go down to give life variety and challenge. In fact, one of these side roads, a serious focus on vim and vigor (but mostly vim), led me right down a primrose path to a project that she absolutely could not countenance: *an action movie.* Too bad for her, she had taught me the joys of "dynamic tension!" But the number one thing about Naomi is she loves comedy; in fact, she likes it more than I do—and with a wider palette. That's how we met, outside a comedy show, one of those shows that only the extremely hip would have known about.

I sure enjoyed the fact that "alternative comedy" was slowly, surprisingly overtaking "club comedy," so there were more and more places to do it—even, much later, in the clubs themselves. Sometime just before we began shooting the first season of short films for *Mr. Show,* I performed on a stage at an architecture- and art-themed bookstore in Santa Monica. I remember my set that night being just like every other set I ever did: sloppy but fun. The best part of the night was meeting a smart young woman who was there to watch the show, and getting her number. I just hassled her as she was exiting the fairly packed room. "Who you?!" I yelled. "Give me number!" I grunted. I wrote number down and waited a month to call her. When she didn't pick up, I left her a message; I did not leave my number. I waited another couple of weeks to try the number again. It took only two dates to realize I'd found my best partner ever, even better than David Cross, if you can believe it.

Naomi Yomtov liked comedy so much that she already knew who I was, and even knew some of my personal story, long before we met. As a talent scout for producers looking to develop sitcom projects, she was a deep-diver in the comedy community and had heard a few of my more self-revealing performances at *The UnCabaret*. She knew I'd had a shitty dad and lots of inner turmoil, and that my response to the traumas of life was ridicule and belittlement. She wasn't a stalker, but it was more than just her job; it was her calling, really. Twenty-five years later, she can still be found in offbeat, beginner comedy stages, because finding new comedy voices is her joy. So long as she doesn't marry another one, I'm good with it.

It was a helluva wedding, way up in Malibu, on a sunny day, an amazing collection of humans—Jack Black and Eban Schletter commencing the ceremony with "Have I Told You Lately That I Love You" and David Cross giving a reading without a single "swear." Ben Stiller brought Owen Wilson as his date, which always makes us laugh to remember. But perhaps not as much as the fact that my mother was told by her priest that she had to sit outside during the ceremony, as it wasn't a church-approved wedding. Ah, religion . . . bringin' people together for centuries!!

After we were married, Naomi struck out on her own, starting a management company. She would, of course, be my manager, after Bernie, and like I said, her greatest joy is in developing raw, incipient talent, and luckily, no matter how much success I might have, part of me would always be that— uncertain, discovering, always risking in pursuit of a fresh, edgy idea.

A brief word about managers and agents. Young actors/comics are very eager to get a manager or agent, and I ask, what for? Do managers make you famous? They don't write the material you'll perform. They don't hire you for projects. Here's what they do: they're a sounding board and they make connections. In a business where there are so many people— layers of contacts at studios and networks—managers try to know a lot of those people so you can focus on being you: an indulgent baby gurgling your special brand of nonsense. A good manager is a partner, is generally supportive (but not all the time), gives advice, but, in the end, says yes to your way forward and makes it happen with the best energy they can muster.

Some managers choose from budding talent, then quietly stand off to the side until the talent buds (gets work), and then they proceed to manage what can be generated from that work. Which is to say, they sign you up and wait around for you to get your breaks. This is a legit approach used by most. Naomi is not like that; she finds new and clever ways to give young clients experience and raise awareness of them. She engineers breaks. She invents opportunities. Managing my career is like managing three beginners all wrapped up in one cute ball of pinging energy. Except I'm not cute.

Having your wife also be your manager can be challenging. Heck, having your wife be your *wife* can be challenging. "Where's my dinner?" "Where's my paper?" "Where'd you go?!" Truth is that, in the fight to make your way through projects, you want the person at home to care about how you *feel* about the project you are currently getting all consternated over, and Naomi is, sadly, a very smart, opinionated, creative person with strong taste who doesn't necessarily love the project I am canoodling at the moment.

"Honey, nobody likes my script."

"Well, neither do I."

That is NOT the exchange you might be looking for if you're me. Bernie always knew what to say: "Fuck 'em, what do they know?" This allowed me to respond, with phony equanimity, "No . . . no, they're probably right."

Over many years, Naomi built her business out with some amazing early clients—Stephanie Courtney, Kristen Wiig, Bill

Hader, and Jenna Fischer, among many others. She has an eye, and she was wise to build out her business, partnering with an ex-agent named Marc Provissiero. This was perfect for me, as Marc provided the balance and encouragement I needed in chasing my fringy, ever multiplying pursuits, especially the ones my dear wife didn't care for. Having been an agent for years, Marc already had lots of strong relationships in the business, which is the great value of a manager: so *you*, the artist, don't have to make "relationships" with "people." Between Marc and Naomi, I have been able to find someone on almost every project who "gets it" and to stay married through it all, the waiting, hoping, failing . . .

"Great Work on That Proposal": Tim and Eric Find Me

The moving sidewalk in LAX Terminal 4 goes on forever in the perfect opening sequence of *The Graduate*, and that can be how the biz feels. Like you are moving but getting nowhere. You're getting compliments from your peers, and execs and heat seekers tell you, "You're really special," "We want to work with you," "Bring us whatever you got" . . . but then, nothing. I know the feeling. So whenever I see someone with talent, if I can say something on their behalf, or help them find a shortcut on their path, I will.

I had an office in Hollywood—usually the death knell for creativity, but I just wanted wall space for posters from my failed movies. It doesn't matter if they were considered "rotten tomatoes"—they cover gouged-out plaster like nobody's business. The only good thing about having that office, besides the ancient A/C unit emitting mold spores that are currently mutating in my lungs, was that I now had an address from which to receive a certain nondescript, odorless manila package from two fresh-out-of-college (Temple University) chaps named Tim Heidecker and Eric Wareheim.

It was a normal day at the dumb office, me staring at the blank page until finally, finally, *finally* lunchtime shows up. I would usually throw out a manila envelope from a stranger. What could be inside? Nothing good. Anthrax? Please, let it be anthrax. I was in my seventh year of pounding failure and I needed the best distraction/ excuse ever—what could be better than "I ingested anthrax; my pilot script for the show you're never going to make will be a few days late!" I opened the envelope and the first thing I pulled out was an itemized bill for the envelope itself and its contents: a T-shirt, a couple DVDs, and some headshots. I didn't even glance at the DVDs, but the itemized bill from a "Tim and Eric" made my day.

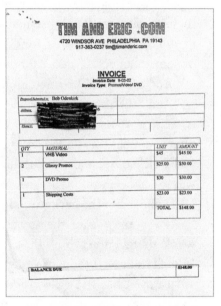

How to jumpstart your career: send an invoice!

Tim tells it this way:

"So I was sitting in New York at my desk job. Eric and I were making these movies. We'd made three or four of them and we had shown them to our friends. People had really reacted positively. We'd shown them at some film festivals. We were feeling really good about it. What do we do? We don't know anybody in the entertainment industry. Zero. I remember walking down the street in New York thinking, 'I should send this tape to some people that I admire.' And there were really five people I thought of . . . I saw a production company logo at the end of a *Mr. Show* episode. I called that number, they said Bob's company is something else. Put me in touch with that number. I called. Got an address from your assistant. I also, at the time, was doing a band called the Tim Heidecker Masterpiece and we had made a record. I sent that first, got no reply. Then we made this tape. And Eric had the brilliant idea to put in our headshots—we had these stupid headshots where, as you can picture, just us, totally inappropriate jogging outfits or something very ironic. And then an invoice."

"And a T-shirt," I remind him.

"And a T-shirt. So the invoice and a DVD went in the mail. A week goes by or something and I'm at work and my cell phone number was on the letter I sent, I guess. And you called and I picked up, and I just thought it was a prank because it was so unbelievable that you were calling. But I heard our DVD playing in the background of the call."

As for my side of the story: "I hadn't even watched the whole thing. I don't think I ever watched the whole thing, just enough to know I thought you guys were onto something."

I enjoyed the T-shirt, a crude outline of Eric in a business suit handing documents to Tim, another office worker, with the caption "Great work on that proposal!" Dry as a windstorm in Death Valley at Christmas in July.

On their DVD were six shorts, which included "The Cat Film Festival"; "Friends," a music video of Tim and Eric capering about to a Broadway-corny song about "You got to have friends"; and a crude animation about a guy visiting the mayor of his small town and pitching him an uninspired idea for restaurants. Two things stuck with me. First, as different as all the pieces were, they all belonged together. They shared a sensibility—a sensibility that was (and still is) hard to nail down. Second, while it was experimental, absurd, and random, they weren't trying too hard. They had a degree of confidence, trusting the viewer that you either got it or you didn't. And it was funny. It was more *funny* than it was weird—the weirdness was funny. Genuinely funny, not *I'm uncomfortable, so I guess I have to laugh,* which I am against.

Their use of "accidental" clumsy moments was something I'd never seen. The "Cat Film Festival" video was the first time I had seen an intentional cutaway *to the wrong person*—the presenter who was not speaking at the moment. It was "meta," but extremely sad-funny. Tim explained the origin of this to me: "Creation is sometimes accidental and then having the capacity to recognize that that's something you want to keep doing and try to do again."

Tim and Eric had an instinct for making a mistake feel "right." They were more absurd than Python but still, always, funnier than off-putting. This special mix can only come from inspiration and instinct. Tim had a good explanation for what is at the core of their choices: *embarrassment.* "The world we grew up in, it was embarrassing to go out there and be putting on a show. It seemed patronizing to the audience, to be 'Hey everybody! How's it going? We're here to have a good time tonight.' That was the last thing you wanted to do—if anything, you wanted to make fun of that and subvert that. It's a humility: you shouldn't be so excited about your ideas. We were making fun of narcissism: 'Hi, I'm Tim Heidecker.' That's like making fun of people that really are trying to do that, that people are stupid enough to believe that anyone gives a shit about what they have to say." Another shout-out to that good old-fashioned midwestern SA (self-abnegation)!

So I called the number on the bill they'd sent and we scheduled a conversation with Eric and Tim, and on that call I asked them what they wanted to do. They wanted a variety show, with room for anything and everything—their very own *Mr. Show.* Well, who doesn't? Seemed like a lot to ask for right off the bat.

I thought that one of their short films, where a not-very-animated guy tells the mayor of his small town about his restaurant, felt nearly like a TV show. It had a setting, characters, and a plot of sorts. Still, it was an extremely crude visual style, but I thought if I could get a celebrity into their demo episode, that could make it stand out to a network. Within seconds, David Cross had gotten roped in—because. The guys made a demo episode and I sent it over to my connection at Adult Swim and *boom,* they had a show!

No.

No, of course not.

I sent it to my connection and he watched it and said, "No."

And it was dead. There weren't many outlets for determinedly static, absurdist cartoons. Too bad, because it was really funny if you could keep yourself from wanting it to be something else, something easier on the eyes.

But.

Eric Wareheim sent a separate copy of the demo to someone *else* at the same Adult Swim/Cartoon Network, a supremely cool genius by the name of Khaki Jones. She saw this homemade animation married to the comedy of human pathetioness and loved it. She pushed it on the top boss, Mike Lazzo. Mike was that truly rare network exec, someone who only knows how to take chances, which is how he established the Adult Swim brand as it is—utterly insane. He said yes to Tim and Eric's vision. So . . . I guess I helped. Sort of. Just not as much as I wanted to.

Tim and Eric came to L.A., set up shop, and began producing *Tom Goes to the Mayor*. Right from the start, they were smarter and harder-working than any other comedy geniuses I'd ever worked with. They knew technical stuff that I couldn't cram into my brain with the best cramming tool available—they knew cameras, editing programs, audio glip-glop, all that stuff. They were better producers than the production people I hooked them up with. The best thing I did was that I laughed at their work, and maybe gave them confidence that they were making something that other people might get. Tim is one of the funniest people I've ever met, and a great presence on-screen, and Eric is a visionary, with a David Lynchian talent for inventing images that strike a deep, subconscious chord. My only fear was that they were making stuff that would only be shown at art galleries that the likes of me wouldn't be allowed into.

I always pushed them to find a story that could be followed, and for *Tom Goes to the Mayor* I pulled in guest stars, not that Adult Swim ever cared about that, but . . . maybe they did. Tenacious D stepped right up, and so did Fred Armisen and Jeff Garlin. Garlin's episode, "Rat's Off to Ya," is maybe the best of the series. Still, while the show worked wonderfully for the guys (and me), in the middle of the second season, Mike Lazzo called and said, "Fellas, this ain't workin'. We should just stop short." It wasn't drawing the eyeballs. We'd never looked at ratings, but I'm sure he was right. Smart guy that Mike was, he immediately added, "But I'll give you a ten-episode on-air commitment for any other idea you got."

And so they got to make the show they had wanted to make in the first place. A sketch show where they did anything they wanted! I'm sure if I'd pitched that first, though, it wouldn't have worked—so strange how that is. I parroted Bernie's advice to David and me: "Put your names in the title, and come out and say hi, otherwise nobody knows who they're watching." They had a couple of titles, "Let's Have Fun Again" tops among them. I mentioned the T-shirt they'd sent me a few years before: "Great work on that proposal!" Man, that killed me. So I suggested, "Something like that—flat and intentionally dull, but a phrase you may have used or heard."

They thunk on it for a short while and came out with *Tim and Eric Awesome Show, Great Job!* Long-winded, a sweaty, clunky gem (usually reduced by fans to *Awesome Show*). I sat in on edits for a while and contributed my voice to their many Cinco brand advertisements, doing my take on the most fake-upbeat announcer voice ever. I also got to say "Great job!" in a marginally spirited manner, which was often placed over some unsettling moment onscreen. I had the best time watching these two develop and conquer and alter the course of comedy.

Tim and Eric's comedy success ended up meaning so much more to me than just an ego boost. My son, Nate, became a huge fan of their work. In his teen years he hit a rough patch that made communication and connection extremely challenging. I was struggling to simply be with him. But he loved *Tim and Eric Awesome Show,* like any smart thirteen-year-old! He got it. Pop culture, idiotic randomness, poop jokes. *Check It Out! with Dr. Steve Brule,* their next big show, starring John C. Reilly, was an even bigger hit with Nate (and me). No matter how rough things were, we could watch a few minutes of Tim and Eric's work and connect. It never failed to lighten the mood a bit. Life is a "tale told by an idiot"—in this case, two idiots—and that can be a meaningful thing to share when you're feeling disconnected or down. In those moments I couldn't believe this thing I'd helped midwife was saving my life in such a crucial way. Maybe Preston Sturges had it sorta right in *Sullivan's*

Travels—and I know *Mr. Show* did the same service for others. One time when David and our crew were doing a live show in San Francisco, an audience member threw a note onstage, wrapped in a dollar bill and bound with a rubber band. The dollar was attached so we wouldn't just throw it out, I guess. We opened it onstage and read a note from a veteran who told us that *Mr. Show* kept him going through some dark days in Afghanistan. We read the note aloud to the audience and had a great moment talking to the guy who'd tossed it at us. It was moving, and, also, we made a dollar doing it.

Comedy . . . keeping people sane for centuries.

Chapter 8

The Incomplete Filmmaker

———

My wife's very first client, the multi-hyphenate Stephanie Courtney, was in an original play in Los Angeles, and that play was a crowd-pleaser. An original play that is a crowd-pleaser? In Los Angeles? If you are not incredulous, then you don't know when to be incredulous. Live theater exists here, but it is always on life support, despite this being a town full of actors, writers, and other stage-hungry beasts. I don't know why. But, look, if you want to do live theater, go to Chicago! Theater rules in Chicago. Enough; off the soapbox. Naomi was going to see a play with the obtuse moniker *Phyro-Giants!* for a *second time,* so I took that as a recommendation. It had a simple setup: four young, thirtyish professionals with money, who are variously engaged in one another's lives, proceed to have a lively, searching conversation about it all. Maybe it doesn't sound like much, but it was full of sharp lines, laughs, and some gently played, surprising sentiment.

Sitting in the theater, laughing along with the crowd, I immediately started thinking about shooting it for film. But that was a tricky proposition. After all, it was four people sitting, for sixty-five pages, so the first question is, who wants to watch that? As a play it worked great, every night a different rhythm, building off audience response—playing funnier or sadder or more surprising, depending on the night. I went to see it a second time and thought about how, watching it live, your eyes wander and catch any character, not necessarily the person talking, and how the actors, whose characters have a hidden and complicated relationship, were always intriguing in their listening and reacting. Maybe I could make it work like that as a film: shoot with multiple cameras, catch glances, intimate reactions. Anyway, for the first time in the history of filmmaking, this kind of thing could be done presentably on the cheap. Digital cameras, home editing—all this stuff was happening, and the writer of the piece, Michael Blieden, wanted to edit, so *cha-ching:* big savings. The actors knew their lines forwards and backwards from months of live performance. I had five cameras going *all at once,* handheld, camera operators crammed together in a huddle, and we shot the sixty-five pages of conversation in two days. That's some kind of record. The performers knew the material so well, we could just barrel forward and then, if a cameraman needed a break or something wasn't quite right, the actors could rewind to literally anyplace in the script I asked them to go to. Michael Blieden was perfect as the curious main character, Melvin. Matt Price was hilariously snarky as his pal with a secret. Stephanie Courtney was funny and sweet, just like in real life, and could kick a dramatic moment's ass around the room, and did. Annabelle Gurwitch did something I'd never seen an actor do (up to that point): she could cry on cue. She brought emotion to the piece and, more important, could play that moment over and over in the exact same spot on every fresh take.

We added some scenes outside the restaurant to open the film up. Jack Black did me a solid and played out a true moment from Michael Blieden's life when he'd worked briefly in a mental health facility, doing intake. Jack was very generous, yet again, and his fame surpassed that of anyone else in the picture at this point, so this was a big favor.

All in all, it was a great, low-budget experience. We called the film *Melvin Goes to Dinner* (2003). I even met one of my favorite artists and friends, Noaz Deshe, an Israeli visual genius, risk-taker, and humanitarian who has gone on to make some beautiful, meaningful films. Making our little masterpiece, I kept asking, "Who's holding camera five?!" Because on that camera, without fail, the images were so compelling. Noaz's framing choices stood out. It was a great experience, and I loved this movie, especially the superb performances from the cast. Now all we had to do was get into Sundance!

This was the year 2002, and Sundance was still, far and away, the hot venue for indie films. If you didn't play there, well, the game was pretty well over. We did not get into Sundance.

"Oh, well, how about that other one, down the road, what's it called? Slamdance! Yeah! That one." Slamdance, the "off-brand" fest, said yes to us, if we could fly ourselves and promote ourselves and, basically, do it all ourselves. But, sure, it would be almost like the real thing. Scrappier. Scrappier is better, right?

I was in for a painful, and probably fairly common, film-fest fuckup.

The Slamdance Film Festival was held in two small conference rooms of an office building in Park City, rigged up with screens and folding chairs for the audience. On our premiere night, *The New York Times*'s reviewer Elvis Mitchell was in attendance! This was a huge deal for us. It was standing room only, which means we must have had more than fifty people in the room. The vibe was upbeat, excited, even though it was a sweatbox before a frame unspooled. As soon as the first image appeared onscreen, I left the room. I couldn't take the scrutiny. I knew the movie had lots of great lines and well-played moments, and that this was the perfect audience for it; it was just too much for me to sit there, hoping every line landed. I also know that I wanted to direct, because DIRECTING IS THE BEST JOB IN THE BUNCH and it was all too important for me. I would just go walk around town while this rapt audience wallowed in our film's undeniable wonderfulness. I walked around Park City, passing all the young, eager filmmakers and the jaded pros—no business saps bright-eyed hopes quite so quickly or thoroughly as the business of film.

After about an hour, I stepped back into the makeshift screening room, expecting to find an audience captivated, but instead I walked into a room of captives, tense and uncomfortable. The audience were leaning forward in their seats, because they couldn't hear the words that the characters were saying. Every sentence had a mangled word or two, if not a complete dropout in the sound. You'd hear the first or last half of a sentence, then there would be a low-volume gargle noise. The thing is, you could hear just enough to allow you to follow the conversation but not enough to be able to sit back and enjoy. What the hell? Did I do something wrong? Was our audio just shitty for no reason? I asked the lone person in the projection booth and he shrugged, "This is how it's been the whole time." The audience was NOT pleased, but they were sticking around. This was a movie that relied almost entirely on dialogue, and so they were leaning forward trying to decipher what little they could. We were sunk.

After they started the projector, the tech dudes had left the building and walked across the street to a diner to order pancakes. I got one of our producers to run across the street to see if they'd come back and ascertain the problem. One of them agreed to come back if it would stop our tearful mewling. The pancake-drunk tech wizard listened to the garbled mess, nodded thoughtfully, glanced at the playback machine, and flipped a switch. Suddenly, crystal clear audio! Something about Dolby and not reading the label on the tape correctly. "Oops—sorry about that." There were still eight minutes of movie left . . .

'Twas fucked.

Elvis Mitchell, the NYT reviewer, was forgiving, but he hadn't really *seen* the film, since he couldn't hear it. Our big moment was gone. Shit. Shoulda done a tech check, that's the simple lesson here, for those of you who want to get credit for this class.

A few weeks later we were invited to screen at the South by Southwest festival, in Austin. The SXSW fest was not yet known as a place to "open" a film; the festival had been focused on music for most of its existence. Here, we were a big deal, and they gave us a high-profile screening in their biggest theater, the beautiful Paramount. I owed it all to *Mr. Show,* which still held sway with the hipsters orchestrating this soiree.

At SXSW they played the film on a brand-spanking-new projector, on an enormous screen, to a nearly full house. It went over as well as any film can. Total love. I'd always thought the movie would play well with young people who could see themselves in the main characters, friends sharing laughs, commiserating over the first deep wounds of adulthood. The audio was crystal clear, and all the laugh lines were heard and laughed at. I called Naomi from the lobby (we had two babies at home, so only one of us could attend). Naomi had been the one who brought me to the play and planted the idea of shooting it; she'd produced it and overseen the stresses of a small-budget film, and the best I could do was share this moment of triumph through a pay phone in the lobby. A festival staffer told me that out of five hundred comment cards that night, there was only one negative. We won the festival's Audience Award, always the best award you could dream of. The people liked it—fuck the critics.

After *Melvin* I wanted to direct another feature. I absolutely fell in love with directing and felt it was the best use of me on a set. The main skills a director needs—problem-solving, story-telling, and ordering people around—were all in or near my wheelhouse. For my next feature I worked hard to set up my own screenplay, adapted from a very entertaining novel I'd picked up in the LAX bookstore a few months earlier: *The Fuck-Up*, by Arthur Nersesian. This gem of a story had been a big seller just out of sight of mainstream success. In it, an un-named protagonist, a young man with high hopes of being a cool guy and writer (who doesn't relate to that?), is kicking around in late-eighties New York, failing at being cool or writing much of anything. As the tale unfolds, in the course of a few weeks and lots of incident, he screws and gets screwed, he loses a lot, he gets beat up, his mentor commits suicide, he discovers that his mentor may have been nothing but a fraud, he ends up in a welfare hotel, and then he ends up on the street, and he is finally saved by the most unlikely, toughest, least phony woman who crossed his path. It's a great story with lots of funny, surprising characters, and a journey of a young artist losing his illusions and finding peace. It made a great screenplay—and is still the best writing I've done, according to my wife.

A wonderful producer, Mary Jane Skalski, who had just had a film-fest success with *The Station Agent*, took the project on and chased the money—which refused to stop disappearing over the horizon. We set to work—I flew to New York and we hunted up actors. Jesse Eisenberg did an amazing reading for the lead character—he was perfect, bringing so much intelligence and feeling to every moment. Will Oldham, an artist incapable of false feeling in his acting and music, was my dream choice for playing the guru/mentor/charlatan, and he was in. An amazing cast was lined up, but damn that money. It just wouldn't come. It was a years-long disappointment, and I still consider it the best project I've never been able to bring to life. I pursued it with the highest ideals and hopes, but wouldn't you know, the film I did get to make was one that aimed, purposely, low-down and dirty.

Prison Daze

"See that, boys? That's Joliet Correctional Center," my dad said as he pointed out the window of the car at the imposing brown stone wall rising up from the midwestern flatness. We were with him for the day, my brother Steve and I. This was before he was completely disconnected from the family, when we were young, and he would do his impression of fathering, occasionally taking us around with him for part of his workday. For some reason we were driving through Joliet, where this ancient horror castle was planted all the way back in Civil War times. Steve and I looked out the window and took in the imposing lockup, surrounded by gentle prairie grass and open sky and gas stations. My dad finished his good-dad lecture. "If you do bad things, you can end up in there." He was right: I ended up in there, and, as in all prison experiences, everyone ended up the worse for it.

I think I enjoyed directing too much and wanted another film too badly to do the simple, first, job of a director—pick a story you really, really love. Something that attracts you so strongly that you will sit with each decision and sweat to make it as great as you can. But I liked this project as a challenge and saw some opportunity to make something offbeat. Plus—and this is core to my choices here—it was a "go" project: they had their funding. And when that happens, there's momentum, a strong desire on the part of the producers to start shooting before that funding falls out of love with the project. Be wary of momentum. Fucking avalanches have momentum.

So . . . how about a movie about prison and its sundry horrors?! A comedy, even?! Take the saddest place on earth, dig in, and mine some lighthearted yuks from it?! It seemed nearly impossible to pull off. In the end, it was. Tom Lennon and Robert Ben Garant, two members of the sketch group the State, a group whose television show I'd envied when I was struggling at *SNL* and they were having a great time on MTV in that gifted passel of clowns (all nice folks, too!), had written a screenplay based (loosely) on the unpleasant self-published manual *You Are Going to Prison*. This is a real book, it exists in the world, and it's real hard to get through, but if you are headed to prison and you want some advice, it's perfect. Its main focus is on how not to be sexually assaulted while locked up. A rough read. Tom and Ben probably dug the challenge like I did. How to turn that darkness into a lighthearted comedy? After all, working with the darkest backdrop can fuel tension and, with some well-placed clownery, big laughs might just arise. Tom and Ben had a story that gave a nod to *The Prince and the Pauper*, thematically. The story was about one cool, hardened ex-con who'd been abandoned as a child, who resents the rich, spoiled son of the judge who'd sent him away, and so he concocts a scheme to get the progeny of his nemesis tossed in the clinker, and for good measure he heads back in himself so he has a front-row seat to the proceedings. Coal-dark. Yet their screenplay was a lot less dark than the source material, I promise you.

I was excited to shoot the project with a seventies B-movie vibe, using visual style from those old films: snap zooms, swish pans, and lots of in-camera energy—like those old grind-house films. I fought to shoot it on sixteen-millimeter film, like a classic Roger Corman biker movie would have been. I was told this was not okay, as distributors would immediately put it in the indie bin. Well . . . so? We did find the oldest thirty-five-millimeter film stock we could get, in hopes that it would be fibrous, speckled, and "gritty." All of the inventive visual exploration was fun to do and did fit the material, but it did NOT save the movie—I think you know this already. The casting was perfect, too, the actors all top-notch. Dax Shepard has a great presence, dangerous and likable, and an onscreen ease that everybody likes in a leading man. Will Arnett is one of the funniest, most agile comic actors alive. Will can play a certain kind of especially dumb innocent; even when he's doing bad things, there is joy in his energy. Chi McBride was the best I'd worked with up to that point. His audition for the role made me embarrassed for my own half-assed approach to acting. Chi nailed that audition, doing a two-page monologue without once referencing the script, and you could have shot it as is. All this good instinct and good talent—and the money to make it! None of this saved the movie. You know who else didn't save the movie? Me. I just made it. The best I could. I only wish all that talent and effort had been for a more worthy cause. This movie *nearly* had a theme. The writers were busy with bigger projects, so there was no time for the reworking, something all films demand. There were some good comic moments, and many that escaped me. A good example is the warden's speech. It was a page or more, in which the warden dryly needled the arriving inmates and presented himself as the ultimate evil bastard. It had some smiles in it, but no big laughs. I brought up for discussion "Can we talk about the warden's speech? I think I might be missing—"

I had not finished that sentence when one of the producers squinted and declared, "THAT is the FUNNIEST THING I have EVER read!" Emphasis on the word "ever." And he meant it. *Okay,* I told myself. *Leave it. Be a COLLABORA-TOR for once!*

Did I need to love every scene in the film? Yes. I did. Because I was directing. But I was only halfway into the project; parts of the job attracted me, but these weren't stories I *needed* to tell, and it shows. The film we ended up with, *Let's Go to Prison* (2006), was abrasive and shocking, not nearly comic enough. Do I need to mention that there was a strong homophobic undercurrent?! Clever me, I thought I could turn everyone's expectations inside out by having the prison relationship turn out to be a good one! Boy, I was off on that in a fundamental way. It's just wrongheaded. You get no points for trying when you fall that far short.

Oh! Something good came from it: one of the background artists was a white guy who had done time in Joliet prison, where we were shooting. This sad sack took me on a tour of the prison wing where he'd whiled away a few years of his youth, and where he had gotten a terribly shitty prison tattoo (the only kind available in prison) celebrating a white-power gang that had promised to protect him while inside. He admitted, defeatedly, that they had done no such thing. Imagine that! White supremacists who don't follow through on their promises! He was working on the movie to raise enough money to have the tattoo removed. I hope he was able to make that dream come true; at least then something good would have come of the whole enterprise.

This is where the true artist stops hustling, sails to Europe, wanders the Louvre, gets a venereal disease, has a vision, and returns to America a changed person with special new insight into his craft. I had two kids, as I said, so I didn't do any of that stuff. Instead, still jazzed by directing, I looked for another petard to hang myself with. I was producing and writing *Derek and Simon,* which HBO was supporting and which was getting better with every episode. Along came the perfect project to entice me back behind the director's chair, megaphone in hand, crazy notions lighting my fire, only to leave me abandoned, naked, alone, and shivering: a sweet-natured little crumpet by the name of *The Brothers Solomon.*

The Brothers Solomon (2007) seemed like a screenplay that made fun of screenplays, specifically buddy comedies of the past two decades. That was my initial reaction and, looking back, maybe I was dead right. It was "meta" to me, though still very funny—but it was hard to see it working for the multiplex. The great, nice, and funny Will Forte wrote it, so it was upbeat and sunny, just like the man himself. The script had a sunny-dumb personality, and after the darkness of *Prison,* I needed that in my life. In the story, Will Forte and Will Arnett played two socially challenged brothers who desperately need to have a baby in order to give their dying father something to live for. The dad was played by the game and good-natured LEE MAJORS!!—sorry for shouting, but I watched a lot of *The Six Million Dollar Man* as a kid. Will had written in the script that the song "St. Elmo's Fire (Man in Motion)" would play many times. For a joke . . . but, like all good Will Forte jokes, a laugh that was both sarcastic and genuine. To me it was the song the characters were hearing in their heads as they lived out their epic tale. Very funny, but, again, self-aware/meta. I handed the script back to the producer who'd given it to me and admitted, "I don't know, I don't think I've got this." I was right, again.

A week later he called me back: "So do you want to direct it? You can cast it. Will Arnett might play the brother. It's a fun movie. Come on, we have the money for it, we're shooting this summer." The producer, Matt Berenson, was and is a genuine, upbeat, hardworking guy, one of the good ones whose indefatigable energy is so very important to making a film project happen. Arnett and Forte teamed up?! That sounded great. Hell, I get to make a movie, and it's a *sweet-natured* one . . .

"Yeah. Sure. I'm in."

I asked Will Forte to write some backstory to justify the brothers' cluelessness; he wrote that the boys had grown up at the North Pole! We needed something so the audience wouldn't think we were making fun of people with brain trauma. Did it help? It did not.

Directors do one thing more than anything else: they answer questions. Costumes, sets, lenses, camera choices, the look and feel?! On this project, I was just guessing in every direction. The script was light-spirited and straightforward, and the character's childlike quality and the broadness of the humor suggested big performances, strong colors, almost a cartoon, which may have been the exact opposite of what I should have done with it. Wouldn't it have been cool to shoot the whole thing in a hyperrealistic, indie film style? I'm sure it would've. Wish I'd had that particular inspiration, vision, for the entire thing—it would at least have been an interesting experiment. Blame where blame is due: I was directing without having a vision for it. I was guilty of being a full-blown dilettante. It's a fizzy little celluloid delight that isn't totally in focus, and that's on me.

Weird sidenote: I have had people come up to me and tell me that one of these films, *Let's Go to Prison* or *The Brothers Solomon,* is their favorite movie—sometimes adding, "of all time." What is that about? Just nerves, I guess: they want to say something nice and they go way overboard. It's okay with me if you like one of them, but please, check out *Chinatown* or even *Planes, Trains and Automobiles* and get back to me on favorites. I am happy to fail again at directing features, but only with something I love and believe in completely, so, maybe never.

The worst part of making these fundamentally flawed projects was reading the negative reviews and endorsing them, wholly. "Let's go to prison IS prison!" someone wrote, and there's me nodding, going, "Yeah, you nailed it." Was it just me bowing to the general consensus—had I lost my ability to know what I even liked anymore? Also, how much of what was wrong with the final product was wrong right from the start? Quite a bit, in my estimation. But that's on me, too. I am eager to stop writing about these painful failures, because I truly deserve the razzies and rotten tomatoes that came my way. I would move far more carefully from here on out.

I was acting here and there throughout these years, but it wasn't my main focus. I was focused on laughing in wonderment and joy at the beautiful kids the universe had entrusted to Naomi and me, to the near exclusion of my bright, slapdash career . . .

One morning I was walking my son, Nate (he remained a baby for almost a whole year), around the house on a "spider walk," looking for the latest webs from the night before. He fit right into the crook of my arm, and we were having a wonderful time soaking in the Los Angeles morning sun when, halfway around the house, a realization hit me—I was supposed to act in the hit sitcom *Will & Grace* . . . today . . . like, RIGHT NOW! I handed my son to the nearest spider and took off. A real actor would have been at the studio gate already, bitching about his parking spot being too far from the dressing room. Instead, I was still in my PJs when I arrived at the studio, unshowered, hair uncombed, the crook of my arm still stinkin' of baby diaper. I dodged into a bathroom and threw some street clothes on, then sauntered into the morning read-through, late but acting like I'd been on time. It was the last bit of acting that I would do for this show.

Rehearsal was a sloppy mess. I didn't know my lines, wasn't really present, which is the first job of an actor—after complaining about the parking space.

Later that day, sitting in my office, writing a screenplay with some *Mr. Show* writers, I got a call from my agent. I picked up the phone and, before he could say anything, I told him . . .

"They're letting me go."

"Bob, I'm calling about *Will & Grace*."

"They're letting me go?" I repeated.

"The producers feel terrible about this, but they think you weren't a great fit and—"

"They're letting me go," I assured him.

"They're letting you go."

"Okay. Have a nice day," we both said in unison, and I hung up and resumed writing. My priority was finding spiderwebs with my son, and it showed in my acting work. I didn't fall in love (like) with acting until years later; it was always secondary to digging thoughts out of my head and putting them on paper to get a laugh—real man's work.

One night in fall 2004, I was walking on a street on the Lower East Side, to see David Cross do a live show at a bar called Pianos, when an exec from NBC sidled up to me and said, "It's between you and Carell! People were watching tapes today!"

I had auditioned for the new, American version of *The Office*. I was a big fan of the British *Office,* where Ricky Gervais played David Brent, the main character, whose desperate hunger for love and attention makes him spew forth with painfully cringey, embarrassing behavior. It made me sweat and want to turn away, and yet I could not turn away—it was too damn funny. Americans don't like cringe laughs so much, so the character mutated quite a bit in the translation. But even more than the specific character, the way the show was made—improvised from a script—was the big attraction. The looseness of this shooting style is the most pure fun you can have as an actor.

I got to enjoy this style of improv-based shooting when I played Gil Bang, a retired porn star, in *Curb Your Enthusiasm.*

"Cook up a few funny, unpleasant stories that a porn star might have," Larry David had asked me in the year 2000. I came up with two stories, both gross and unfit for dinner party chatter. The one they used on the episode, about a finger dipped in Tabasco and inserted anally to supercharge an erection, did the unpleasant trick. When people ask me if acting is "fun," well, *this kind* of acting is fun! Larry is the one who came up with the line "the house that cum built," by the way, so send all compliments his way on that.

As much as I wanted the *Office* job, I didn't feel too bad about not getting it. Carell was perfect in the role, and I had so many projects to drive into the dirt, and laughs to be had along the way. One trick for surviving Hollywood's beatdown is to keep making new things in spite of every "no." To somehow stay in touch with the joy that brought you into the game. I never stopped getting on stand-up stages or doing one-off shows, like San Francisco's yearly Sketchfest, with some collection of friends. As always, the fringe was where I felt most at home, and it was there to rescue me from the abyss.

A Pipe-Hittin' Member of the Tribe: Saul Is Born

I was sitting at my desk at Raleigh Studios, the warm Santa Ana winds whistling through cracks in the clapboard siding that Charlie Chaplin himself had hammered (poorly) together. I had somehow discovered that I'd gotten myself in a financial hole, which was quite an achievement, considering how steadily I'd worked and how humble my indulgences are. Basically, I splurge on ice cream and that's it. But at the time I had a business manager who mistook me for a prizefighter, and suddenly I was signing a loan for nearly a million dollars just so I could continue living in the house I lived in and go to this claptrap office to make more claptrap. One fine day I was looking at two piles of scripts side by side on my desk; one stack was feature films generating interest, and the other was TV pilots I'd been sent to consider auditioning or writing for. I'd skimmed all these scripts thoroughly, and it was a strange thing to become aware that *not one* of the scripts in the movie pile was as good as the worst script in the television pile. I wasn't being sent movie "gold," understandably, but, more important, TV was climbing to new heights. After *The Sopranos* and *The Wire* and, more recently, *Mad Men* and, hanging in the background, *Breaking Bad,* it was shockingly clear that high-quality writing was leaning toward TV in a big way. This was 2009, January or so, and the future of deeply considered characters and complex plotting was laid out right there in front of me in these two stacks of writing.

I'd been working on a pilot about a minor league baseball team. *The San Diego Snakes* was a vérité comedy, single-camera style, written with Reid Harrison, a friend who knew sports better than I did. I've always loved the dramedy of minor league baseball life, and I'll read any memoir on the subject, because it's guaranteed to be filled with comic characters, dashed dreams, sacrifice, hope, and baseball. FX had backed our efforts, but we were struggling. We wanted to shoot at least part of the show among real minor leaguers in real ballparks. Tricky.

We'd had some conversations with some rich fella who had his own private league. Not a private team—a private *league,* four teams in the Southwest—but the layers of legal challenge and expense just to do an offbeat comedy show were daunting.

I had become an even easier no for the network suits. If my assistant told me I had a call from the network, I wouldn't even pick it up. I'd just yell back, "Tell them it's fine, I understand. Thank them for taking it this far."

In the midst of this limbo, I got a phone call from my agent at the time, who said, "They're going to offer you a part on a TV show, and please, you should say yes to this one. It's good."

Angels sang.

Nah, none of that happened. It was just another day, and I was suspicious of this so-called "show" and this "part" . . . some dumb sitcom, maybe? I'm just going to have to say no, which I wasn't supposed to say anymore, according to my new business manager. I asked him what the part was.

"It's for a drama. They want you to play a lawyer, a low-class, bus-stop-bench-ad, dealmaker type, kinda shifty."

Right. Sure. A version of Stevie Grant, whom I'd played on *Larry Sanders* years before. More of the same. I hesitated.

He carried on. "You should do this one, it's got good writing. This is the kind of part that people win Emmy awards for." (He came close on that prediction!)

"What's the show called?"

Breaking Bad.

"I'll call you back."

The clouds parted, God poked his head out, and he pointed at me and said, "Do it!"

Nah. First I was going to do some research. I had heard of *Breaking Bad,* and I vaguely recalled the image on the billboards—a guy in his underwear in the desert? I would phone a friend, see if anyone had actually seen it . . .

"Are you kidding me? *Breaking Bad* is the best show on TV! You've got to say yes!" urged my writing partner on the *Snakes* pilot, Reid Harrison. Reid was the first person I called, and I needed to call him anyway to discuss our dying show. I didn't expect to hear this effusive response. Not many people had seen *Breaking Bad* yet; the first season had been cut short by a writers' strike, and it was overshadowed in its early days by *Mad Men.*

"Sure, then, I'll do it," I told Reid. Look, I probably would have done it anyway, just to pick up the coin, but it was real nice to hear that someone whose taste I respected loved it this much.

I told my agent, "I'm in." They wanted me for three or four episodes to serve their story needs, but I could only commit to three, because I was already penciled in for an episode of *How I Met Your Mother,* where I had a recurring part on perhaps the happiest set I've ever been on in Los Angeles.

A word about *How I Met Your Mother.* Those people had to be on something. Everyone was too happy and kind. I'd never seen so many smiling actors. *HIMYM,* as it's acronymically called, was in season 3 already, well into it, when I made a few stop-ins, so where were the exhausted, jaded, entitled celebs? Nowhere to be found. It was the most gung-ho, upbeat set I've ever been on. I didn't believe it at first, but after a few visits I believed it. The best people ever, and happy to be right where they were.

Because I wasn't available for all four episodes of *Breaking Bad,* Vince Gilligan needed to invent yet another character to do some story work, so, on the seventh day, he created Mike Ehrmantraut, and found the perfect actor to inhabit the irascible sweetheart fixer, the great man Jonathan Banks.

Okay, now the clouds parted, the Mormon Tabernaclers yowled, and a pig winged it across the night sky.

Fortuitous happenstance.

But let me tip my cap to my brief hell of bankruptcy: it softened me up. That pit of fear that took up residence in my gut for about two years when I had a young family is something I can still draw on to kick my ass and take action when needed—for instance, when acting, or voting. I was intimate with deep uncertainty and wanted to move away from the feeling. This rough patch also helped me greatly as an actor. I now had a "sense memory" of fear: my nerve endings had received a thorough scouring and were ready to come alive onscreen . . .

Chapter 9

Breaking Bad

———

After coolly muttering, "Sure, I'm in," to my agent regarding the job offer, I did not think I was signing up for a big and fundamental acting gig that would change my life. *Breaking Bad* was not even close to a hit at this point. In fact, I figured there was a good chance almost no one would see what I did on the show—outside of my friend Reid. It was just a cool little sidetrack. At least I wouldn't have to stare at blank pages for three days! I had the excuse of focusing on my lines and my acting, and taking in some quality Albuquerque cable TV in my hotel room, where I did get to watch a deer-hunting-themed channel that had a show that was really an advertisement for all kinds of things that help human hunters cheat in their effort to slay these beautiful, innocent, oversize vermin. The channel even advertised a camouflaged golf cart with thick tires for driving your lazy ass silently through muck, parking, waiting, killing, then loading out your prize dead animal. Remarkable.

The part of Saul Goodman did make me smile, though. Saul was big! And showy! He talked a lot, too. Wow, diarrhea of the mouth. So many lines, but I was certain that before shooting, his many rambles and runs would be rewritten down to a nub. Peter Gould was listed as the writer. Vince Gilligan gives Peter tons of credit for the invention of Saul, for the character's comical and grandiose run-on rants, for his panache. I read the script and didn't understand everything that was happening (because I'd never seen the show), but I liked it. They were trusting me with all this dialogue and razzle-dazzle, trusting me to hold the focus, and I hadn't even auditioned! Honestly, I wondered if they had the right Odenkirk. Oh, well: if they didn't, their problemo.

Vince and I talked the next day, and he started in in his genteel southern manner, "Gee, Bob, well, it sure would be great to have you . . ." *Please,* I'm thinking, *get to it. Nobody is honored to have me.*

I interrupted Vince's niceties. "Tell me about this character."

"Sure, well, he's a bus-ad-type lawyer, but he's actually good at what he does, he's capable, and . . ." Vince stands out in Hollywood as a considerate, soft-spoken, humble person, but also as an artist with genuinely high standards, the maintenance of which he is willing to sacrifice for. Vince is so good at what he does that he has no need for bombast or stroking his own ego. His work leads the way, and he drives from the backseat, calm and confident, or at least putting up a damn good front.

Anyway, being Mr. First Thought = Best Thought, I had no time for his drawling humility and I interrupted him:

"I have an idea for his hair! What if he has a comb-over on top, mullet in the back, cleaned up on the sides?"

Vince chuckled. "I think so, yeah, that could work."

There . . . I'd made my big contribution, and I guess it proved to both of us that we were on the same page about this Saul Goodman clown. Vince carried on talking, I carried on agreeing with him. I started thinking, *Oh, man, this could be fun.*

Like I said, I figured Vince and Peter had chosen me for the role of Saul because I'd played Stevie Grant, the agent on *Larry Sanders*. There are similarities between these two scammy fellas: the fast talk and serving their own interests above all. But I learned that they chose me because they were fans of *Mr. Show*. This is kind of amazing, considering that *Mr. Show* was full of broad, loud, dumb, and crazy characterizations, as compared with *Breaking Bad*'s calm, grounded, and subtle ones. *Which scene from* Mr. Show *recommended me for this?* I wondered. Was it the sad sack who kissed elephants' asses as a part-time job? The guy with the British accent who beat a woman with pans and then jumped out a window? Maybe the TV detective who waved a "crime stick" at the camera and shouted, "CRIME!" I could never figure out which. It was the sum total, I guess, and simply the fact that I could bring some funny energy to a show steeped in darkness.

In that first script, Saul talked up a storm. In the comedy scripts that I was used to, dialogue pops back and forth, and anything that runs even a little long gets thinned to either joke or setup, not much in between. So I did not bother to learn my lines yet, figuring they would be cut way back. But a few days before my shooting was to start, I received the "blue page" rewrites. Blue is the color of the third rewrite, or fourth—I can never keep track, but it's pretty final. You should definitely memorize the blue pages, young actor. In my blue draft, only one word had been changed from the script I'd first read a week or so ago. I had a lot to memorize, and also some thinking to do about drama acting, because up till this point in my life I had given it the amount of thought a mouse puts into farting. In fact, I had written the lines in *Mr. Show* that went like so:

All acting is is jumping up and down and yelling and screaming a lot.
　　—High school guidance counselor MOE PHELPS

And that's true, to a point, sir.

Acting is pretending! Simple, right?

The bottom line for me is: once you hear the word "action," the goal is to have some sort of "there" there. A sense of your character being caught by the camera in a moment of their life, and that the life we are catching a glimpse of is somehow greater than that moment—bigger, more dimensional. Like Del had done when he got up and improvised that one time in a class: he brought a world to life around him; he wasn't just a mouthpiece or an attitude. There are many ways to do the work, many different approaches. Most actors are working consciously, using their particular version of Method acting. Others just have disastrous internal lives that they let leak onto the screen, turning their inner turmoil and frailty into sweet dollarinos. I'm a little of both. Of course, there's more to it than that, and yet, not much more. Acting is a trick, and you can get better at tricks with practice.

Whatever your approach, it helps to begin by learning your lines.

I was intimidated, but pretended not to be while preparing for that first go-round at *Breaking Bad*. I started, like a writer would, by reverse-engineering the script, taking apart the dialogue for text, subtext, rhythm, humor, and just who was this guy? Saul Goodman proudly tells Walter White that this is all a "front," and he seems quite happy about it. Saul (aka James McGill) is gaining Walter White's confidence by entrusting him with a secret: "Just between you and me . . . I'll tell *you* the truth." And he's a wiseass. "Pipe-hittin' member of the tribe," and all that. So the stakes are low for him, he's having fun with this game. Peter Gould had written Saul with . . . maybe not wit, but wisecrackery, and louche swagger. What the script didn't tell me, the costume did: outrageous, showy suit, loud tie, big cuff links, neon socks, and then there's the hair: comb-over, as discussed, and with highlights in it! I found, as I dissected Saul's run-on sentences (we're kindred spirits), that he was sizing things up moment to moment, trying to hook his mark and thinking on his feet.

The sheer bulk of words was intimidating, though. I asked the universe, "Who wants to listen to another person talk that much?" "Well," the universe responded, "some people *are* fun to listen to." At the time I started shooting on *Breaking Bad*, I was on my third listen of the audiobook of Robert Evans's showbiz bio *The Kid Stays in the Picture*, as read by the author. Evans was a raconteur, scallywag, and spinner of stretched yarns, his voice a cocktail of aged whiskey, honey, and self-satisfaction. He had a fair amount in common with this Saul character, so I rehearsed my lines in an imitation of Evans's lilting, cliff-hanger-laden style. Anyway, it was fun to do, so I was entertaining myself in the process. Dynamic pacing! That was the key. As the years went by and I continued playing the character, I kept this little trick up, and it has served me well. Thanks, Evans—ya made me look good, kid.

Saul was the first role I'd ever done where I didn't take out my pen and try to rewrite. On most comedies, it's considered good to know *most* of your lines, *pretty much* in the right order, and you are encouraged to "have fun," as in: MAKE IT FUNNIER, *please*. Garry Shandling himself, worrying every single line of *Sanders*, was always encouraging me to pitch lines in the show. I didn't take the bait: I knew how much brain sweat had gone into what we already had, and I didn't want to put any of my pitches under the master's microscope.

Breaking Bad, I suspected (because I really wasn't sure yet, because I hadn't watched much of it), was writing on a very high level of precision, so I stopped myself as I raised a pen to make "some notes" on the script. This was a crucial moment. I would treat this project in a fundamentally different way from all the comedy I'd done my whole life. To respect the word, and let the character talk in sometimes strange constructions. This way I might end up losing *myself* even more, because Saul was someone who didn't talk like Bob Odenkirk. I let the words be just as they were and worked hard to memorize them just like that, and when I hit a phrase that didn't flow from my clumsy mouth, I worked it until it did.

In the first scene with Bryan Cranston, Saul, in this moment opposite Walter, is clearly a kid on a joyride. Bryan grounded the whole thing so I could be nuts. He also gave me the confidence to lose myself. Bryan doesn't need me to tell you that he is one of the greatest actors alive, as well as one of the kindest, most generous and fun professionals in this business. A scene partner doesn't get better than Bryan. In fact, all of the *Breaking Bad* cast were total pros who sensed they were making something that could rise above, and I think Bryan deserved great credit for setting the tone and standards.

I had fun doing those initial scenes. Nobody told me to "play it bigger," and I felt dialed in. I remember especially liking the sense of the camera being up close, allowing the smallest choice to come across onscreen. There's more shouting in comedy, and it was real nice to be able to whisper. Somewhere in the middle of shooting that first scene in Saul's law office, after a verbal run of Saul's flimflammery, a crew member, lost in the scrum around the camera, shouted out, "Can I get a job on the spin-off?!" And everybody laughed.

A Smile Full of Sand

About a week and a half later I was again back in Albuquerque, on my knees in the desert, a gun pointed to my temple and a comb-over/mullet combo hairpiece flapping about in the wind. It was 2 A.M. and a sandstorm was whipping particles into our eyes and mouths. The character of Saul is rattling away in Spanish while Jesse and Walt pressure him to help Badger stay out of prison. In writing Saul's desperate plea, with its references to guys named Ignacio and Lalo, Vince Gilligan and Peter Gould were unknowingly laying the groundwork for another TV series to come, years down the line, but no one had an inkling of that.

I particularly loved shooting that scene. The situation was so fantastic. A giant crane holding a brilliant artificial moon high in the sky, Bryan and Aaron and me, three grown men, waving fake guns, crouched over a shallow grave at 2 A.M. This was show business as conjured by some dreamer, staring at a poster of *Chinatown* (I'm talking about myself). I love it when it feels like you're with a pack of folks getting away with something outrageous, unjustifiable, *out there*. Between takes, Bryan, Aaron, and I would hide out in the Winnebago to escape the sandblasted cold. Smiles all around. The life. Kids playing with costumes, emotions, and imagination.

I'd say one reason I enjoyed playing Saul was that *Saul* enjoyed playing Saul. The audience liked him times ten. He brought light to the doomed universe of *Breaking Bad,* or at least until things went bad for him, too. The offstage story I had for Saul in the context of *BB* was of a hollow man, like my dad and his pals. After hours, Saul's life is strip clubs, alcohol, and golf on the weekends, of course! A garbage life. A big fat zero. That was all the backstory I needed at that time.

Overall, I tried not to psych myself out about the shift I'd made from sketch comedy to this world of dark drama. Like I said, in comedy I was often asked to "play it bigger." But no more. There was something Zen about the experience, losing yourself in the moment—even if the moment was fraught with tension, frustration, manipulations. The kind of writing I was suddenly getting to work with was loaded with subtext and drive—worthy of every ounce of my attention.

I don't know if the joker in the crew who wanted a job on the spin-off got one, but he may have, because much of the crew of *Better Call Saul* was drawn from *Breaking Bad*. At the time, I laughed at the notion of a spin-off, along with everyone else, and just enjoyed the ride as *BB* continued, slowly, then quickly, to become a massive worldwide hit and marker of the best that television drama can be.

The Eighteenth Beatle: *Breaking Bad* Fame

Breaking Bad was, and will remain, the biggest cultural phenomenon of my earthly idyll. The confluence of zeitgeist, technology, and sheer creative excellence gave that show escape velocity. This was something to think about, to try to fit myself into. The cult fame from *Mr. Show* suited me fine. I knew my fans, generally speaking, and they knew me the same way. That was my brain up on the screen, so yeah, they kind of did have a connection to me in a meaningful way. It was nice. Being a part of the *BB* juggernaut was another level, and I could enjoy it only with a healthy dose of compartmentalization: far more attention, but as far as I was concerned, I was collaterally "famous." I was a bystander who got caught up in it, that's all. The love and appreciation was for the show itself, and that core cast, of which I was a satellite.

Somewhere in my second season of *Breaking Bad*, sitting in the makeup trailer one morning, going over my lines, I asked Bryan Cranston, "So. Gus is . . . your friend, right?"

To which he replied, "You've never seen this show, have you?"

Aaron Paul and me at the big *Breaking Bad* final episode
event. He's wearing protective gear to keep his ego in check—
totally unnecessary, as his heart has always been in the
right place and his feet on the ground. Me . . . I'm wearing
diamond-studded underwear and it hurts.

Well, he was right. I had two little kids at home, and the one
time I'd started playing an episode, one of those kids walked
into the room right before someone named Krazy-8 was about
to be dissolved in a bath of acid. I decided I couldn't watch the
series until something like that wouldn't happen. I eventually
got around to it after the third season.

The success of the show was gradual. During seasons 3 and
4, *Breaking Bad* was a damn good job but not a career-
changer, not a world-beater. In those middle seasons, if I mentioned the show, the chances that anyone had seen it were not
high. Netflix began streaming the show online around season
3, and in the course of season 4, *kaboom!*—it took off. The
wave of attention grew, and kept growing. On the eve of our
sixth and final season, the whole cast went to San Diego

Cranston and me after one of his acting "lessons"—he only hit me a little.

Comic-Con to do a panel, sign things, and be big shots—as close as I would come to feeling like a Beatle in '63, especially walking around the San Diego party streets, tagging along with Aaron Paul, so much younger and less jaded than the rest of the cast. Aaron was eating it up, running from street corner to street corner, trailed by shouting, excited zombies. We went to party after party—never spending more than a few minutes in any crowded place, because the fun was in between, walking the streets, feeling the heat. It was all great to experience from one step removed. At that same event, Bryan Cranston put on a meticulously realistic Walter White mask and walked the floors of the convention, unrecognized. Bryan, more than anyone I know, handled success with grace and a sense of humor; it never changed him, but he intended to make the most of it.

The show had its final episode play on a big screen at the Hollywood Forever Cemetery, a star-studded event with a massive projection on a mausoleum wall. Spread out on the field were cast and crew members and their families, and famous fans, including Warren Buffett. He's a real nice fella. The good vibes of the project carried through right to the end, and beyond. Around the world, people were tuned in and came away thrilled and satisfied at Vince Gilligan and company's majestic, striking climactic moments. I can't believe I got to be part of the journey. I certainly expected no more excellent blood from this particular turnip.

The four years that I was involved in *Breaking Bad,* I was a part-timer: my character popped up here and there, and I was pretty sure Saul was going to get knocked off at any moment. He would have been the perfect character to take out—big enough to matter, not big enough to change the core story. Every time I was sent a script, I looked for Saul's death scene. But it never came.

Meanwhile, the jokes about a spin-off continued. In season 3, I was in costume as Saul, wandering the office next to the studio where we were shooting, and Vince asked, very seriously, "What do you think? Do you think there's a show in Saul? Because I think there might be."

"I have no idea." I said. And I didn't.

I spent no time considering it, since I had no control over it.

Saul was fun to watch in the context of *Breaking Bad*'s story, where every other character had their life on the line and he was just trying to make a score and crack jokes. But who the hell was he outside of that context? A schemer? A fast-talker with "situational ethics"? He might have made a good Republican candidate, car salesman, or exactly what he was: a lawyer. But he's no hero, and, by my estimation, awful hard to root for.

I kept busy making cool things and being a dad. I was an extremely involved dad. Here's me: "Let's do this, let's do that! I made food for you—please pretend to like it." A helicopter dad. Little kids make me laugh, so I was in it for the entertainment value. Professionally, I kept scribbling and doing guest parts on mostly fun TV shows. *How I Met Your Mother* put me to work, and so did a great film, *The Spectacular Now*. I developed a show for myself with Tom Gianas. I tried to slow down and prep this one more than most, a reaction to so many crash-and-burns. Maybe if I dug a little deeper before pitching, I would come out with a project that could go the distance. This was good thinking, but taking my time backfired in this instance. Lesson: DON'T TRY TO OUTSMART PROVIDENCE.

Human Interest was the name of the show. Tom and I developed a single-camera comedy with a knot of pain at its core. I would play a crabby, alcoholic, and estranged father (my dad) whose job as a human interest reporter for a national weekly news program took me to far-flung places and put me up close with humorously bent people. The title was both literal and ironic, with my misanthropic character going on a journey of self-discovery. I pictured him alone in bland chain motels when he wasn't interacting with stridently weird, damaged people who somehow had it more together than he—the big celebrity—did. Sort of *Groundhog Day* crossed with a Chris Guest movie—a fun mix, my sweet spot. But, after months of preparation and laying careful groundwork, another show beat us to this premise: *Jon Benjamin Has a Van*. It was uncannily, frustratingly, similar. Jon, one of my favorite performers, played a human interest reporter traveling America, hanging out with screwballs. The only difference was I was going for a more "downer" vibe. America loves downers!! Anyway, way too close. This kind of "great minds" facsimile pitch is a weirdly common experience. Someone pitches or, in this case, sells something that is so close to your screenplay/show idea/autobiography that your project feels totally undercut and pointless. It hurt—I actually needed the work for the first time in a long time—but the fact that I liked all those guys so much softened the blow. At least they'd be making a show I'd want to see.

So we had to drop our idea before it was even pitched. At this point I was feeling jinxed. I was exhausted with cooking up TV shows, and entered a gun-shy headspace that might actually have been a good thing. I started to lose projects in the weeds of preparation. Some of my collaborators probably ended up feeling burned after months of development; I was more apt than ever to let things fall away—incomplete, unpitched. All I could do was warm up, never step up to the plate. I might have quit altogether if I'd had the money to do that, but I didn't. And thank God and Saint Lucifer that Vince Gilligan and Peter Gould were walking the sidewalks of Burbank, striving to make the wiseacre remark "Can I get a job on the spinoff?" into a reality.

Listen to the Children: Saying Yes to *Saul*

A few months after the final episode of *Breaking Bad* played, I got a call to meet with Vince and Peter at the Chateau Marmont to discuss a Saul spin-off. The Chateau is a classic Hollywood place: you can sip gin and tonics and imagine Marlene Dietrich and Cary Grant hitting on themselves in a mirror. Now, dismiss those romantic La-La Land images and picture three pasty white men wearing khakis, seated at a corner table, discussing a TV show and trying not to order the cheesecake.

"What do you think about a show built around Saul?" Vince asked me, *again*.

I'd known that this lunch meeting was on the calendar for weeks, so I had tried to take the notion seriously. Tried and mostly failed. I shared my one big thought: "Well, the first problem you'd have is to make the character *likable*." I hoped they didn't take this as an insult. After all, Peter had invented Saul with Vince. Vince, being the overseer of the *BB* universe, had personally, and with great care, masterminded every choice in that paragon. They probably liked Saul just as he was, a lot more than I did. I liked playing him, but that kind of person? Con man? User? Not so much. But, I figured, "Let's not beat around the bush—after all, this is Hollywood, nobody has time for bullshit!" . . . Wait, no, that's the *only* thing we have time for. I'm always getting that equation backwards. I'm not a very good ass-kisser, so I uttered this conversation-stopper, and we hadn't even ordered lunch yet!

Vince and Peter hesitated, but only briefly. They seemed to agree that the Saul we'd gotten to know in *BB* could be difficult to root for, but also, both felt there was something more there, a person of interest behind the front of Saul's flimsy character. They told me that they'd been wandering the backstreets of Burbank asking the question "What kind of problem does *becoming* Saul Goodman solve?" An interesting question, whose *Jeopardy!* response might be "What is deep-seated self-hatred?" The judges might also accept "What is a feeling of abandonment?" It seems to me Vince Gilligan likes nothing more than facing a nearly impossible storytelling quandary, and then, along with Peter Gould and a select few trusted minds, solving the riddle: What makes an interesting person tick . . . and then go "boom"? Vince puts himself into a corner, then digs himself into a hole in that corner, then solders it shut, and then he tries to find a way out. From this self-inflicted struggle have emerged two great television shows.

One thing that Peter and Vince had going for them was that the audience had never seen Saul "offstage"—when he was not in his chosen costume: sleazy lawyer. The character was, to a great extent, a blank slate. At that moment, they didn't seem to have much nailed down at all—and Vince made it clear that their thoughts were wide-ranging, saying, "We don't know if it's a half-hour comedy, or maybe an hour-long procedural . . ."

"Sure . . . why not?" I thought—and probably said out loud. It still all seemed so far-fetched, and I was satisfied that I got a free burger at the Chateau out of the deal. "Guys, if you think there's something there, then there's probably something there, and I'll be happy to do it," I shruggingly concluded, not helping in the least. They went back to the drawing board and life went on.

After that, I had time to jam in one more numbing creative disappointment, a pilot with Eric Hoffman entitled "Incompetent Husbands," to showcase my friends David Cross, Jeff Garlin, Jerry Minor, and Andy Richter, and myself. Eric and I had been thinking about that opening diner scene in *Reservoir Dogs*, where the bad guys are arguing about Madonna videos, and what if it was a bunch of suburban dads and you're just hanging out with these incompetent, unnecessary men. I was sure it would *sing* when we held a read-through with this blazingly talented and perfectly cast group. But it lay there like the proverbial rotten brown egg. Perhaps the script wasn't stellar, but it's hard to tell, because no one seemed to give a shit. Every single person showed up as a favor to me. Lesson: NEVER ASK YOUR FRIENDS TO BE IN YOUR PROJECT. HIRE STRANGERS WHO NEED A GODDAMN JOB!

A LIVE TOUR saved my spirits, as live performance is wont to do.

Lesson: WRITERS, ESPECIALLY COMEDY WRITERS, SHOULD ALWAYS BE PUTTING THEIR WORK IN FRONT OF PEOPLE. Get those laughs. Or call up them crickets. When you write comedy, you need to have that audience in mind, sitting right there, eager to laugh, or scowl and grunt disapprovingly. Doing brief live tours had become a lifeline in my lost wandering through these Hollywood development years. This tour was me, David, Brian Posehn, and a couple of ringer sketch actors we picked up in each city to perform some quickly rehearsed scenes. The night began with a riff about how David and I couldn't use the name "Bob and David," or "*Mr. Show,*" because we didn't own either one (true) and HBO had sold the rights to a traveling theatrical group in South America (go for it, HBO). So we put big papier-mâché heads (of ourselves) over our real heads and danced along with a pre-taped opening audio track playing "The Mr. Show Experience." We started the tour in New York, and by the time we'd made it to Portland we were ready for the Big City. *New York, here we come!* . . . Oh, that's right, we *started* in New York, when the show was still rough around the edges. See how we did that? How we undermined our efforts with counterintuitive thinking? Little advice for you: Counterintuitive thinking only works in Malcolm Gladwell books.

But it was a good show, lots of laughs, like this wonderful sketch about our founding fathers:

> HOST: Okay, let's talk about the economy.
> America's in real trouble.

THOMAS JEFFERSON: That's because you're paying
your slaves!
BEN FRANKLIN: Not paying slaves is a great way to
fire up the economy!
GEORGE WASHINGTON: That's how we all got rich.
We called it "The Slave Factor"!

It was some months later that I got a call from Peter and
Vince: this show about silly old Saul was a go. Really? It had
moved out of the in-joke category and now was a legit quandary. They had settled on two things for sure: it would be a
one-hour drama, and it would be shot in Albuquerque.

Albuquerque . . . That's what you call a showstopper.

I had two kids and, like I said, I liked looking over their
shoulders—this would be very hard to do from seven hundred
miles away. Heck, I was the soccer coach for three seasons and
I helped out a lot at school, and I had all these TV shows to
watch self-destruct. Who was going to cook my kids meals
with oatmeal, spaghetti, and a hammer?

My helicopter parenting was not ready to land just yet, so I
said no to the offer of starring in a TV show about Saul Goodman. Marc Provissiero counseled me on this decision; Naomi
had taken herself totally out of the mix, not because she didn't
like the project—she loved *Breaking Bad*—but because she
simply didn't want to put pressure on me one way or the other.
In this case, she wanted to be my wife and partner and let
someone else do the status/career math. Marc, like any good
manager, felt I should lean toward saying yes to an extraordi-
nary opportunity, but I didn't budge and he had to pass along
my big fat no.

"What the hell?" you ask. "Don't you want to be a star?!
Isn't that why you got into show business?"

Well . . . NO.

Haven't you been reading this goddamn book for hours now?! I don't give a shit about that stuff. I am in this to entertain myself. Here's how much fame I need: "just enough" and no more. You seem like a nice person, but, seriously, read books more carefully next time.

Marc passed my no along to the studio on a Friday, and on Sunday the studio called him back just to check if they'd heard that right. He then called me and asked if my no meant no, or if it was some kind of squirrely negotiating tactic that even he hadn't been included in. I explained to him, "Yeah, I meant it." I repeated my reasons, number one being my kids needed me for a couple more years of annoying dad duties. He listened and said that he would pass the second, emphatic, and yet humble "no" on during working hours the next day. My son overheard this conversation, and after I hung up Nate said, "So are you saying no to that show?"

"Yep."

"Well," he told me, "you're going to disappoint a lot of people."

"I'm going to disappoint a lot of *strangers*," I clarified.

"Well, some of them are my friends."

We talked about it and he said, "Go do it, Dad . . . We'll take care of things at home, and we can take a break from those three meals you make that we love so much."

Later that same day I'm driving my daughter Erin somewhere and this unbelievably composed and mature kid at thirteen, who grew up in Hollywood, asked me some questions about this show that I'd turned down, the most piercing being "If you made the show, and it was bad, how bad would it be?" A very clever and forward-thinking concern for a thirteen-year-old.

I did the math. Peter Gould and Vince Gilligan writing and,

no doubt, a bunch of *BB* people coming along for the adventure. I answered, "It wouldn't be *bad;* the worst thing it would be would be an 'interesting experiment.'"

She took this in and said, "You should do it."

Having already turned it down and now getting their go-ahead, I could reconsider the choice without pressure, and my thinking changed.

The biggest reason to say yes to this offer was what I'd learned from the Del Close School of Trying Crazy Shit. Do something hard, something that you will probably fail at, something that tests you and excites you and takes you places you didn't know you would ever go to. Buy the little brown bottle with the label worn off and swallow it (metaphorically speaking). If the kids were really okay with it, well . . .

The next day I called Marc and said yes to the part.

The Cranston One-Step Acting System

What would this show be, though? How would Vince and Peter solve this "likability" problem? Peter told me, "We were fascinated by the Saul we met in *Breaking Bad*—and blown away by your performance—but when we thought about centering a show on him, we realized there was something missing. Vulnerability. Saul, as we knew him, seemed to be happy and complete in himself. He could be frustrated, he could be physically hurt—but what was driving him? Where was the itch he couldn't scratch? First of all, we made him an underdog, struggling to make ends meet, living in the back of the nail salon. That was a start. But we needed something else: we needed someone for him to care about. And that was when we conceived of Jimmy's older brother. At first, we thought of Chuck as a burden for Jimmy. An unreasonable shut-in Jimmy had to protect. A responsibility. Someone who Jimmy wanted to please. And that, we hoped, would help Jimmy have the vulnerability, history, and human connection that was so hard to see in Saul Goodman."

Wow. That's some deep diving into what makes a person tick. Behind the many layers of this Saul con man was Jimmy McGill (his real name), someone who loved someone, so now we, the audience, could love him for that.

As the shooting start date for the first season approached, I asked Bryan Cranston if he'd give me some insight into the challenge before me. Being the best guy ever that he is, Bryan said yes and we met at a coffee shop in the Valley. It was cold in L.A. (it can happen), but still, we sat outside, because inside the coffee shop were ten people writing screenplays, and it's not good to be around that if you're a recognizable face.

I hit Cranston with the big question: "How do you do it?"

Cranston nodded, sipped his tea, and went into his best John Wooden: "Well, Bob, you got this. You're going to be fine. You've got Vince and Peter and the crew behind you, and everything you've done has built up to this moment—"

I stopped him. "No, sorry, I mean, I know I can *survive* it—I mean, I wrote, acted, and produced my own show for five years—but . . . *how* do you do *this job*? What does your day look like?"

I was too dumb to know I could use a pep talk. I'd said yes already, and they were well into writing scripts. This was happening, I was in whether I thought I could do it or not. I just needed some conception of how an actor prepares. A real actor, like Bryan.

Bryan got it. He gave me a summation of his daily schedule on *Breaking Bad*. "You get up really early, get to set, and start running your part. Then, at lunch, you memorize lines for the afternoon scenes—don't eat too much, you want to keep your energy up. Then, before the shooting day is done, you ask craft services to make you a sandwich or something for your dinner—they'll be happy to do it for you, and so you can take that home and focus on learning your lines for the next day."

"What about weekends?"

"Well, I usually went home to L.A. on weekends. I learned my lines at the airport and on the plane; that way I could relax a bit more when I was home."

"So basically, you learn lines, rehearse, act, eat some food, learn lines, act again, cram some more food down your pie-hole, then learn lines, fall asleep, and on weekends you don't stop working?"

"Yeah."

"So you just work all the time."

"Right. Work all the time and you'll be able to do it."

This was what I needed to hear. No trick to it. Just a lot of elbow grease.

"Can I call this 'The Cranston One-Step Acting System'?"

"Sure. Now let's blow this joint before anyone finishes a screenplay."

Chapter 10

Drama!

————

Better Call Saul would have been intimidating to take on if I'd thought about it for too long, so I didn't. I just got down to work, line by line, scene by scene. Surrender was the only way forward. That first season was something I barely survived at times. It beat me up and left me by the side of the road, gasping for breath, but I gave it everything I had—and I was surprised how much of me it took.

I pretended not to care about the enormity of the task. The first rule of acting: Act like you got this! I put on a good show of being confident, or simply not caring too much. I cared a lot, and I was intimidated. I lost my voice in the first weeks of shooting. I am sure stress was the real reason, but the good doctors at the UNM Hospital showed me some kind of nodes on my throat, and the only fix was to stop talking. How to do that and play Saul Goodman? I limited my yammering to vocal exercises whenever I wasn't acting, and kept my head down. Good thing I had Rhea Seehorn and Michael Mando to hang out with: they're both talkers, so they could fill that space, plus they are astute students of thespianism, dramaturgy, emotional bloodletting for the stage, and they gave me many insights into the spirit and mechanics of our work. The team spirit of *Breaking Bad* carried over wonderfully to *Better Call Saul*.

This was quickly a cast of great friends. We hung out. We

Me, surrounded by talent—my secret to success.

talked through everything regarding the show, and our personal lives, at length. Patrick Fabian has seen the ups and downs of the acting life and has risen from the fire better, stronger, faster, but above all kinder. Rhea takes this shit (acting) seriously, and this particular job required and rewarded that approach. We are partners in the resolute, all-in effort to bring Jimmy and Kim's complicated, sad, sweet, doomed, enabling relationship to life. And we laugh together a lot—she's funny "like a guy," which is to say she can be critical, she can give it and take it. (She shares this jocose manner with another fine actress named Meryl something . . .) When Rhea walked in to read with me for the role, her smarts and inner strength were on display, and those qualities have made Kim Wexler a formidable and layered character.

Banks, the pro, rolls with the punches and is always there for everyone, but brooks little nonsense. I, on the other hand, traffic in nonsense, so we're well-matched for fireworks. He saves being peeved at me for when we're on camera and I love it. Mr. McKean is an actor of gravity like few others I've shared the screen with. Hilarious, too . . . and with an abundance of acting experiences to draw on. Michael McKean raises everyone's game, but I especially owe him for boosting my own focus and presence in character. Vampirically, I leeched his power and presence when we shared scenes; I'm not sure if that's something an acting class can teach you—it has more to do with having a competitive gene and a brilliant scene partner. Giancarlo Esposito is another pro, with the longest, possibly most varied résumé in the bunch. Giancarlo shows up ready to shape-shift into Gus Fring, a stone-cold creature, the opposite of Giancarlo's warm and empathetic nature.

A word about Michael Mando. Michael's life story is worthy of explication, too much to do here. He grew up in Canada and Sierra Leone and the Ivory Coast, he speaks French as his first language, and whenever he's speaking Spanish he's faking it like a pro. His acting heroes are Brando and Pacino, so he brings power every second he's onscreen. Offscreen, he's insatiable in his interests, with talent radiating in every direction. Mando is an inspiration. I love every one of these people, and if they just want to hang out for five months every year in Albuquerque and *not* do a show, that'd be fine with me.

If Saul Goodman talked a lot in his brief visits to *Breaking Bad*, he's nothing compared with Jimmy McGill in *Better Call Saul*. Three-page monologues happened regularly, and in the second season, a five-pager: a scene where Jimmy is calling a rigged bingo game and tells the old folks a story about the time he dropped a "Chicago sunroof" on someone (shat through their car's sunroof), which had serious consequences when he got caught. My God, the writers trusted me with all the twists and turns of emotion within these verbal pileups! Why?! Not for me to know; just "head down, dig in." Maybe this helped me—somewhere in the first season, I wrote a little note to my-self: "Every line is emotional." Which is not entirely true, but let's say it's mostly true—or at least it's a good guide to finding the purpose of all of Saul's chatter. I am always looking for the emotional underpinnings of any line or moment in a scene—so I'm not just memorizing lines, I'm memorizing feelings, which stick inside you deeper. But you need to know the lines, too—they just tend to come easier if you're following the emotional journey. This is all shit I'm sure I would have learned if I'd taken an acting class or two sometime in my life. Take note: unlike Saul, Jimmy McGill in *BCS* is full of feelings, desires, hurt, and hopes. Jimmy is a tangle of raw nerves, while Saul, his later self, is a shell game—hollow, with a pea-sized soul that disappears whenever you look for it. Conversely, Jimmy in *BCS* was fighting to share himself, not to hide himself. He'd made a choice when his brother, Chuck, saved him from a big jail sentence—he decided that he would straighten out, put his heart into it, set his hopes high, and become a good person, someone his brother would be proud of. It was a fool's errand. When this becomes apparent to poor Jimmy, then, slowly, bru-tally, the seeds of Saul are planted: he won't get fooled again. Instead, he'll take out his revenge on the world, get his share, through "situational ethics" and scheming.

The writers toil over every word, and we actors approach their efforts with great respect. As perfect as the writing is when we get our hot little hands on those scripts, there is much to be worked out and understood before the shooting starts. I think this is where this cast and crew shows its high standards and love of the project. Every moment is taken apart and que-ried and, as much as is possible, understood. And every depart-ment brings all their skills and sweat to every moment—and *why*? Because the audience. Because there's an audience out there who will watch every detail and appreciate every choice and inspiration that makes it to the screen. Once again, the audience wags the dog (the show people). This job is hard, and I love this job, and I know people around the world will appreciate every detail that we get right! They watch oh-so-closely.

I remember once, during *Breaking Bad,* Bryan Cranston stopping the shoot to get on the phone and take apart a choice Walter White was making that didn't fit for him. It was a long and involved argument, and in the end, according to Vince, he felt Bryan's instinct was the right one. This kind of commitment, on the part of the writers and actors, is what makes these

Rhea Seehorn and me about to embark on a hike full of chatter about our characters and acting and subtext and all that actor stuff. You don't want to be there, trust me.

two shows work: everybody brings their A game, nobody lets a line go by that doesn't track, and we trust one another when we're asked to go somewhere fresh, dangerous, uncertain.

I found that I enjoyed taking acting seriously—it was a change of pace from ironic, broad comedy acting that is perfectly fine for silly-ass sketches. When David Carr, the legendary journalist for *The New York Times,* visited our set during the first season and asked me, after an emotional scene between Jimmy and Chuck, how I "did that," I let him in on my only secret weapon.

"I know exactly how I did that," I said.

He nodded, ready for my big acting theory . . .

"I have a poor sense of personal boundaries." Indeed. A shortcoming in real life, one that causes me to overshare or blurt out hurtful commentary, but when you're acting it can give you the freedom to leap cavalierly to raw and difficult feelings. It's my only superpower. If I'd had a choice, I would have picked flight, but I'll settle for this—emotional bluntness.

Saul Survivor

All this "emoting" was draining. I got pummeled by the sheer amount of Jimmy's deep feelings in that first season. I hate to admit it, but if you've ever wanted to hear an actor whine, get ready, your moment has come!! I was surprised to find that there is an emotional toll to a role this big. For six months, my personal worries were compounded by Jimmy's woes—his complex web of personal hates and loves, his hopeless fight for acceptance. It wore me down. Luckily, my wife and my daughter had picked out a wonderful dog at the pound, a Staff terrier–German shepherd mix named Olive, and hanging out with her was medicine for my shaky nerves after months of nonstop *emoting*. I was never a dog person, but if you're in a bad place, hang around a good dog for a while: you'll feel better. Thank God for Olive: without her I would have had to consider shaving my head and becoming a drug addict . . . but I'm saving that for after this book gets its ass kicked.

I can tell you the exact moment it occurred to me that I might be about to get rotten-tomatoed to death on the world stage. I was heading into a grocery store on Vine Street in Hollywood to buy eggs and a variety of potato-based chips, and way, way up over the building I was walking into, they were putting up a four-story image of ME as Saul, standing in the desert facing a swinging pay phone. *Hmm,* it finally hit me, *EVERYBODY is going to watch this.* I mean, if you saw *Breaking Bad,* well, you were at least going to sample *Saul. Oh, geez . . . I hope it turns out all right.* My heart told me I'd probably get destroyed no matter what, so I was very surprised at the warm reception the show received.

I've never done so many interviews as I did for that first season. They sent me around the globe. In London, I stayed in one of the nicest hotels ever—imagine a Trump hotel if Trump had nothing to do with it—about a block and a half from Mr. Buckingham's Palace. Good thing the digs were so sweet, because I only got to leave once. The rest of the time I was sequestered in a room talking to a long line of journalists from every country. It was an ego boost for the first few minutes, and then exhausting, and then a shame: there was London outside, waiting for me to walk around and be delighted by, but there was no time for delighting. Time only for answering five questions that would be repeated every hour for eight hours. Imagine your favorite movie star, and now picture them in a hotel room talking about a character, a fictional character, for hours at a time. No wonder they throw in their political point of view—they're losing their minds! I survived the PR tour, but it was an eye-opener, another glimpse into what the real stars do with their lives.

Questions about the show were hard for me to answer, seeing as how I didn't write it and we didn't want to spoil anything. I couldn't pontificate on where it was all headed, or why anything happened. I could only speak about it like any fan, and yet I was expected to speak at length. I was very happy to find that people were upbeat and open-minded about *Better Call Saul* before its premiere. I expected skepticism and knives out. That was not the case. I attribute this welcoming interest entirely to *Breaking Bad*'s being so damn good and not overstaying its welcome. People wanted more of anything that was even in the ballpark of that great show.

When I look back on the state that first season left me in, I think about those hours hanging out with Olive, feeling shell-shocked at the dog park. It's hard to admit that I was shaken by this work; I mean, it's just acting, right? I think it's the sheer amount of time you spend being someone else, as well as the depth of turmoil they'd written into the character of Jimmy McGill/Saul Goodman, that got to me. Of course, I imagine my nerves and stress about how the show would be received was about equal to Vince Gilligan's and Peter Gould's before we shot anything. . . . But those guys are gifted with foresight; I'm more *in the moment* (brain-damaged). They went way out on a limb, trusting me to explore such deep human complexity onscreen. I'll tell you right now, this opportunity, *Better Call Saul,* was the biggest break of my career by a fair margin, and I'll never be able to repay the universe, or these two gentlemen, for it.

Seven Too Many: The Birthday Boys

As part of her never-ending quest to find new comic talent, Naomi sees more comedy in a year than is good for a person's aura. She notes her favorite sketches and actors and invites them to do their material at a benefit show every New Year's Eve day. *The Not Inappropriate Show* is for all ages, because, just like its title, the sketches are not inappropriate for a family to watch. It's a great event and a good use of all her effort, plus we get to interact with some excellent up-and-coming talent as we put the show together every year.

One group that was invited back a few years in a row, the Birthday Boys, looked like they had that special something that would make for a good TV show: a shared sensibility. This is remarkable, because there were seven of them. That's a lot of brains that need to line up for a sensibility match to occur. They wrote consistently funny stuff that was apolitical. Supremely silly. Bob and Ray territory, but mixed with a focus on storytelling tropes of television and film, so . . . a touch of *SCTV*. *Mr. Show* had David and me grinding axes, and *SNL* always had the week's top stories covered, so I thought there was room for their ebullient shenanigans. Most young comedy sketch groups have multiple axes to grind, which is fine—we all like a well-ground ax—but these guys lacked prickly anger. One big drawback: they were seven white guys. But I thought that since they were funny and likable, and churned out the laughs reliably, well, I'd run it up the flagpole. Ben Stiller's company, Red Hour, saluted. This makes sense: Ben's comic oeuvre lines up with the Birthday Boys' main obsessions.

Between seasons of *Saul,* I got to resume commanding a comedy writers' room, my favorite place to be. I didn't want to alter their sweet goofiness, but I tried to get the boys to "relevantize" their material, connect it up to something identifiably floating in the zeitgeist. I pushed them to reach out and try to connect. I'm not sure it helped, but we made some very funny half hours of TV. IFC had had good luck with *Portlandia,* so there was an audience for offbeat comedy, and I felt we were in the right place. We were given two seasons to win people over, but we couldn't find the audience. The guys, each one of them talented either in writing or production or performance, were a joy to work with, and there was very little argument. It was a good team. One of my favorite sketches illustrates their gentle loopiness. In it, Mike Mitchell plays "September Santa," a portly, Santa-ish fellow who climbs through the window of a family's home, chuckling "Hoo hoo hoo" cheerfully. He then explains that he's "like Santa, but for a different month," and proceeds to distribute No. 2 pencils to the good boys and girls, who are nonplussed. Satisfied with that reaction, he politely bids adieu and leaves the house through the front door. Come on now, that's great stuff. Oh, well.

In the end, I agree, and I think they do, too, that seven white guys is too many white guys to have in one place, ever, for any reason. Much as I liked what they did, we should have tried to re-form the core group in such a way as to appeal to a wider audience and not be so easily brushed aside.

There would be more—and more triumphant—returns to sketch comedy. I needed it, and heck, *Saul* only shoots for five months out of the year. So, in 2015, David Cross and I put the band back together, because there was a sketch I wanted to fix.

Still Silly: *W/Bob & David*

All the stuff that doesn't work sticks in my craw, and my craw is full up. There were a few sketches from *Mr. Show* that didn't live up to our standards, and I had an idea for fixing one of them, so . . . time to put the band back together.

The failed comedy sketch that called to me was named "Waiter Spill" (season 4, episode 4), a waste of good TV time in which I played a waiter who spills a dinner on a business-man played by John Ennis, who gets upset, then I apologize, then David comes out as the manager and offers to pay for half the dry cleaning bill. Half! Inappropriate, but hilarity does not ensue. Mirth ensues—barely. We didn't have too many of these lifeless dogs in *Mr. Show*—one or two per season—but somewhere in the intervening decade, I had figured out how to make it funny. Because it should have been funny—we were a comedy show! Here is how it should have been:

"Yeah, but *half*?! That's not fair! You should pay for the whole thing!"

"Point taken. Fine, we'll pay for the suit, and the meal, but I get to wear the suit on weekends."

"Sure, but . . . No! I'm not *sharing* my suit with you!"

"Okay. Then I get half your meal . . ."

"But I'm hungry!"

"Well, the customer is always right. How about this: I'll give you my jacket and pants to wear until you get home, and I'll wear the soiled suit, we'll both eat half the meal off the floor, and I'll give you five bucks to drink a bottle of Tabasco in one gulp."

"No!"

"All right, then, you can drink it in three swigs, but NO MORE!"

"I don't need five bucks!"

"Twenty bucks! And you have to swallow a goldfish!"

It's not important to get a sketch "right" unless you're me, and I am me, so I was bothered enough to want to create an opportunity to revisit this utter nonsense gone awry. Luckily, in the intervening years Netflix had arrived! Hooray for the great and wonderful Netflix, headed by one of the biggest *Mr. Show* fans of all, Ted Sarandos. David and I, and the whole amazing group, regrouped and magic ensued, all inspired by my desire to fix a bit of nonsense that needed fixing.

We couldn't use our old name or we'd be sued, but HBO and Universal agreed not to break our legs if we used only the less recognizable part. Netflix was fine calling this new show *W/Bob & David,* written that way, in abbreviation. Seemed like a fresh take on our old crew. Our staff of *Mr. Show* writers—Brian Posehn, Scott Aukerman, Paul F. Tompkins, Mark Rivers, Dino Stamatopoulos, Jay Johnston, Eric Hoffman, and Bill Odenkirk—all said yes to sitting in a room prying laughs out of one another. This was a surprise to me. Aukerman had since cornered the market on absurd brilliance with *Comedy Bang! Bang!* Paul F. Tompkins had a full dance card, with the most and funniest podcasts going. My brother Bill was pulling double duty at *The Simpsons,* writing and directing. Dino had his own empire of cutting-edge projects, including the recent Oscar contender *Anomalisa.* But everyone wanted in on this double-fisted comedy-reunion death match. The same went for the actors. Jill Talley, Brett Paesel, Tom Kenny, John Ennis, even the world-famous Mary Lynn Rajskub (famous from 24 . . . the TV show 24; she wasn't twenty-four years old, that would have meant she was four when she started on *Mr. Show,* stop distracting me with math!). They all said yes. But could a bunch of old comedy minds make spirited, angry, trenchant comedy that makes you almost-think, but then laugh instead? We could and did.

We met at my wife's office, took five minutes to exchange pleasantries—"What's for lunch?," "Yeah, when's lunch?," "Is lunch here yet?"—I shared my rough scripts, and within seconds they'd punched 'em right up into Shinola. It took no time to be back on solid ground. Spoiler alert: we did have lunch, with Prilosec or some other intestinal balm, afterwards . . . and

The *Mr. Show* core writers and cast reunite for Netflix in 2015 to prove we're older but still funny, but mostly older. You see me, Mark Rivers, Paul F. Tompkins, John Ennis, Brian Posehn, David Cross, and Jay Johnston.

then wrote a sketch about Prilosec and how it makes it possible for you to "eat like a baby with money" all your life.

In one of the best scripts of that first bunch, a loudmouthed liberal (David with shaggy David Crosby hair) is pulling up to a DWI checkpoint where he plans to use his phone to video himself getting harassed by "the pigs." At the checkpoint he finds an even-tempered, hardworking cop, played by the pitch-perfect Keegan-Michael Key. Keegan's cop is just trying to do his job and keep the traffic flowing, and is not up for an argument. David's social justice warrior can't believe he isn't getting a rise out of the cop, so he is forced to return, again and again, trying every tactic to provoke a reaction and get some tasty video. After busting a taillight, soaking himself in beer, and simply being unrelenting, David's wishes are fulfilled: he gets a beatdown from a cop who "gets it" (Jay Johnston, back in fine form). David's character is thrilled to get maced in the face until he vomits, because he's gotten what he came for. Yes, it's about the current political climate, where people are so deeply invested in their hatreds that they will do anything it takes to confirm their biases. It's harsher on liberal stridency than on conservatives; we are liberal people, but like all good liberals, we hate ourselves. But this sketch, of all our sketches, THIS ONE gets called out, and Netflix nixed the entire episode to avoid any hassle. It was called out for having a use of "black-face." Hmm . . . I couldn't even remember that it had black-face in it—I had to watch it again to be reminded that David's character, frustrated that he couldn't provoke a considerate, hardworking African American policeman, decides to darken his face as an extreme provocation. He crosses a line, and this succeeds for him in provoking a reaction—from a white cop. Oh, and the fact that blackface is the final straw implies that, yes, there is bias in American policing. Whose side are we on? We are on no one's side . . . We aim to tease everyone, equally.

"All comedy is critical"—John Cleese.

It is. There isn't a good joke alive that can't be found insulting or insensitive by someone. Amazingly, there's a sketch *within* the four episodes we made for Netflix that comments on this very phenomenon. In episode 1, David plays a film producer screening clips from a new reboot of *Roots* where, in order not to perpetuate demeaning stereotypes, the plantation workers are not called "slaves" and are shown getting paid for their work. Like the best *Mr. Show* pieces, the point of it is hard to boil down, and yet David's character logic is perfectly reasonable in the context of our time. As the new producer of *Roots,* he is being reasonable and sensitive, but then . . . what is *Roots* without the slavery? It's pretty stupid and laughable. Please do check it out, a vision of the future.

A lot had happened in the sketch world since we took our ball and went home. Dave Chappelle, Amy Schumer, and others had blazed new trails with pointed, personality-driven shows that were strong on funny character riffing, and far less concerned with structure or a core joke, or any kind of comic concept that existed outside of the performance. *Key & Peele* seemed to care the most about structured sketches, and it's my favorite of the bunch for sure.

One of our *Mr. Show* writers, Mark Rivers (who'd imagineered the great "Wyckyd Sceptre" scene back in the day), had a gem of a live sketch in our second go-round that I consider one of our best. It's inspired by the short story "The Most Dangerous Game"—with David and me as idiots on a deserted island. David's rich guy plans to hunt me, and I keep trying to even the odds. He admits that the hunt is unfair, and I end up with his shotgun, his clothes, and the run of the place. Dino wrote what we, at the time, thought was the most dangerous sketch, a film about a misogynistic guy who keeps using the C-word to talk about the women in his life, and each time he rants about a "cunt," the lady in question suddenly appears right behind him! As if by magic! And she is, understandably, enraged. Turns out this is a superpower, which he then enlists in search of a lost child, so he is a hero, briefly. It turns out to be the sweetest sketch ever written with the word "cunt" in it—I dare anyone to try and beat it.

Also, I did get to rewrite that old sketch, but we took it in an entirely different direction. John Ennis plays the aggrieved businessman who enters his local dry cleaner's to pick up a suit that had food spilled on it (in a failed comedy sketch twenty years earlier!). He collects his garment, only to find that it has *more* food stains on it than when he dropped it off. The lazy clerk (played by me) explains that the dry cleaning receipt makes it clear that the shop claims no responsibility for stains that happened *while the clothes were in the shop*. However, the ticket also offers compensation in the form of a trip to see a Broadway show. The scene transforms when the businessman, unable to take the time to visit Broadway, agrees to write an entire Broadway show with the clerk and owner of the dry cleaning shop. Trust me, it makes perfect sense and, frankly, should happen in real life more often.

Thus we have a montage of three characters: Ennis as the businessman, David as the store manager, me as the clerk and owner of the shop, writing a new Broadway show based on a terrible idea, which was based on a poster for a Broadway show that appeared twenty years earlier in the background of another *Mr. Show* sketch. The poster is for *Rooms: The Musical,* about a house where the rooms individually come to life and SING! And so begins the tale of the making of a Broadway baby. We shot our epic montage in a truly backasswards manner, with David improvising lyrics, John pretending to play the piano, and then all that footage was dumped in Eban Schletter's lap and he had to put music behind David's singing but also have that music fit John's meaningless piano gesturing. Impossible, you say? Not for this musical genius. Eban delivered magic. The finished piece is a triumph of lunatic teamwork that I hope you will waste five minutes of your time on one rainy day.

W/Bob & David is top-notch to me, as good as *Mr. Show* was years earlier. I feel that no one in the creative department had lost a beat. The writers were full of fresh, sometimes dangerous ideas, based on what was happening right now. Together we were still chasing that gold-standard sketch, with great structure, surprise, and opportunity for funny performances. We achieved it a few times in a short run, but it could only be viewed by critics and audiences as a reunion, a revisitation. It did not make waves, nor rope in a fresh audience. Bottom line: sketch comedy is the province of young people who love ideas over everything, and hate watching older people do anything. I get it. But it was nice to feel like we still had it, even if no one wants it from us anymore.

The next time David and I found ourselves onscreen would be when a Hollywood icon whose last name begins with "Spiel" and ends with "berg" insisted on it.

Killed to Death

WENTWORTH: Who the fuck are you?
MILLER: Who the fuck am I? Detective fuckin'
  Miller, fuckin' homicide.
WENTWORTH: Taft is dead.
MILLER: Yes. He was killed. To death.

That's some sweet-ass dialogue. Eric Hoffman, a *Mr. Show* writer, handed me a script for a film called *Girlfriend's Day*, soon after the show wrapped. Eric had written this comic tale, a riff on my favorite film of all time, *Chinatown,* with a pal, Phil Zlotorynski, and I loved it. It was the perfect tone for me: screwball. The best thing about it was that the main character, a down-and-out greeting card writer, Ray Wentworth— romance cards being his specialty—was someone I could play for years to come. I would need those years to get famous enough in order to pry open someone's paws and get the fundage. Fifteen years after I first glanced at the pulp pile containing the verbal sparring and bloody nonsense in proper screenplay form, I had finally achieved the necessary Q rating to pull off this grift. I got to make the movie. The story is a humdinger, you oughta see it! Few have. In the bloody tale, Ray hasn't had a romantic thought or feeling in years, ever since his wife left him. The governor of the state announces a new holiday—Girlfriend's Day—along with a contest to see who can write the "most romantic card" in the state. In order to write it, Ray first has to fall in love and feel something again. Of course, big-money people want the card, and there's murder and intrigue and Ray gets punched in the face a lot.

Michael Stephenson directed with steady aplomb and didn't skimp on the bonhomie. Amber Tamblyn was kind enough to play my love interest, the woman who "tricks" Ray into feeling "in love" once again so that he has the raw materials to write a romantic card. Amber, being married to David Cross, had to act in it as a friend. I've been in her position many times before and I sympathize. But I needed her talents and what was she gonna do about it?

Naomi helped us pack the frame with great actors, Natasha Lyonne, Stephanie Courtney, Alex Karpovsky, and Ed Begley Jr. among them. Stacy Keach delivered a fantastic, evil, two-page monologue telling my character of the bloody, painful origins of greeting cards. This scene comes right after David Sullivan and Toby Huss, as two ex-racists, threaten to give me a paper cut "on the pee hole." This is a movie for everyone! Anyway, it made me laugh, and that has always been the REASON, don't you get it?! (And here picture me grabbing you by the lapels like Dennis Hopper in *Apocalypse Now*, wild-eyed, insistent, with a commitment Rasputin himself would envy, telling you how it's "nothing and everything—don't you get it?!" Because that's how I feel about the little bugger.)

Somehow we got David Lynch himself to read the three-line intro to the film, one that informs us that greeting cards are a three-billion-dollar-a-year business (true). Mr. Lynch's voice was the perfect tone-setter for our cracked comedy noir.

Does a tree make a sound if nobody is around to hear it? Does a movie make anyone happy if you don't click Play and watch it? *Girlfriend's Day* was my experiment to find out.

Never Tell Me How to Act Again

In the wake of *Better Call Saul,* some wonderful roles came my way. The first was in Noah Hawley's reimagining of the feature film *Fargo* as a limited television series for the FX network. Naomi told me this was happening and, like anyone else who'd seen that feature, my first thought was "Don't mess with a good thing!" She handed me the pilot script, and by the time I got to page 9 in my reading, I realized it was perfect for an extended story. Hawley had done a masterful job of adapting the tone of that great film, its dry gallows humor, and building a fresh story around it. It's a world that is fun to hang out in, with characters who are comically human, sweet—except for the bad guy, played by the keenly mesmerizing Billy Bob Thornton.

I played Bill Oswalt, a stubborn, simple fellow who refuses to see the evil in the world—not a great quality in a police officer. Bill would eventually show a deeper understanding of his own shortcomings, making him sympathetic and not just pathetic. I was familiar with the accent from childhood—but I was careful not to overdo it, which is the most common mistake actors make, I think. The only time humans speak with an unwavering, intense regional dialect is when they're actors in movies, trying to win awards. In real life, dialects come and go. It's when you try to apply the most intense version of the regional intonation across the board that you go too far and become a joke.

In Calgary for *Fargo,* I got to meet one my heroes, Keith
Johnstone—the prime mover whose book *Impro* was
a pilot light for me. He's a legend in my mind, and a
kindly, mad genius.

We shot in Calgary, Alberta, Canada. It's nice there, if
you like your outdoors as cold as hell. We needed snow on
the ground from November through April, and they had it. I
loved it for a change of pace, and I appreciate the Canadian
POV, I shoulda been a Canadian. I appreciate their point of
view on America—appreciative but kept at arm's length. One
day on location, filming had to be halted because it was forty
below and some of the electric cables had snapped like tooth-
picks. I hung out with Martin Freeman every chance I had. I
liked his surly English sardonicism—even when it was turned
on me. I'd been trained up by *BB* and *BCS* to engage at length
with the writers and my fellow cast members on every aspect
of the scene before us that day. Lots of interaction, argument,
brainstorming. I was still new to the mercenary professionalism of more experienced thespians. At one point I had a
scene with Martin, so I suggested (apropos of nothing) some
backstory between our characters that he could "use if you
want."

"Maybe your guy could kind of . . . resent me for something, or . . . maybe we had an interaction in the past that informs your anger here," or some such cloddish notion.

Martin squinted at me as though I weren't entirely visible and then (and please, say this to yourself in his clipped British accent) plainly stated, "Never tell me how to act again."

Wonderful delivery—cold as an Alberta breeze in February. Let it be noted: we got along really well when I wasn't giving him "pointers."

Arriving on film sets over the next few years, I was continually surprised by what a solo endeavor this acting gig was. While the cast can be very friendly and social, once you hit the set, you're on your own. Very little to no rehearsal takes place outside of the day of shooting on most sets. This is not the case with *Saul,* but I get it—that's the deal everywhere else. Acting is a far more solitary and risky endeavor than comedy writing, where "the room" is always going over your stuff and, hopefully, contributing to it.

Fargo had a fantastic cast: the charismatic and intelligent Allison Tolman, the supremely friendly Colin Hanks, and the immensely likable Gary Valentine. The part was fun to play, and it got better the longer it went on. Noah's writing showed me what to look for in a great character: simply put, *growth.* In *Fargo,* the blinkered Bill Oswalt eventually shows a glimmer of self-awareness, and it surprises and makes him a person worth caring about. Self-awareness makes characters much richer. Everyone has at least an inkling of their worst character traits, no matter how well hidden they are in public. When you show this self-awareness peeking through, people recognize it. Other actors may count lines (really, not naming names, though), but I did not go into showbiz to do math. I count layers and laughs and I'll settle for either.

W/Bob & David & Steven

My ability to analyze a script and find my bearings in a role improved greatly thanks to the crucible that was *Better Call Saul*. I would need that confidence for my next gig. The intimidation factor I had to overcome had nothing to do with the actual work of acting. It was sheer fame-blindedness that fucked me up.

In March of 2017, I got a phone call from my manager and agent, both on the line with a proposal for me: "You've been asked to leave show business" is always my assumption, and I have my answer at the ready: "Nope. Tell 'em I said nope."

But it was, in fact, the opposite. "They" wanted to pull me in deeper. A certain "Steven Spielberg" was offering me a plum role in his upcoming film, entitled *The Post*. My agent and manager both had smiles in their voices: this was exciting news, and nothing but great.

"Uh . . . could I think about it?" was my response.

They didn't like this "tack." But my hesitation was based on a series of rude, selfish, gimlet-eyed suspicions. It sounded all too perfect, and I jumped to assumptions: first, that I was being asked to play yet another shifty lawyer/agent, and I'd been there and done that. So I wanted to read the part before I said yes, because, as cool as it would be to get to act for Steven Spielberg, it would be dumb and uninteresting to play that same sort of character again. Really, I was just trying to buy time so I wouldn't be swept up in their euphoria.

But Naomi and my agent wouldn't hang up the phone without a yes, and I'm glad they felt that way. My scowling guesswork was wrong: I was being offered a beauty of a role, perfect in so many ways for me, the best of which was I got to play a real person who, once I knew his story, was someone I wanted to portray and share with others. From 1947 till 1974, Ben Bagdikian was a hard-nosed reporter who spoke truth to power, no matter who it rankled. He was a troublemaker with strong standards and determination, and people who knew him personally told me he swore like an Odenkirk, which is to say, a lot. His father may have been a minister, but he was a man of principle who didn't have time for bullshit niceties. My kind of guy.

Anyway, I did say yes on that phone call, overwhelmed by good advice. I did not read the script first; I didn't even have the part described to me. I just trusted everyone and it worked out. Imagine that.

I was comforted a few days later when I was talking to David Cross on the phone and he told me *he'd* taken a part in a Spielberg film. This was becoming shady. Did we both have IDS (imminent death syndrome, *Mr. Show*, episode 104)? It must be! I was dying, and this was a prank to make me smile one last time. Actually, smiling turned out to be the biggest challenge awaiting me.

David took the part, I took the part, and the big-screen *Mr. Show* reunion was on.

> **Impostor syndrome** (also known as impostor phenome-non, impostorism, fraud syndrome, or the impostor experience) is a psychological pattern in which one doubts one's accomplishments and has a persistent internalized fear of being exposed as a "fraud."
>
> Not to be confused with Capgras delusion, in which a person believes that a loved one has been replaced by an impostor.—Wikipedia

I had both! A whopping dose of impostor syndrome about me being in a Spielberg film, and a touch of Capgras delusion, too, wondering if that could possibly be my old pal David Cross standing four feet away from me on this set, or has he been replaced by a doppelganger who is just as funny? Oh, maybe Spielberg's an impostor? An incredibly kind, smart, generous impostor.

Of course, the truth is simple: this is showbiz—we're all impostors! Damn good ones, too.

Truly, the casting director of *The Post*, Ellen Lewis, had done a sterling job of it. Everywhere I looked, I was surrounded by excellence and perfect pitch. In fact, Ben Bagdikian looked like a twin of my grandfather, and I, with the color bleached out of my hair, looked like Ben (not counting the formidable schnoz). It was a passel of pros, and yet, almost to a man and woman, everyone was identically afflicted: between takes, off and on through the day, someone would ask someone else, "Can you believe it? Steven Spielberg is talking to me. Aren't you freaked out?"

The other person would reply, "I'm totally freaked out. And, no, I can't believe it."

To which the first would add, "I mean, come on, he's *Steven Spielberg* and I'm . . . *me*."

"You're *you*?!" the other would say. "I *wish* I was *you*! I'm *me*."

David was able to stay cool and make jokes. Me, I was thrilled to be there, but really, really off-balance, with an almost Tourretic urge to blurt out something undermining:

"Look, 'Spielberg,' is it? I've never *seen* one of your so-called movies, but if this Hanks fella is going to give my character shit, then my character has to WIN the argument. It's in my rider."

"Hey, Steve-o, do we need all these lights? I look ugly if people can see me too well."

I got indigestion from swallowing snarky comments. My

psoriasis bloomed. So I was mute and tense, which fed into the awkwardness. It wasn't just about the fame factor. I was intimidated at least as much by the niceness of Mr. Spielberg—the guy radiates decency. Then, to make matters nice-worse, you got Tom Hanks standing there doing his Tom Hanks impression—the good guy of all time. I was seriously in a niceness pickle between these two. Shit, why not throw the Dalai Lama in there while you're at it, make me melt like the witch in that old movie . . . I can't remember the name.

There was a further distraction happening. Without fail, during blocking (that's where you work out with the actors where to stand during the scene), Steven would always say, "Bob, you go stand nearer to David." Or, "David, move closer to Bob." What the hell? Was Spielberg the world's most famous, most closeted *Mr. Show* fan?

I'd look at David: "Is this really happening?"

David would shrug back: "Do you want to tell him?"

We were both concerned that if Steven ever found out we spent all those years standing side by side on a television show, it might put a little dent in the fictional universe he was so carefully constructing. But we let it go on, not wanting to push back on anything, hoping that no one would notice. It was a good plan until someone noticed.

Acting tip: LEARN YOUR RANGE.

For instance, I can't really smile. God didn't gift me those particular muscles. My face can go from scowling to deep thinking to concern . . . there's no easy joy accessible.

Early on, I think it was probably my second day on set, Steven Spielberg asked me to smile for the camera. On take one, I did my best. This wasn't a simple shot; the camera was on a dollying crane with a large crew huddled behind it, and there was a coordinated movement to the whole thing. I needed to hit my mark *emotionally.* As part of the triumphant final sequence, the presses rumble in the basement of the building and my character knows his work came to fruition. He's happy, okay? So he smiles. Steven leans in and asks me to "smile for the camera." And I'm thinking, *Did Steven Spielberg just talk to me?* and then he calls "Action" and, like a six-year-old at Walmart on photo day, I freeze up. Worthless.

"A smile, just give me a nice big smile." He made a simple gesture with his fingers, indicating I should utilize the muscles in my face to make the corners of my mouth turn upwards.

You got it, I thought. *Watch this!* On take three, I hit him with the biggest, most grotesque and forced smile ever made by a *Homo sapiens*–related object. Real *Joker* shit. He cut in the middle of my doofus grin.

"No! Stop! Not that! Just a smile . . . just a good smile." He was trying not to be mean, and I was giving myself a little pep talk: "*Fuckin' tone it down, idiot!*"—my best impersonation of Stanislavski.

Take four and I finally got it right, and Steven said, "Great— print that!" To which I shook my head in frustration. Steven sensed my scowl. "What's the matter, Bob, didn't like it?"

"I did not," I said.

"Okay, let's give him one more."

I just wanted to feel good about it before we moved on. This happens all the time on *Better Call Saul:* you work with the director to find the core components of the scene and then, once the director is happy, you do one more. Now that you've got it, you can relax, and then maybe (usually) you'll do an extra take that's even better. I wanted to feel that it was right.

Heck, I'm no Daniel Day-Lewis, and I never will be if I don't get some damn practice!

We did another take. I didn't like that one, either, and said so.

Okay, hold up, Steven Spielberg has an entire feature film to shoot, he has to move along. So he called me over to the monitor and showed me the take before the last, the take that he liked. While it was playing, he showed me *exactly* where he would be cutting into and out of the shot. He'd be using about four seconds total. And it was "perfect," in his words. I nodded, took one more look at him, wondered where I got the stones to argue with Steven Spielberg and if I could return said stones for a refund, and said, "Thanks—I'll shut up from here on out."

I think he appreciated that.

On *The Post*, I was getting a glimpse of perhaps the hardest thing a character actor has to do: acclimate to everything in a flash. Ascertain the temperature, tone, and thrust of the piece and find your place in it. Fit in. Both on camera and off, find a shared vibe with a group of actors from differing backgrounds, all working for a director you may have had only a brief chat with. I had met Steven a few weeks before we shot, at the *SNL* finale party, and it was a perfectly fine, normal, relaxed interaction until I started talking about Bagdikian, whom I had researched by reading his autobiography, and Steven's eyes glazed over within milliseconds. He did not want to get into my character work. Okay, I get it. But making the adjustment, feeling out the set, getting on the same page, and being confident in it—this is a real trick that I think the best, most experienced character actors are proficient at. It's not easy, but I'm getting better at it with time and that most powerful motivator, shame.

Steven proudly informed all of us that he never used storyboards, and from what I could tell it was true. He'd show up on set, walk around a bit, have the actors do a rough version of the scene, contemplate his options . . . make a few adjustments, and he'd have it. With the fewest possible setups for the most impact, he would have sorted out the scene, blocking, camera placement. Using actors' movements and fairly simple dollying moves, too. Economical, tight, and with maximum value. It was really something to see. Magic. "The fun for me is solving problems," he told us, and filmmaking is a great business if you like problems.

For a brief phone-call sequence where my character, Ben, is tensely chasing a story and using multiple pay phones, Steven came up with a mix of long-lens shots and a handheld camera up close. Making phone calls tense, watchable, and a little comic was the mission. He had the camera orbit me as I'm shaking, dropping coins, trying to remember the phone numbers that will get me to my connection. I may not be a great smiler, but boy can I flail. After a good take, Steven came running over to get me: "Get over here, you've gotta see this!" He took me behind the monitors to show me the take.

He gleefully declared, "It's great, it's just like a seventies film!"

I'm thinking, *A seventies film? You mean, like, it's* Spielbergian—*well, you know who you are, right?!*

I did *not* say that. I was just so happy to have made him happy.

I may have even smiled.

A few days later the penny dropped.

"Oh, my God, it's Bob and David!" screeched someone behind the monitors.

Zak Penn was the shouter. Zak is a *Mr. Show* fan from way back, and at that moment he was on the set of *The Post* because he was the screenwriter of *Ready Player One*, which Steven was editing simultaneously with shooting *The Post*. Steven was alarmed at Zak's outburst, and Zak breathlessly explained, "That's Bob and David, they're—they had a show—it was great—you got 'em back together and . . ." and then Zak started crying and slammed the door to his bedroom so he could write in his pink journal.

Steven asked him, "Hold on. Do I have a problem here?" Exactly what David and I had worried about and kept to ourselves—would audiences stop enjoying the film about a serious moment in our nation's political life and start looking for comedy sketches to happen? Zak reassured him that the cult of fans who might react as he had was very small in number (*elite*, I mean). So no, no problem.

This film, while it's a small part of my career in showbiz, was one of the best and most important experiences I've had. Being around Steven's verve was a reminder of why we do what

Even when David and I go out in our "old man makeup," invariably *Mr. Show* fans ID us and we're forced to pose for photos.

we do. Of the fun to be had in the challenge. Somehow, Steven showed up with the energy of a kid making his first film every single day. He was discovering something new all the time, and figuring out a scene brought him so much joy. I hadn't seen that kind of joy on a set in a long while. There is so much tension for all of us in this business, trying to get projects made, wanting to do it right, trying to get ahead of problems—Spielberg did all that, but with joy. The joy you felt when you started doing this stuff. It's something you forget about until you're in the presence of it. Sandler brought that same thing when he came to *SNL*. Del Close, back in that apartment in Chicago thirty-four years before, having quit on his steadiest gig ever, starting anew with a show that even he didn't have a handle on . . . had that same energy. That's the thing I'm always chasing, inspiration with a palpable strain of risk.

On the occasion of *The Post*'s final large ensemble scene, Steven toasted us all with champagne and told us we were "his favorite ensemble" (I bet he tells that to all the ensembles). Everybody exhaled and gave each other pats on the backs. Walking through Central Park afterwards to the informal wrap party, talking to my wife on the phone, I teared up. I was so moved by the comradeship, the rediscovery of the excitement of filmmaking. Shooting *The Post* refueled my spirit in wonderful ways I won't soon forget.

The set of Greta Gerwig's *Little Women* was a reprise of the professionalism and good energy of *The Post*. I felt less out of place this time, and again, I liked the guy I was bringing to life! Good ol' Bronson Alcott. He was nuts, in the best way! His mind went in a million directions at once—he was one of the original Transcendentalists, and he barely made a living out of spouting opinions and getting carried away with his notions—I could relate. Kindred spirits we were. It was a delightful project from beginning to end. Greta had the ability to make a movie with big feelings, many characters, some grand, sweeping cinematography of fields and city streets, but the sprawling nature of the project never got out of her hands. The focus stayed on the people and the strong feelings at the film's core. Working for directors like Greta and Steven and Alexander Payne on *Nebraska* is a dream—they give you plenty of room to hang yourself, then they gently but firmly remove the noose from your nervous neck and help you dial in. *Nebraska* had the added joy of working alongside Bruce Dern—and that meant I got to have long dinners with the legend, hearing stories of his work with Hitchcock, or scrabbling together films in the seventies with Corman and that crew. I lived for Mr. Dern's funny rambles, traipsing through the weeds and lilies of his illustrious, wide-ranging career.

Bruce Dern, a great actor, raconteur, and spirit, and I'm there, too.

So I got to make some very sweet films, full of heart and imbued with empathy for the human condition. What to do next? How about the most unsweet, dark, and rageful cinematic showpiece I could cook up?

Sans Irony

My brother-in-law Luke sent me a screen grab of an ad for *Better Call Saul* playing on his hotel television set. He was in China at the time. We had just finished season 2, and I thought: So, in this city in China (Zhengzhou, to be exact), they are watching the escapades of a second-rate lawyer and his personal psychological traumas? More important, they're watching me? Hmm . . . This got me thinking, always a dangerous prospect.

I knew that people were watching all around Europe and Latin America, and I wondered if there was a feature I could make that would appeal around the globe as well. Most of the screenplays I have written were aimed, like my sketch comedy, at me and people exactly like me. Offbeat-comedy nerds. Could I pursue something with a far, far wider appeal? What, exactly, might that be? Well, there's only one kind of feature that fits that bill: an action film. Action plays around the world: everyone relates to the wish fulfillment of kick-ass action sequences. But hold on . . . *me,* in an action film? The comedy writer pondering where to aim the next spitball? The ice cream eater with a hatred of all heightened movie heroism? The guy who, with his pal David Cross, actually attended a film festival by request but *only* if they'd agree to screen Steven Seagal's *On Deadly Ground* so that we could be on mic the entire time poking fun at it for an audience of hipsters? Yes. That me—it would be a ludicrous, unpredictable, outlandish proposition. I was starting to warm to the idea.

There was some deeper logic to it. The character I played in *Saul*, Jimmy McGill, is an earnest striver who keeps getting knocked down and getting back up again. His heart and pride keep pushing him to take chances to pursue his caprices, and he is driven by an unhealthy dose of retribution. In short, an action hero—just without punching or shooting anyone . . . yet (we're still making the show).

A further realization came upon me: a bloody action film would be a nice little fuck-you to the pat arc of my journey from comical clown to tolerated dramatic sideman. *The Post* had been a great challenge and joy, but, looking ahead, it was going to be character parts for me forever and anon. Which is fine, but . . . For some weird reason, the action genre allows for leading roles for all types of people. Rage knows no age, as they say in the Bible.

Right from the start, I was proposing an action film played *straight*, a total embrace of the genre, without irony, winking, wisecracks, comic distance of any kind. Otherwise, well, that just seemed like a cop-out.

But there was more to this twist than some kind of career maneuvering. It had an embarrassing, all-too-personal undercurrent.

I had some rage to "work out." My family had suffered two home break-ins in the recent past, and they had left a residue. A nasty one. I carried a lot of baggage, doubts about how I'd handled these invasions into my family's peace and security. I was proposing this kind of incident to fuel the character, a more real-feeling person than the main characters of *Taken* or the *Bourne* films—all very satisfying, but I didn't see myself as that perfect killing machine. More like a sweaty, struggling, unreliable killing machine.

To be clear, I was pretty sure I'd be laughed out of the room upon suggesting myself as an action lead. But anything for a laugh, right? At the same time, I had begun a passion project about the story of David Carr, the *New York Times* journalist I'd met a year earlier. It was a heroic story of overcoming personal demons and taking down public demons. David was an antihero, something the viewing public had shown great affection for, only he was a real-life one. His personal saga, told in the memoir *The Night of the Gun,* would give me a chance to play out so many themes I cared about: alcoholism, recovery, Catholic shame, and anger that is put to some use—in David's case as a muckraking journalist. Also, I just liked the guy. We hit it off in the very brief times we had to chat. I was certain that Hollywood would want this story of an amusing, dangerous rapscallion and his journey to redeem himself before they would want to watch me beat the crap out of a bunch of bad guys in a rain of retrograde violence and a shower of shotgun blasts.

I was wrong on that.

When I floated the idea of my kicking ass onscreen, my manager Marc Provissiero was the first to say, "Could be . . ." My other manager, Naomi, was the first to say, "I hate action movies." Don't forget, she's also my wife, so more on this later. Marc stepped up, and he began a strange, years-long campaign that produced exactly the kind of film I imagined I might do. Something that might give the good folk of Zhengzhou a reason to hit the multiplex.

Braden Aftergood, who'd recently had success with the excellent *Hell or High Water,* sparked to the notion of me as a good dad/badass. We found a few writing teams—real screenplay scribes with real résumés who also wanted to take on the challenge. But everyone slow-rolled the action histrionics. People were proposing some kind of indie version of an action movie. Understandable, I guess, since I was such an offbeat hero type. But I wanted the full monty. Big feelings, seething rage, brutal violence, screen satisfaction. The real question was, could I blow my *self* up? I wanted a script that started with real feelings but then grew bigger and bigger into the grandiose and operatic. But no singing, of course. No real opera. Yech. Give me ear-splitting gunfire over that awful warbling any day.

Derek Kolstad was the key. Derek had created the *John Wick* franchise of action films, each one topping the previous with impossibly fantastic screen action. A mythic world of bad guys in sinister, dark shadow organizations, assassins chasing each other through a fabulous imaginarium—you can never have too many assassins! Derek himself is a smiling teddy bear who knows and loves action films with the ardor I have for sketch comedy. He easily references scenes, dialogue, and plot points from obscure action flicks from countries I've barely heard of. He liked my simple notions for the character, and his imagination took off. In his telling, Hutch can't help himself; he HAS to pursue revenge on whoever broke into his home, and in acting on his darkest impulses, he disturbs a hornet's nest, bringing more danger upon his family. His impulse to fight back creates more problems, problems he secretly yearns for. He's a damaged guy, but if I played him right, relatable . . . at least at the start.

Derek's outline for the film is what finally pushed the project forward. We were lucky to lure Kelly McCormick, a producer who knew the lay of this land better than any of us, having produced many action films, including the latest, greatest one, *Atomic Blonde*. She and David Leitch were starting a film company dubbed 87North, and when they signed on, well, this thing started looking like it might one day come to fruition. Wow. Okay, I guess I'd better learn how to throw a fake punch.

I had a long way to go. Now, I didn't strictly *need* to do my own onscreen fighting. There are stunt doubles who do this for a living, but that was not the deal for me. I was doing this as a personal challenge on many levels, one being physical. Plus, in my favorite action films, which include Jackie Chan's early work and also *Atomic Blonde,* the lead actor is fighting *in character.* It's old-fashioned, maybe, but . . . that's what I wanted. Grit. Pain. A recognizable character in trouble, not an unstoppable fighting machine—I wanted to be *stoppable.*

And then, this most unpredictable project found the perfect director.

"I want my first American film to be an action thriller starring a comedian with a shotgun," Ilya Naishuller, a gifted Russian director told his agent. So shall it be. Ilya was another supremely perfect addition to the team, and he didn't even mind that the Russians were the bad guys. His first feature, *Hardcore Henry,* made on a shoestring, was a story told entirely in first-person point of view. *Hardcore* was embraced by action fans worldwide.

I got a lot of laughs from learning to fight. Laughter from myself at the expense of myself. For such a long time, it was as sad and ridiculous as I knew it would be. Believe me, I wondered if it was just a midlife crisis, my own, that I was being forced to participate in and watch from an embarrassed, head-shaking distance. Please . . . it had to be more than that. What drove me was the feeling that I was pushing myself, this one quality of acting I really get off on—being someone VERY different from me. Now do I sound like an actor? Well, I may be in the process of becoming one.

Kelly McCormick connected me to a guide, teacher, and fight guru named Daniel Bernhardt. Daniel is the premier stunt actor going, and he's such an abiding soul that he was willing to put up with my sluggish journey to competency. You know him from that amazing fight opposite Charlize Theron, or his wonderful acting turn as Ronny in the TV show *Barry*. Daniel had his work cut out for him, but he never flagged and never laughed at me to my face, either. This must have been very hard to do.

Daniel is one of those amazing people in showbiz whose talents far outpace the attention he's received. A rare condition. He was born without a top-notch PR team, how sad. In the course of hours and days spent at the gym, he helped me put my body to work—to stress-test what remains of my comedy writer's physique and raise it up to screenworthiness. Thanks to Daniel, I know the rewards of pushing yourself, the fun of a choreographed, brutal beatdown, and I have a two-pack. That'll do for me.

Took about two years, but eventually Daniel was telling me to slow down my moves so they'd read better on camera. Being instructed to slow down made me feel like I'd gotten to where I needed to be, ready for action. Good thing it takes so long to get a movie made; I needed every minute.

Ilya had an insight into the darkness of the main character. "He's an addict and he's deprived himself of violence and given himself no other outlet—so he can't help himself." What I liked about Ilya's point of view was that it explained the lengths to which we were going—truly an orgy of retribution on the part of the main character. Hutch is cracked, and his damaged psyche gorges itself on the forbidden fruit: revenge. One of our touchstones for Hutch was the lead character in *Oldboy,* and of course those classic Bronson films.

Getting into shape wasn't the greatest challenge of shooting *Nobody.* It just took time and focus. A bigger challenge was guns. I'm not a gun guy! But I trained with real guns and real

Daniel Bernhardt and me in Berlin. I'm the
star of the movie. Go figure.

gun guys. Mark Semos, a Navy SEAL sharpshooter, helped me
gradually get familiar with handling these death contraptions.
Mark focused on safety, because he knows, firsthand, the purpose and impact of guns. I think the word is "killing." Later, as
I met more "gun people," things got . . . more casual. I found
that the folks who were recreationally into guns were the loos-
est when it came to safety rules and general carefulness—they
were "playing" with guns and, of course, were the most stri-
dent in their gun love.

So, yeah, guns make me nervous, and that's a good thing.
The second greatest challenge to this part was acting the hero
without the crutch of irony.

There were funny lines in Derek's script, but they weren't

funny to the character who was saying them. As planned, I had to put my heart into the lines, no winking, no self-deprecation. I've never played a character more different from my true self—and mind you, I played a dancing tooth on *Mr. Show*.

The night before I was to fly out for the shoot, Naomi and I had a delightful dinner with the Idles, Eric and Tania, and Matt and Morgan Walsh—comedy was well represented. There you had Monty Python, Upright Citizens Brigade, and *Mr. Show*. Eric was his funny, brilliant self, and he brought me a booklet from the group's big O2 Arena reunion of a few years before. I made him sign it. This was the nerdiest thing I've ever done. Matt and Morgan and the Idles were all mystified by my story of heading out in the morning to be an action star. I wonder if they just thought I was drunk on my one mojito. "Yeah, yeah, you're going to go shoot an action film in Canada tomorrow—who isn't?"

We were shooting in Winnipeg in October 2019, and it was freezing on the night we shot the big fight sequence on the bus (legendary by now!). This was two all-nighters in the brittle cold with a gang of excellent stuntmen and me finding my way through. It was nearly as much fun as any comedy writers' room, but the references were different . . .

"After I punch Kirk in the head, then you come up behind me and I'll throw an elbow in your nose, and then duck a punch and grab that bottle and slam it across your face!"

"Yeah, got it, but instead of throwing a wide hook across Daniel's face, you should pound him with a hammer fist—and then you can catch me with a knife in the back just before I land the second punch."

"Okay, great, and remember, throw me HARD when you throw me into the panel."

"I thought I did throw you hard."

"Harder—I need the energy. Don't worry, I'll be fine."

"Great!"

"Great!"

A few hours in, I looked over at Daniel Bernhardt, my good friend at this point. He was reclining between takes and had a big smile on his face—a smile that featured a fair amount of blood—and he looked back at me and said, "It's like being a kid, right?"

It was, indeed. If we did it right, it looks violent and intense, but making this film was pure fun.

Nobody was, like all film projects, a whirlwind of discussion, uncertainty, teamwork, laughs, and last-minute, fingers-crossed decision-making. I've never seen a film so supercharged in editing—good thing we had some phone calls taking place onscreen where story points could be added or amended. All in all, except for waving guns around, which is sometimes a hoot and sometimes just plain disturbing, it was an adventure and a challenge. I've never been part of a film with a darker heart that was made with more love and good energy. *Nobody* was a project I pursued, and in every important way it came out as I imagined it might be, and that is rare. I have no way of knowing how it will be received, but I've been left with a lot to process and some new perspectives. What more could I ask for? In case you're wondering, I still haven't won my wife over on the project. The "better angels of our nature" may be the ones we want leading us forward, but the worser angels are the ones that we seem to want to watch onscreen. Does anyone want to watch a miniseries about a kindly, gentle, straight-talking lawyer prudently acting with patience, empathy, and deliberation? Hell, no! Give us Saul Goodman, his brittle ego, his resentments, his self-serving manipulations! The actor's command to "love your character" can be hard to hold to; we often play damaged people doing dastardly things.

If I'm particularly skilled in one area, it's being able to risk:

I can step right out onstage and suffer crickets and rotten toma-toes. Can a cricket pick up a tomato? Someday. This might be the biggest gift of my early improv-based training: learning to grab your junk and jump.

What's Next

A few months after finishing *Nobody,* I resumed work on *Undone,* for Amazon. *Undone* is a passion project for everyone involved. Unclassifiable, it's an exploration of mental disorders, ancient beliefs, and the complicated web of secrets that a family can hold. As the main character experiences shifts in her reality, the viewer goes on the same journey. This work, by the brilliant Kate Purdy, is beautifully unique. Like many things I've been associated with, for the people who connect to it, it will be a deep connection.

We have our big final season of *Better Call Saul* still ahead to shoot. Nothing will outdo the uncertainty and dangers of season 1 and our first step into that unique world and these very particular characters. Now we're going to try to stick the landing. The experience has reshaped me fundamentally, and I am still learning to walk as Jimmy/Saul through the desert, without water. For the record, I did NOT drink my own pee in episode 508, but rather I ACTED as though I were drinking pee. Thank you. Thank you very much.

I've teamed up with a smart TV exec, Ian Friedman, and we're pursuing many projects—some broad comedy, some dark drama, everything in between. It's a numbers game, if you haven't figured that out from this book, but it's also not. Every single project I work on is one I believe in and that I believe the world needs to gaze upon. Sadly, most will stumble and col-lapse far short of their mark. Marc Provissiero and Naomi

Odenkirk are my managers; please talk to them if you want me to appear in your movie that you're doing for charity about sexually transmitted diseases as told by the disease itself. Marc and Naomi and my wonderful agents at William Morris Endeavor, including but not limited to Esther Chang and Doug Lucterhand and Greg Hodes, are my "team" at this point, and that will change with time and tide. That's okay. The key here is that you know, young actor-writer, that it takes a fucking village, so *make more friends than enemies*. We're not curing cancer here . . . We're a distraction, which is inarguably key to life on earth, because life on earth is so bleak and painful and the only and best response to that is to LOOK AWAY! We're

Shooting the shit with Judd Apatow and
Dave Rath backstage at Largo at the Coronet.
Any backstage with funny people is still my
favorite place in the world.

giving people something to look at while they're looking away. It's a good job.

My idea of a dream week would go as follows: two days acting in a drama, three days writing and acting in a comedy, and two more days of half drama, half comedy each—and one long night shooting an action sequence on a cold bus in Winnipeg. No weekend required.

How To

"How do you make a break happen for yourself?" asked a young woman of me at Second City in 2019.

I really wanted to give her an answer. A yoga pose she could do every morning. A pill she could take. A crack she could smoke.

Do a lot of different things to increase your chances . . . Hmm, no. Then you might spread yourself too thin.

Do one thing constantly until you are the best at it . . . Obviously not the lesson of my career.

I settled on the truth: "You can't. You can't make your own break." She was not happy to hear it. Sorry, kid. But if you care about doing the work, if it rewards you, *just to do it,* you will probably be all right.

Overall, I've had more gains than losses, and this is possibly due to the fact that I've had good peripheral vision, an ability to spot some light breaking through off to the side, not always where I've been looking for it.

It's January 2021. Chicago's getting hit hard with snow tomorrow, my sister Maria, who still lives there, just shared with me. The Bears look like they might put up a fight in the waning days of a crap season. Those snowdrifts will be gray slush in about three days, and those nitrogen-cold winds will camp out for the next two months. With the coronavirus pandemic still

Backstage before interviewing Eric Idle for his
autobiography with my childhood pal Steve Meisner.
Our minds blown.

shuttering theaters, restaurants, and people in general, well,
poor Chicago is looking at a more forlorn and bleak winter
than usual. Rough stuff . . . But I'm excited about what's next.

Just like Del thirty years ago, in his cluttered shitpile apartment, I am stepping over stacks of books, chasing ideas that I
can see fluttering in the corners of my mind, catching what I
think might just be vivid glimpses of greatness, if only I can nail
it down. When this book comes out, I believe this pandemic
will be receding, and I think receding fast. Young people will
be opening new theaters, there will be new ideas, fresh energy—
too much energy—and it will be great and I'll be happy to be a
part of it. Things are changing, and I hope they are changing in
the direction of opening up more and more. Opening up to
new people, new visions, new ways to share our humanity and
to make fun of ourselves. My wife read an early version of this
book and mentioned that I should say something about "white
privilege." Well . . . isn't that kind of the backdrop of the entire
book? You can't read a page without reading about the privi-

lege I have had—the privilege to believe it's possible to make something happen. I've certainly shared my doubts, my skepticism, but, taking into account that I have never wanted to conquer the world, it's clear that I've always believed good things might happen if I just hung in there and showed up with my best effort. This is a privilege everyone should have, of course. I've taken full advantage of it and am happy to fight for others to have the same privilege.

I got very lucky running into Del on that day. He was at a turning point, which was the key to his frame of mind—it helped that an old friend of his just happened to be passing through right at the same moment. I think I would have kept on going down this road if I'd never had the balls to bother him in that bookstore, but he put a point on it for me. We were more alike than different: socially awkward idealists with sad hearts, immature men whose response to life's disappointments was ridicule, with an eye out for something hopeful and great, something new and exciting, a means of escape, if only for a moment, from this dim-witted, slapdash saga. Both of us eager to be the idiot who narrates the tale of sound and fury around us. He may have uttered incomprehensible nonsense in between hacking his lungs out, but the thrust of his spiel held true in my life, turned, as it was, on that fortuitous meeting. As Del triumphantly shouted at me through a cloud of marijuana smoke on that arctic Chicago day in 1983, "Signs and portents in the sky! Eclipses of the moon and fireworks!"

Acknowledgments

So many people to thank.

Ben Greenberg is a great editor, because he didn't start crying a million times whenever I'd submit another terrible draft. Ben, thanks for wanting me to do this and for suffering through it all. Marc Provissiero, for the encouragement and reading early drafts and your good counsel. Ian Friedman, also for championing this pulpy ragamuffin. Thanks to my beautiful, smart, hardworking wife, Naomi, and my brilliant kids, Nate and Erin. Dad's not working on his book anymore, so you never again have to engage in this conversation: "I'm working on my book." "How's it going?" "Not good." We all win.

I couldn't remember much without these good people and the time and thoughts they shared with me: Adam Resnick, Brent Forrester, David Cross, Jeff Garlin, Steve Meisner, Tim Heidecker, Tom Gianas, Mark Beltzman, Peter Gould, Steve Rudnick, Leo Benvenuti, Robert Smigel, Dave Reynolds, Paul F. Tompkins, Brian Posehn, Beth Lapides, Todd Glass, Ilya Naishuller, Jack Black, Daniel Bernhardt, Kim Howard Johnson, Bill Odenkirk, Conan O'Brien, and Judd Apatow. Special thanks to Claire Partin for contributing personal thoughts about the early days.

Other friends who gave me great encouragement: thank you, Rhea Seehorn, Patrick Fabian, Michael Mando, Meg Grgurich, and Melissa Heiman.

I have been incredibly lucky to have a few great writing partners who made me better than I am by far. I apologize to you, dear reader who reads every last goddamn letter of every word in the books you pick up, including the dumb acknowledgments, that I was not able to rope one of these pals into co-writing this with me. Tom Gianas, Robert Smigel, Tim Thomas, Eric Hoffman, and the great and wonderful apple-of-my-eye cherry-on-top razzle-dazzle primo-magnifico-cheezerino lyin'-Ted-Cruz great-ball-of-fire of all time now and forever amen David Cross.

Index

About the Author

———

BOB ODENKIRK is an actor, comedian, writer, director, and producer. Odenkirk got his start in sketch comedy in Chicago and went on to write for *Saturday Night Live*. He's starred in AMC's *Breaking Bad* and *Better Call Saul* and has written and starred in the sketch-comedy cult hit *Mr. Show*. He's also written and produced a number of television shows and directed three films. Recently, he has appeared in the action film *Nobody* for Universal.

About the Type

———

This book was set in Sabon, a typeface designed by the well-known German typographer Jan Tschichold (1902–74). Sabon's design is based upon the original letterforms of sixteenth-century French type designer Claude Garamond and was created specifically to be used for three sources: foundry type for hand composition, Linotype, and Monotype. Tschichold named his typeface for the famous Frankfurt type-founder Jacques Sabon (c. 1520–80).